A Year With Angels

*A year in the life at
Tierra Madre Horse Sanctuary*

Alexis Roeckner

Copyright © 2014 by Alexis Roeckner

All rights reserved. No part of this publication may be reproduced, distributed, or transmitted in any form or by any means, including photocopying, recording, or other electronic or mechanical methods, without the prior written permission of the publisher, except in the noncommercial uses permitted by copyright law. For permission requests, write to the publisher, addressed "Attention: Permissions Coordinator," at the address below or email sealofterspress@gmail.com.

Sealofters Press, Inc.
1061 East Indiantown Rd, Suite #104
Jupiter, FL 33477

Sealofters Press, Inc. was established in 2008 as a publishing alternative to the large, commercial publishing houses currently dominating the book publishing industry. Sealofters Press, Inc. is committed to publishing works of educational, cultural and community value.

Table of Contents

Foreword i
Prologue iv
Summer 1
Autumn 115
Winter 251
Spring 313
Epilogue 323
About the Author 331

For the angels

the ones that run

and the ones that fly,

For the volunteers

the ones near

and the ones far,

For Mike

who was loyal till the end,

For Marti, Trace, and Bre

who will be, too

and

For Jim

my last two-legged hero

Foreword

By Jim Gath

Author and Founder of Tierra Madre Horse Sanctuary

In the late springtime of the year 2009, my life - & our horses' lives changed.

And they changed for the better.

Because, at that time, a young woman came to Tierra Madre Horse Sanctuary early one sun-splashed morning. The date was June 1st.

And on that fine morning, the young woman – Alexis Roeckner – told me that she was soon to be a senior in high school & needed to undertake a major senior project. And that her idea was to make Tierra Madre & our horses the subjects of that project.

She would work each & every day, all summer long – mucking stalls & paddocks, cleaning & refilling water tubs & buckets, grooming horses, walking horses – doing whatever needed to be done around the ranch.

I instantly agreed. After all, it's not every day that someone lays an offer like that in your lap, right?

Well, over the next few months, Alexis became an integral part of the Tierra Madre family. She not only worked hard, but she got to know each of our horses as well as anyone has ever known them. Love affairs developed between Alexis & dozens of horses.

Tierra Madre Horse Sanctuary is a 'forever home' to horses that - in their prior lifetimes - had, for the most part, been abandoned, neglected, injured or abused. And, sometimes, we face the ultimate act of love: that of having to send them on to The Great Herd.

And, during that summer, we lost two members of our four-legged family. And Alexis was right there with them until the very end. It's never easy for any of us, but for a high school student, Alexis exhibited a degree of love, compassion & courage that I've seldom encountered, even in the most mature adults.

Oh, sure – we had our sad times. It goes with the territory.

But we also had wonderfully happy times that summer. We'd all laugh & splash each other with water & spray each other with hoses & pig out on the occasional junk food snack & talk about - & hang out with - horses all day long. And Alexis was right in the middle of it.

Now, I really don't think I'd realized it at the time, but Alexis was writing a daily journal about all that went on here that summer. I was finally entrusted with reading some of her journal entries - & I read them over & over. They were that good. They were heartfelt. They were insightful. They made me laugh out loud & they made me cry. Goosebumps weren't uncommon.

Over that summer, I began referring to her as 'The Faire Alexis'. And, to me, that name has stuck for several years – to this day, as a matter of fact. Why? Because she's like Tierra Madre's Guinevere: beautiful, kind, smart, generous & a whole lot more.

So, do yourself a favor.

Read this book.

The Faire Alexis' book.

Like she changed my life & our horses' lives - for the better – she & this book just might do the same for you.

Peace.

Out.

Prologue

I had been volunteering at Tierra Madre Horse Sanctuary for many months when I heard the following phrase spoken by one of my fellow volunteers that would come to summarize every thought I would have about the ranch forevermore:

"This place *does* something to you."

And that was it. Those were the perfect words. The words were as close as one could possibly get to describe the miracles that occur on a daily basis at this sanctuary.

I always tell people that Tierra Madre is no ordinary ranch and that its horses are no ordinary horses. Here in the vast stillness of the Sonoran Desert, they are allowed to thrive and simply be horses. They are given respect, attention, and all the love they can soak up. The ones that walk through our gates fearing humans are given distance until they are ready to trust, and those that come to us with broken hearts are shown such tenderness and compassion they learn to give their souls to humans again.

I started volunteering at Tierra Madre Horse Sanctuary on June 1st, 2009. It was the summer before my senior year in high school, and as a graduation requirement, each senior needed to complete one hundred logged hours of community service and write in a journal about his or her experiences. Each day after I was done volunteering, I sat at my computer and wrote for hours about the horses and about what had happened at the ranch that day, each entry surpassing the required length by far. As I wrote more and more throughout the year, I came to realize that I was telling a story, a story about the most incredible animals on Earth, a story that needed to be shared with the rest of the world. This book is that journal I kept from June 2009 through May 2010. This is their story.

If there is anything I have learned at Tierra Madre, it is that life goes on in more ways than I could possibly describe. Once a chapter ends, another story begins. I am tremendously grateful that I had the opportunity to do something that changed – and keeps changing – my life for the better. Even after this journal ends, there are still countless stories to tell and richer experiences to be had.

And for the life of me, I am still trying to put those adventures into words.

Alexis Roeckner

August 2014

Author's note: These are the true accounts of events that occurred over the course of one year at Tierra Madre Horse Sanctuary. Some names have been changed to protect the privacy of our past and current workers and volunteers.

And he said unto the horse, "Trust no man in whose eyes you do not see yourself reflected as an equal." ~ Anonymous

Tierra Madre Horse Sanctuary motto

Alexis Roeckner

Summer

June 1st, 2009

I now know humans as "two-leggeds". And horses? They are my saviors.

My new mentor asked me a question today: if there was a huge pasture filled with grass a hundred feet away from a horse, and a smaller, more modest patch right next to him, which one would the horse graze from first? Instantly I replied, "The bigger one, because there's more grass to choose from. Right?"

Wrong.

Jim Gath knows a lot about horses, more than the average breeder or handler or every-day rider would. In the four hours I was at his ranch today, I saw him interact with his "kids" and saw how they responded, and I felt the energy of a bond that was more than friendship pass between them. There are twenty-nine horses at this horse ranch, this Tierra Madre Horse Sanctuary, and all of them have different personalities and beautiful souls and gifts and lessons to teach to the rest of the world. And he knows it. Jim knows it.

Lesson number one: horses are prey animals. We "two-leggeds" are predators. Horses react on their "flight," instinct when it comes to that age-old flight or fight intuition, and we who have eyes on the front of our heads rather than on the sides are the ones that go straight into battle. To see a connection between horse and human, prey and predator, so strongly built on trust so that this animal of prey lovingly places his forehead against that of a two-legged's and sees that person as an equal... that is something too beautiful for words. This goes especially for these horses. These incredible animals have been neglected, misunderstood, injured, unwanted, abandoned, and in some cases, horrendously abused, at some point in their lives.

Horses are also herd animals. A herd is two or more, and here at this ranch, we two-leggeds must be the *itancan*, a Native American term for "leader". We must have the inner confidence to know that whatever we say will be obeyed without question. In a herd, the rest of the horses, called *waunca* (a Native American term for "follower" or "one who listens"), follow their leader with absolute faith. And that's what we're doing here. Building, building, building trust. It is all about the trust.

Back to the patch of grass.

Horses live in the here and the now. Jim said that the earth is moving through space at a tremendous speed and we won't be in the same spot tomorrow, physically or mentally, for that matter. Two-leggeds tend to have regrets and think about the past and the future too much. Horses, on the other hand, live in the present, only focusing on the hour, minute, second of the day they are in.

In answer to the question I got wrong: that little scrap of grass, the one that is right next to the horse? That will be eaten first. Why? Because it's there, right there, in the now, right in front of nibbling lips and a sniffing nose. That huge, luxurious patch of grass in the distance and in the future can wait. And it does.

Why can't we two-leggeds be like that?

I started out today mainly by following Jim around with the grain buckets as he introduced me to his "kids". When we got to Heighten, he said that his and Heighten's relationship go way back, back to the 1840s where Jim was the horse and Heighten was the rider. He laughed as he said that's just how he felt and that's how Heighten felt, too, even if it seemed really messed up, but I could sense the connection they had and see the truth in the statement. I could sense all of the connections, really.

Jim said a lot of things that made me see things differently than I had been viewing them. And I soaked it all in as well as I could.

Anyway, other than getting lost on the way over to Tierra Madre Horse Sanctuary, I think I did pretty well for a first day. I mainly mucked out stalls, which I was fine with because even though I'm sure I was awful at mucking, I got to meet a few of the horses personally. Moose "Moosie" rubbed his head up against me either in greeting or to scratch his face (I'm thinking it was the latter) and studied me as I cleaned out his stall. I think I must have passed some inspection because he twitched his shoulders in something like a shrug and walked over to his water bucket. Moosie is one of Jim's particular favorites, I think, and I can see why. The beautiful horse has so much wisdom in his eyes.

While we were over by Moose's water bucket, Jim showed me how to fashion "squirrel savers" out of twine. Apparently, squirrels occasionally fall into those huge water buckets the horses drink out of and can't get out, so he leaves little knotted ropes for them to save themselves should they get into trouble.

Who would think of the squirrels? That added touch to the water buckets continued to convince me that I had found the right place for volunteering.

I also learned that Sweet Boy has a chime fashioned out of horseshoes that hangs outside his stall, and he nudges it with his nose when he wants a treat. If I am within the box surrounding his stall, I learned, I am obliged to give him one. It's fair game.

And Ted. I like that horse.

I was cleaning out his stall and the huge cart I had to haul out of it was very heavy. I got it to the edge of the stall where the ground dipped into a little trench, then the wheels sank down and were instantly stuck.

I yanked at it. It didn't budge.

I tried again and again and again to pull it out of the tiny ditch while Ted sauntered over and looked at me with mild interest, obviously wondering what in the hell I was doing there if I couldn't pull a cartload of fresh horse feces (the mannerly way to refer to it, I learned). I glanced down at the wheels that were rooted down into the dip, then back up at the big Thoroughbred, wondering if he was mocking me.

"It's stuck," I told him expertly and he snorted in a, "Well, duh," sort of way.

By now he was so close to me that I could lean forward slightly and rest my forehead on his, which I did. We stood there for a moment or two, heads close, then Ted breathed gently through his nose and I leaned back, looking up at him. And I stepped toward the cart again, picked it up, and in two good tugs had dragged it out of his stall and into the dirt.

Now, I knew before today that horses were incredible animals. I knew that they understood the earth's stories and they knew how to live in ways we two-leggeds have never heard of. But now I am convinced that there are more hidden lessons within them, more unspoken words in every ripple of movement, and they are here to teach us.

A few more things I can't forget:

Chance was the only horse that really caught my eye. He has been horribly abused so whenever anyone comes near him he is extremely agitated and nervous and snaps horribly. But he's so beautiful. He's a big, golden palomino with a white mane and tail and a white star on his face. If only that was the only white on him... the whites of his eyes show, too. When we were introduced we studied each other for a moment before he pinned his ears to his skull and glared at me, blowing air from his nostrils and pounding at the dirt with his hooves. His message couldn't have been clearer: "I don't know you, I don't trust you, I don't like you, and I want you away from me."

How could I not fall for that poor horse that has seemingly never known kindness? I hope I can help show him what it is, and that he learns.

Mike is the black and gray ranch dog that is very protective of Jim, the horses, and the property. He barked at me for a good half hour and shifted uneasily when I was near, but Jim assured me that he would calm down once he knew I wasn't a stranger. He said Mike was doing very well and had eased up more quickly than usual at the end of my stay.

I also met Sam, Jim's right hand man that lives on the property with his wife and helps Jim care for the horses. He is quiet but very nice, and seems to understand the horses almost as much as Jim does.

I only worked the morning but I'll be back tomorrow. Bright and early. I think I'm going to like this place.

June 2, 2009

Today's adventure was pretty interesting. I met Joy, a fellow volunteer and a college med-student, who helped me feed the horses. She was very sweet.

Mike barked at me a couple of times and took a snap at me when I walked by him suddenly, but by the time I left the ranch he was thrusting his nose into the palm of my hand and looking up at me with gentle eyes. I think we've made progress.

I scrubbed out the water buckets for Guess, Bella, and another pretty chestnut mare whose name is escaping me at the moment. I helped Joy bring RustyBob and Diamond "Little D" out to the pasture. I love leading horses and walking with them.

I also had the lovely task of mucking out Sweet Boy, Sedona, and Moosie's stalls. I got new bedding for Moosie, too, and scattered it in his house.

Sedona is so fun. When Sweet Boy rings his bell and gets a treat, I always get an extra one for that big guy. I stayed with my head close to his and he took my hair in his mouth and nibbled lovingly the whole time. My hair's going to need a wash but he's a sweetheart.

I have to say, Chance has really captured my attention. He snaps at everyone who comes near him but I can't help walking up to his stall and just gazing at him. There is something so breathtaking about his spirit that I just want to be next to him. He was let out in the pasture today. Joy got the halter on him and he was fine for a while, but once he was let loose, he is wild and reckless as the wind. He and RustyBob played out in the pasture and Chance galloped and bucked and reared and plunged with the pure joy of being out of his stall. He was dancing the whole time.

Before I left I went to see him in his stall again. And in his eyes I saw a little of everything. Anger, exhaustion, hatred, uncertainty, weariness, and that glimmer of a question that every horse in that place must have asked at one point: "Can you help me?"

Today as I drove back home, I remember how shocked I was to see the cars flying at me when I had to make a right turn. I was startled back into reality, but only for a moment.

I'm gone now. I've gone into this beautiful world of horses and friends and laughter and faith and hay and slobber and sweat and excitement. This world is unlike anything I have ever been in before, and there is no way I'm ever losing the feel for it again.

June 3, 2009

When I drove into that ranch today, my third day, I felt like I had been doing so my whole life. The horses whickered in greeting and Mike only barked at me for five minutes or so, then he calmed down.

I helped feed (I'm getting better at memorizing who gets what) and then mucked out stalls for a little bit. Ted is officially my love; he would barely let me move in his stall when I was cleaning it for want of petting and kissing. He would put his head up against my chest or just stand as close to me as he could get. When I had to leave he would pound the stall door with his hooves and raise his head as though to say, "Huh?"

He's a good boy.

I helped bring Akira and Mr. Steve Vai out to the arena, too. Akira is a pretty little paint mare; Jim calls her "his angel". Mr. Steve Vai was a little nervous with me but he got better as the day went on. He's a very handsome horse; he's a bay with a little white stripe down his forehead, with a black mane and tail, a slender neck, and inquisitive eyes. He and Akira got along well in the arena.

Oh, and I'm hoping Chance may be getting used to me. I walked past his stall today, talking to him as gently as I could, not looking at him and turning my back and swishing my hair as though I could care less that he was there. He calmed down after a few minutes, but not before snorting and tossing his head, pawing at the ground and laying his ears back. I would have liked to stay more but it probably would have irritated him if I had been there longer, so I left.

I hung out with Kiss today, too. He lives in the big field with several other horses. He laid his ears back as well but he meant no harm; he kept butting me in the backside so that I actually stumbled at one point, as if he was trying to say, "I don't know you, but if you can handle this I guess I can accept you." Big, black, eighteen-hand Bentley was like that too. Oh, and M'Stor. Good old M'Stor tried to eat out of the bucket when I went to feed little

Rusty. Poor Rusty – he has a couple of bedsores and he is so thin and he can barely walk, but there's something very calming in his eyes yet something very sad and profound. Either way, he is a sweetheart.

I saw the horses paint today as well. We went to a couple of them and Jim would put a paintbrush under the horse's halter and guide him so that he (or she) pained onto a canvas. I got to carry it around. Joy carried the bucket of paint while Sam took pictures and gave the horses treats. It was fun. The paintings are sold to raise money for the ranch.

I offered to bring water and carrots on Friday. I have to work tomorrow and I'm beginning to wish I didn't have to!

June 5, 2009

Well, there truly is no "typical" day at the ranch, but I guess one could say that it was more or less normal. Mucked out stalls, helped feed, spent some time with Ted. Bentley's leg had to be cleaned and re-wrapped, so I held his lead rope while Jim and Sam did that.

It was really breezy and cloudy today and I swear it was less than 90 degrees outside. We were pretty shocked. But it felt nicer than the usual blazing heat.

Today in Jim's blog he talked about how helpful I've been but how most kids my age don't want to volunteer and can be very spoiled. Well, even if my school didn't require it I have a feeling that I would still be at that ranch, by fate or by choice, I'm not sure. But I love it more every day. When I got home I went straight to clean the kitchen after I ate lunch rather than just flopping somewhere or going right to the computer. I felt motivated.

I fear that kids my age could care less about whether or not they make a difference, whether or not they have goals and dreams and hopes and ideas. That's why I don't fit in with anybody. It's because I want to be something more than just average. We teenagers are so stereotyped and so spoiled from our luxurious lifestyles that we start to take everything for granted, and we don't think about the future other than to wonder if the most popular kid in school will ever ask us out.

You know something? That pisses me off.

But I'm not going to focus on how the rest of the teenagers in America live. I'll live in the here and the now, just like everybody at Tierra Madre Horse Sanctuary. I know not to take hot water and clothing and good food for granted. I think the horses have helped me realize that. I think they are helping me to become somebody worthwhile.

They know.

They know what I want to do, who I want to be. They know that I think being in Ted's stall with his head against mine is more valuable than a Juicy purse or going to all the good parties.

My mother complained about how badly I smelled of horse poop when I walked through the door today, and said aloud—jokingly—how she couldn't imagine people would want to be in the same room with me. You know something? I'd rather be at that ranch, smelling of horse poop, equal to the horses, than be with people like that.

June 7, 2009

Today I sort of wanted to sleep in rather than wake up early. You know we're more than a week into summer and I haven't slept in once?

Well, anyways, as always I was glad that I had dragged myself out of bed and driven over to the ranch. Seeing all of those horses, happy and secure, grazing in the field and in their stalls... it gets me. I don't know what it is and neither do they. But there's a hidden energy there at that place and I love being a part of it.

I guess I should describe the ranch somewhat. There are seven or eight horses that live out in the pasture that is to the right of where you pull in. To the left of that little road there's the open arena, the one where Jim lets horses go two by two to gallop and buck and play and live. There's a little house connected to the first stall in the "barn" area, where Jim lives, then another stall. In between Moosie's and Sedona's stalls there's a big space called the "breezeway," for a tack room and chairs for us to crash down in when the chores are done. Then there are three other stalls (Ted's is right next to Moosie's and in between CharlieHorse's), then perpendicular to those are the line of horses in separate stalls starting with the girls: Guess, Bella, and Jani, then it goes Heighten, Hudson, Mr. Steve Vai, Akira, Mistah Lee, Diamond "Little D", RustyBob, and ending with Chance. Chance's stall is next to a round pen and is separated from the main gate by a little wash.

Anyway, today Jani's "Mom" came to visit. Her name's Ginger and she has a couple month old son named something like "J.B." She walked around for a bit with Sam's wife Sally while I was filling one of the water buckets in the pasture. Kiss (the king of all love bites) came over and played with the hose. Now, lots of people underestimate the power of horses. Heck, Bentley (one of the biggest horses on the ranch) came up to me today and rubbed his head against me playfully and his force knocked me into the fence. It didn't hurt, but it startled me. But anyway, once Kiss had a hold of that hose he was not going to let go unless he wanted to. We had a fun game of tug-a-war, anyway. And he nipped me all over – the love bites. Horses always nip at each other in play but they are more equipped to handle strong horse teeth than we two-legged are. Long story short, I think Kiss walked away pretty full of himself because I had to duck every time he came at me for fear of getting hurt. And for some reason I like him. He's very full of spirit.

I helped feed, muck, and water as usual. And as I was doing the chores, cut off from everyone but the horses, a thought came to me.

Horses truly are prey. To get one of them to trust one of us, a predator, a threat to their survival, is an incredible thing. True, they're stronger and faster than we are by far. But we are natural-born predators with a tendency to kill things we shouldn't. An everyday horse discovering trust and eventually having affection for two-leggeds is amazing.

But an abused horse? A horse that has known nothing from two-leggeds but hatred and cruelty, a horse that has grown to loathe every human that walks near it? A horse like that surrendering its body and soul to one of us and learning what love is?

That is something beyond words.

And I've seen it. It happens at the Tierra Madre Horse Sanctuary. Every day.

And I hope that it will happen everywhere else so that someday, trust will be something every horse holds within them again.

June 8, 2009

Auction.

That is The Bad Word at the ranch.

Sure, everyone swears like a sailor there so lots of "bad words" are thrown out a lot. That's something I actually like about the place. Everyone is real; nobody bends to society's rules on language. But

I have begun to notice, especially as I ask Jim or Sam about everyone's stories, that there is only one word that drains the life out of a person's eyes at that place.

Auction.

See, a lot of the horses at the ranch came from these markets, these auctions where unwanted horses are sold to the highest bidder. These bidders can turn out to be good owners or people who are trying to save them from the last category of bidders: the killer men. These are the people who buy horses in order to sell them at a higher price to those who run slaughterhouses.

At these auctions, the horses purchased by killer men are bought for their weight and size – the larger the horse, the larger the price. Because horse slaughterhouses are illegal here in the U.S., horses are mostly shipped to Canada or Mexico (Mexico being more common around here) in tiny trailers once they have been picked up at auctions. They're crammed in with several other horses so that none of them can move. They're there for days at a time, standing without food or water or exercise. Once they arrive at these slaughterhouses, they enter whole new levels of hell. They are slaughtered.

Murdered.

I'm not a hateful person. I've mostly forgiven the people in my life who have done me wrong. I've accepted them. I've moved on.

But there are people like those auctioneers, these slaughterers, people I don't even know, that I would just like to understand. For the life of me, I can't figure out why they would shoot, stab, and mangle the life out of a beautiful animal like that.
I can't.
I'm grateful that killer men didn't buy the Tierra Madre's horses that were showcased at auctions.
Moving back to the ranch...
Ted told me he wanted to go out in the arena today. I reported this to Jim. And five minutes later Ted, bucking and rearing out in the pasture, was happy as a clam. As I gathered sawdust for Moosie's stall from the pile across from the main gate, that horse watched me from the arena and followed me around as well as he could as I walked. When I was mucking out his stall today he rested his head on my shoulder.
He's my overprotective boyfriend of sorts. But I love him.
For some reason I was thinking back to the days where I would wonder whether or not horses really do have different personalities. For a while I thought that most horses just kind of stand and chew and toss their heads and have the occasional different temperament... I actually wondered whether or not they could be truly different. Of that I am guilty. And looking back at the twenty-nine horses at Tierra Madre now, I know I was seriously wrong.

June 12th, 2009

You know what I was thinking today?

I was mucking out the stalls as usual when Ted and CharlieHorse were let out in the arena. Sometimes they go right after Sweet Boy and Sedona have their turn.

Anyway, Ted ran like crazy. Out there he was twisting and turning and galloping so gracefully across that pasture that I stopped for a good minute or two just to watch him. The sun rippled off of his dark coat and the wind – courtesy of this incredible weather we've been having – raked through his mane and tail so that they were like his wings. And I was thinking that there is just something amazing about watching a horse run of its own accord, watching their legs fly across the land and their heads plunge and their hind legs kick. Ted's sprint made my breath catch in my throat as I watched him.

It was beautiful.

And it was natural, too. There were no runways involved, or obscene amounts of goopy make-up, or fancy clothes or perfect hair or expensive handbags. None of what the rest of the two-legged world calls beauty.

Here at the ranch there is so much natural beauty I can hardly write about all of it. The way Rusty's eyes flicker every now and then after he was neglected and abused for years. The way Kiss— once so shy—grabs the hose when I fill the water and plays with it.

Bella's nose perfectly pressed against my palm. Akira pushing her forehead up against Jim's in utter devotion. Chance taking a bit of hay from my hands with barely any hesitation. The way neighbors drop in to say hello.

And the Moose.

Moosie is what Jim calls "The Medicine Man," and I agree wholeheartedly. His eyes are so deep and thoughtful and when he looks at someone . . . I swear that horse can see someone right to the core, past all of the different layers and right to the center of what makes a person what they truly are.

Well, that just sounded lame. But it's true.

Anyway, Moosie had his hooves done today. Jim and Sam took off his bandages from his front hooves and put different kinds of ointments on them as well as the padding and the lifts. The lifts on his hooves force more pressure to be distributed rather than have all the weight pressed down on one tiny area – especially the front. Wow, I almost have no idea what I'm talking about. Jim knows just about everything about every horse in that place and any illnesses or complications that goes with them. I don't even begin to understand everything.

When I drove away today, it hit me that every day when I drive away from the ranch, I am always aware of the fact that I am being forced against my will back into two-legged civilization. I have been pulled into this amazing sanctuary's world and am never coming out again.

June 13, 2009

Today I met Sam the Volunteer. I didn't have to muck out the stalls because he and the other Sam were doing that, so I got to do the NoFly! Doing the NoFly requires you to go to each horse and put liquid on his or her face and legs. This liquid has-fly repellant on it that keeps flies away. That was pretty fun – each horse has a different reaction and it was exciting to really meet each one in that way. I was told to steer clear of Chance – not that I needed to be tipped off. Chance wouldn't let me get anywhere near his face (it doesn't help that the only way I can go into his stall is if I'm willing to be trampled). His ears were flicked back even though I talked to him as soothingly as I could, and I offered him a couple handfuls of hay as a peace offering. Then I reached out in an attempt to pat him. I put my hand on his face for about a millionth of a second before yanking it back in fear of getting it ripped off; he didn't react but that's only because I think he was just shocked that I had dared to touch him.

Still, that was amazing.

When I was walking away and looking over my shoulder briefly, his ears weren't laid flat on his face; instead they were perked up and he was watching me go. When he saw that I was looking at him, however, he pinned his ears to his head again, snorted, and turned away.

I think we're doing well.

M'Stor and I had fun today; I went into his pen to do the waters and we played around for a bit. He chewed whatever piece of me he could get his lips on while I threw my arms around him or patted his face. He loves to nibble. He is a very sweet and courageous boy... a few years ago he broke his leg on the racetrack and might have gone to the slaughterhouse had somebody not made the effort to save him by sending him to a horse sanctuary. Jim told me that apparently M'Stor could barely walk for months and fought for his life. He fought well, because he walks today with no limp whatsoever. His hooves are lousy, but otherwise he is happy and healthy.

Today I also rode Venture! Jim rode him around the arena bareback to demonstrate how they used halters with reins rather than bridles and I asked if I could do it, as I had not been on a horse in over a year. He said yes so I vaulted on Venture and rode him bareback for a couple of minutes. I just about died and went to heaven.

I noticed that lately I've been driving much more slowly and carefully than my usual wild speeding. I wonder why...

But you know what I think? I think that the kids are teaching me how to slow down and live in the here and the now. I think that what they've been saying is starting to sink in.

I love them for that.

June 15, 2009

Do I dare say that Chance and I are progressing?

After I did the NoFly and the waters and mucked a couple stalls I went up to him with a couple handfuls of hay. He grabbed each one as he always does, hurriedly and forcefully, as though he expects me to turn around and hit him, but later on I noticed how he barely touched his lips to my hand it was almost like he was trying to be gentle. Jim told me that if he ever got too aggravated to turn away and never look him in the eye, and to offer the back side of my hand at a vertical angle. I tried all of these—I have been trying all of these—and as I walked away his ears weren't so flat on his head.

He's a good boy. He's so beautiful, so proud . . . so angry. Hopefully someday that anger will start to melt away.

Right after I left on Saturday Jim said he had one of the biggest scares of his life.

John coliced.

Apparently that boy was going to die. They said they had the doctors coming and on the phone and everywhere and John couldn't get up and that he wasn't going to make it.

But he did.

Jim's cutting back his feed. He thinks that he both ate too much at once, and that the stress of being the pasture's herd's itancan was getting to him. Solo, his best friend, accompanied him to the round pen where they hung out for a little while. John's doing better—in fact, I wouldn't have even guessed that he was sick had I not read about it in the blog. I'm glad he's okay. I'm so glad Jim knew what to do.

As I went to fill Big Charlie's water I saw a little floating thing on the surface. I thought it was a piece of wood. Looking closer, I realized that it was a bird. The poor guy must have fallen in and couldn't get out.

It's amazing how my detail to other life has sharpened since I started volunteering here. I hardly ever glanced at rabbits or lizards or birds. I preferred to focus more on the bigger animals, like dogs and cats. And horses.

But after I saw that bird floating face down in that water today, I'm starting to realize just how precious life is for everybody, no matter how small a creature might be. I was so sad when we chucked that little bird over the fence into the desert. Sometimes life is cruel.

I did the NoFly for Rusty today. When I went in his stall I saw about fifteen flies buzzing happily around his head. He just stood there, taking it in, robbed of energy to do something about it.

When I took his fly mask off and put the liquid all over his face with my hands, he stood as patiently as any horse ever could, and then closed his eyes in mental exhaustion when I went to spray the NoFly over his legs and flanks. He didn't try to follow me with his eyes like most of the horses do. He stood there, facing ahead, trusting me to do what I had to do to get him better. And after I put his fly mask back on, he lowered his head and pressed it to my chest in gratitude.

I felt my heart twinge.

This was a boy who was neglected for years, a guy so thin from abuse that I could have put my arms around his stomach and had my hands touch if I wanted to, a horse so speckled with bedsores and some other scrapes that it was all I could see at first when I met him. Not his eyes, not his face, not anything else . . . just the wounds.

And here he was, letting go of his well-reasoned doubt in that simple, graceful movement. It was overwhelming. It was and still is like nothing I could ever describe.

Slayer follows me from his pen right next to Rusty's and M'Stor's whenever I'm around, his head out to rub against my arm or leg or face or whatever he can get close to. M'Stor snorts loudly if I leave without patting him and letting him nibble at my hair. And an hour later when I went into the pasture today to say hi to Kiss they all came running. Well, maybe that was because I had treats in my back pocket.

But still.

Trust is the thread that weaves everyone together in the ranch. Without it everything falls apart. Without it there can be no healing, no friendship, no fun or happiness or different personalities or love.

And these guys trust me.

Even Chance perked his ears up briefly when I was with him. Even Bella and Min stood still as I put the NoFly on their faces and Guess finally let me near her head and Hudson rubbed his head against my side when I turned to leave his stall.

They trust me.

They trust me.

They trust me.

And knowing that the thread has begun to form, in this moment, in the here and the now, that is enough.

June 17, 2009

A few observations:

Before I started volunteering at this ranch, I used to ride at another ranch, a place that was devoted to getting its students to the show ring. When I rode once or twice a week, I would come home – and yes, this is strange – smelling normal. I would have been around horses for an hour or two and yet the only things that would smell of horse were my hands.

Now when I come home from Tierra Madre I am completely emitting a ranch-inspired stench. It's not just my hands, it's my hair, my face, my clothes, arms, legs, boots. My boots are the worst. My mom makes me keep those in the garage. She'd keep me in the garage, too, I think, if I didn't have to eat and sleep.

When I was riding before at the riding center, the biggest accomplishment I thought I could make was to have a horse respond correctly to different seat positions, to various rein instructions, to weird foot placings on the flanks.

Now, the triumphs I do – or help do – at this sanctuary are so much more than that.

And I definitely don't mind smelling like horse poop.

Another observation: Jim is as Au Naturel as one can get. Today when we discovered a huge ant problem in Moosie's feeding bucket he dumped them out on the concrete and instead of spraying them, he got out white powder and dumped it over them instantly. The ants started crawling away. When I asked what the powder was Jim said it was finely crushed oyster shells, a natural and painless way to get rid of unwanted critters and insets. I was astounded. Usually people just spray bugs and move on. Not Jim. He doesn't want poison where Mike or the horses could get at it, and he doesn't want to kill anything he doesn't have to.

Overall, it's amazing how natural the place is. "Tierra Madre," means Mother Earth in Spanish, and Jim said that it was crucial to live up to your name. Otherwise, you're just a good-for-nothing liar.

And another random but awesome thing: after a brief discussion with Jim before I had to leave early for a dentist appointment, we've come to the conclusion that the hippies will rise again. He and I share the same hippie mindset.

Here's to all of the anti-war protesters like Jim and I and all the horses there. Here's to no guns, for no hatred, for love and integrity and truth and everything reflected in the horses' eyes.

Here's to Slayer and M'Stor, who asked as I walked toward my car, "Hey, where are you going, Lex? The fun's about to start!"

Here's to Mistah Lee, who rolled his eyes as I put his flymask on but let me do it even though he was eating.

Here's to Sweet Boy and Sedona, who want those treats *now* and will be bound and determined to fight until they get them *now*.

Here's to Moosie, who shrugged and just moved over a couple steps when we moved his food bucket due to the ants.

And Here's to Chance, who was a tiny bit calmer with me this morning when I said goodbye. Or so I hope.

Oh.

And Here's to Jim. For someone that I think actually understands me.

June 18, 2009

Where to begin?

Well, it's been an interesting day today. Did the usual stuff. You know, mucked out stalls, did the NoFly, helped feed, and got attacked.

Yes, attacked. Briefly, anyway. By Chance.

See, I think I spooked him, or pissed him off... or something. When I went to do the NoFly for him he behaved pretty well. He even let me spray some around his eyes when he was eating and his head was down (through the railing, of course). I walked past his pen a couple of times, talking, as I always had. And then I made the mistake of pausing and leaning up against his stall wall and turning my back to him. And he nailed me, all right. Right in the back of the neck. I saw him move over, quick, out of the corner of my eye, and before I could think I felt a searing pain just under my hairline and an agonizing prickling as he ripped at my hair. The thing that got me though, as I jumped away and faced him again (and I don't know how I managed to keep using a soft voice), was that he tossed his head and utterly glared at me as though to say, "You keep away from me or I'll do worse next time. I don't like you and I never will, two legged!"

I seriously felt close to tears. Here I had thought we had been making progress. Well, we still are, I guess. Maybe. I gave him a couple of the leaves he loves before I left and he looked at me somewhat uncertainly before taking them, which was weird, because he always grabs them. Then he watched me leave uneasily. Sweet, cow-nose RustyBob flicked his ears back and glanced over at Chance before pressing his nose to my hand.

One positive thing was that I got Mr. Steve Vai to take his NoFly. It took a while and I walked around the stall for a bit before I got it on his face but he let me do it. He trusted me enough to let me do it. That was really something.

Even with me finally getting Mr. Steve Vai's NoFly on his face, I felt sad for the rest of the day. I felt sensitive to everything around me and it didn't help that I got lightheaded from the sun while I was watching Bentley get new shoes. Ted knew, though (as well as most of the other horses do, I guess). He wouldn't let me clean his stall for want of thrusting his head near my shoulders and neck and snorting softly and I eventually just buried my head in his mane while he stood still. I like my personal space, so it was the strangest but nicest feeling, to have someone so close, guarding and shielding me. It was as though Ted was fully aware of the fact that I'm unwilling to let anyone protect me.

Slayer is the same way. He is so beautiful that sometimes all I want to do is gaze at him. He's a light bay with a black mane and tail and a white star on his forehead. His legs are darker than the rest of his body and very elegant. His eyes are liquid and all-seeing and his neck is always arched and proud. He lifts his hooves happily when he walks. And he loves me, or so I hope. When I go to feed Rusty he always trots up to me gleefully and thrusts out his nose in greeting. I would kill for ten minutes on him.

And Moose...

I have to admit, it's taken a while for us to connect. Everyone has gone on about him for as long as I've been there and while I respected him greatly and he would stand and respect me, we haven't really made a connection. And I think I know why now: I can't make connections without fully trusting and letting down my barriers. And Moose knew. The other horses understood it as well and they mostly would come rushing if I offered them the palm of my hand. But Moose took his time, just as I took mine – just as I still take mine – until the day where I would be in such a moment of weakness that I would surrender and make the first move.

That day was today.

Moose made it seem like such a graceful thing, surrender. And coming from someone who has tried to avoid it her whole life, that is a lot. So today as I finished doing Moose's NoFly and was walking out his stall door, I hesitated and looked back at the beautiful, regal horse almost helplessly.

And he looked at me. He just looked at me.

There was something so deep, so profound in those eyes, something that truly, for the first time since I had met the Moose, made me feel as though he could see past everything else inside of me and see what I truly was. As though my soul was being searched and seen... and accepted.

I stood there for a moment. Then I dropped everything, ran to him, and threw my arms around his neck. He stood patiently.

"Thanks, Moosie."

"No, not at all, Lex. Not at all."

That Moosie.

He knows me.

And what's more, *I* know me.

I've stopped wearing makeup for the most part. I don't care what other people think anymore. I drive slower. I smile more even though I'm sad right now. But I will smile soon. I know it. They all know it. Especially the Moose.

Thanks, Moosie.

June 19, 2009

Well, today was a better day.

I did the usual: helped feed, mucked stalls (Ted would hardly let me work again) did the NoFly. CharlieHorse seems a bit more comfortable around me. He's a lot like Rusty in that sense: he just sort of hangs out, lets me do my thing, then waits until I leave to continue contemplating life. But as Rusty has come around for me, CharlieHorse is now, too. He put his head over the stall wall to see me when I was mucking out Ted's stall (or attempting to). The little sweetie.

Chance watched me when I came down the row with the NoFly, ears flickering occasionally but never laid back on his head. And while he was distracted with food, he let me put it over his eyes while he ate. I was very careful to not go near the spot I had been in yesterday. There's a lovely red scar on the back of my neck now but hardly a bruise. I guess that's good. I deserved it, anyway.

Hmm . . . I did the waters over by Tarzan's big pasture and M'Stor played with the hose for a while. He's very convinced that he's the itancan of our horse herd. And Slayer came over to say hello. He's my special boy.

It was funny; today we got our horse manure bulldozed into a big truck bed so it could be taken away – some of it, at least – and Suze, Bentley, Solo, and Kiss ran over to where John was when they saw and heard the big machine coming. John looked up at them as they seemed to scream, "John! John! What the hell is that? What's it doing here?" and he just shrugged and I could hear his reassuring: "It's all good, guys. It's just some big machine and it won't hurt us. We've all seen it before." John's the king. Nothing scares him.

Solo, John's partner in crime, pawed at the ground and looked back at the herd and replied, "That's it, guys. Exactly what I was going to say." Best friends Jericho and Venture, the other two in the herd who were out in the big arena at the time, snorted and rolled their eyes. But everyone calmed down.

I've got a list of things to get at the grocery store where I work. I mentioned to Jim that I was only getting so many hours and I was thinking about getting another job and he thought for a second before offering to pay me part-time for my work. The words were barely out of his mouth before I started telling him no.

I told him I would have found a way to them eventually – by choice or by fate, I guess – had my school not required me to do community service. He told me I was an angel.

No, I thought to myself as I walked from stall to stall at the end of the day, patting noses, rubbing foreheads, gazing into reflective eyes, *I'm the one who's surrounded by angels*.

June 20, 2009

Today was unbelievable.

I didn't have to muck out stalls, or do water, because Sam the Volunteer was here (I helped feed though. I actually got to do Mistah Lee's and Akira's complicated breakfasts by myself). No, instead I got to help with the riding lesson.

See, Jim doesn't usually do riding lessons but at the open house Tierra Madre had about a month ago, a special needs kid, Ben, won a lesson in a raffle. So he came today with his twin Evan and their adoptive parents. They were all very sweet. Evan didn't talk but I chatted with the parents. They asked questions about the ranch and I was so proud to answer them. I was proud to help with Akira, too (who Ben rode) and they seemed to think that I was an old pro when it came to horses. I assured them I was not. All twenty-nine kids are still teaching me.

The lesson went great and I talked to Ben for a little while. He was so descriptive when he was talking about the hurricane he had seen coming through Arizona (!). The mother jokingly told me she was going to hook me up with her son. Jim chucked as they left. I rolled my eyes.

I finished the NoFly (and mixed it up, too) when the four of them were gone. I also had to brush Hudson down, because he had a bunch of mud on his face and his sides. When I went out to where the herd was, Bentley used me as a scratching post for his head while Suze ran for cover when she saw me with the gray bottle. When I was over there, Heighten and Hudson (best friends forever, those two) got loose on their way to the arena and ran around in the wash area where all the plants were. I missed most of it, but apparently it was a good show.

When I got to Rusty's stall I saw that he had his head low and up against the fence. His eyes were downcast. Maybe he was just sleepy, but I felt a lump rise in my throat, just looking at him gazing at the ground in an almost hopeless manner. I took his fly mask off, which makes him happy, then spent a couple minutes just patting his head and kissing his nose. Slayer poked his head through and touched noses with him briefly, and I got the feeling that I was with spirits that truly cared about me, ones that don't judge or scoff at what I do or how I look. The three of us stayed there together for a while. Three old friends. Like we had known each other forever.

When I went into Slayer's stall and Rusty went back to his hay, we stood there facing each other for a minute or two. Usually when I go to pat the other horses they toss their heads once or twice (or won't let me touch their noses at all) before jokingly thrusting their muzzles at me. There's none of that with Slayer. He looked at me trustingly as I reached for him and there was no hesitation in the way he placed his nose in my palms.

Even before today, when I had always stopped to pat him and he would poke around in whatever bucket I was carrying, I had felt something. Somehow, as I threw my arms around his neck and he let me bury my face in his mane today, I know that our understanding will remain, in many ways, unwritten.

He knows me. And that is the beauty about these horses. They know me without even needing to spend time with me. But with Slayer (and I would really rather call him by a different name, but I love him so I will accept it) I feel as though we've been together in past lives, like we were once eagles flying together over undiscovered land. Or he was my rider and I was his horse once upon a time (like Jim once said about himself and Heighten). Maybe when he followed me around his stall today with his nose to my hand, he was remembering the time when I followed him.

Well, I'd follow him. I trust him so much.

June 21, 2009

Something happened today that was absolutely breathtaking.

Slayer was let out into the arena today. He bucked and reared and plunged and neighed with happiness as he bolted everywhere. Jim, to my delight, brought out the saddle. But it wasn't meant to be. Jim gave Slayer the choice of being ridden or not, and he chose not to let Jim put the saddle on him. Jim said, "Okay, baby boy," put the saddle down, and went in to play with him anyway.

Jim walked to the center of the arena as Slayer began to race around again. Somehow, someway, their movements melted together as Slayer began to circle around Jim and Jim turned around and around, facing him as Slayer moved. They went in a circle, going one way, until Jim raised his left hand and turned, and in perfect harmony with his actions, Slayer turned and went in the opposite direction. This went on for a while. Then Jim stopped and so did Slayer. He turned his back to the horse and Slayer crept up beside him, ears flickering, trying to catch the unspoken words that seemed to be floating in the air between them. Jim turned and focused on the horse. For a moment or two they stood there, silent, motionless – then Jim began to walk away with his arm held out slightly.

And Slayer followed.

That horse followed him around through twists, 180 degree turns, everything. It was flawless, magnificent, amazing. So much trust and strength in that connection... I can't even think up a way to describe it that gives it justice.

It was simply heart-wrenchingly, breathtakingly beautiful.

Another thing that was beautiful was my walk with Mistah Lee today. Mistah Lee and I go for a walk every day I'm there. This beautiful white horse had arrived at Tierra Madre with a broken hip several years ago, and although he overcame the impossible by healing at his older age, he needs to be walked several times a week so his hip can get gentle exercise. He loves getting out of his stall to sniff at the brush in the wash and nibble at palo verde seed pods that have fallen on the ground.

When we passed Chance's big pen, I think Chance heard how I was talking to Mistah Lee and when we passed him without looking or speaking to him at all, Chance trotted up to the edge of the fence and stared. His ears weren't back on his head; instead they were pricked forward. His eyes weren't filled with the usual menace. One of his ears twitched when I snuck a glance back at him. And as Mistah Lee and I walked on he let out a long snort as though declaring, "Well, I didn't really care to speak to you, anyway."

But I had seen his actions beforehand. Later on I went to give him some leaves and he took them greedily, ears pinned to his skull again. But whenever I leave his ears go right back up, and the tension I feel in the air is gone. When I sneak a glance behind me as I'm walking away, four out of five times his eyes are on me.

You know what I was thinking today? The horses are kind of like students in a classroom. I'm not quite sure where these thoughts came from, but I began to really notice how different each horse is and compare them to the typical high school classroom.

Moose is the teacher. He's wise and thoughtful and knows things the others don't. When he looks at a person, he sees every part of who they are.

Ted is the athlete who tries to show off to get the girls' attention, but he's a team player when he's talked into it.

CharlieHorse is the guy in the corner who is always shy but nice enough, just wanting to get back to his artwork or his homework or his food.

Sedona and Sweet Boy are the best friends who are lost in their own world, helping each other with homework, playing football after school.

John is the football star. He knows what he wants but doesn't push people around to get it; he earns it. He's also the leader of his gang and is on his way to being an excellent teacher eventually.

Solo is John's partner-in-crime. Second-in-command and somewhat of a bully, he repeats whatever John says and makes sure the orders are carried out.

Venture and Jericho are the best friends who are in John's gang, too, but they would rather play with each other and go off in their own world than listen.

Suzie is respected by everybody in the gang and she does what she wants, but, when John lays down the law she lowers her head and obeys.

Bentley is the big, loveable guy in the crowd. Huge but harmless.

Kiss is the last member of John's gang. He used to be part of the popular crowd but since he is new to the group he is well liked and accepted, even if he's on the bottom of the totem pole.

Tarzan is the boy who just wants peace and quiet. He doesn't want anyone too close to him because he doesn't trust easily after his terrible ordeal, but he is learning to like one or two people.

Rusty is the sad, quiet boy who is learning to love again. Horrifically abused by others, he is learning to accept everything for what it is.

Slayer is the playful but kind guy (and Rusty's best friend, I think) who would take tacks from the teacher's chair if others placed them there, and he tries to reach out to those who need help. He loves to be loved.

M'Stor is the kid that likes things done a certain way and he doesn't enjoy people taking advantage of him. He loves and thrives on attention.

Big Charlie is the big tough guy that everyone's afraid of, but he is really harmless. He would teach poetry to the little kids on Saturdays.

Min is the scrawny boy everyone teases, but he is someone who isn't afraid to throw a punch to protect his honor. His number one priority is to protect his dignity at all costs.

Guess, Bella, and Jani are the Clique. Guess is the beautiful, headstrong leader that tells them what to do but Bella has her own mind and often refuses to do whatever needs to be done. Jani is just along for the ride and content to be part of the team so long as she gets her time alone.

Heighten and Hudson are the big, tough football stars who laugh a lot and are really friends who care for one another. They show affection and joke around, as they are the "cool" kids, Heighten more so than goofy Hudson.

Mr. Steve Vai is the softie. He's shy and artistic and looks around at the world through big eyes and while there are those who know how to take advantage of his meekness, everyone loves him.

Akira is the angel. Teacher's pet but mischievous in her own way, she finds a place into everyone's heart eventually.

Mistah Lee is a new teacher. He's wiser than most but a little too laid back to be in control just yet. But he'll learn and he knows it. He's got a lot of confidence.

RustyBob is the roly-poly who asks everyone for food but is sweeter than anything and is cheerful no matter what. He shrugs a lot and goes with the flow and is happy to be in his own world.

Diamond "Little D" is the princess. She squeals a lot when the boys come but inside she's coy and eager to love and be loved.

And Chance...

He's the new boy who walked in with second-hand everything, newly escaped from an abusive family and still wondering whether or not he'll be liked or safe.

All in all, a very diverse classroom.

When I went to say goodbye to Slayer he played with my car keys. I dropped my water bottle and he bent to pick it up curiously. I love that horse. I still feel like we've known each other before, in past lives.

We good, Slayer.

We good.

June 23rd, 2009

It rained today!

Well, it sprinkled slightly as I was filling the waters, twice. That counts, right?

Today I had to muck out stalls because Sam the Volunteer wasn't there but that was all right. Joy came for a while. She got to do most of the NoFly first but I still got to do the row starting with Guess and ending with Chance.

When I went to fill Moosie's water I found about three thousand ants crawling around in his feed bucket, so I got that out of there (squeamishly) and put down the crushed fossil shells that serve as a natural "poison" for killing bugs with exoskeletons, or something like that. Jim made fun of me because when I told him the feed bucket all but fell apart when I was getting the ants out of it I must have looked nervous about breaking something, but apparently that thing has been wasting away for eight months. Sam sarcastically informed me of the company policy: you break it, you bought it. Jim said the thing was worth eight cents.

I went out to the pasture with some treats and of course all the kids all came running. Slayer kept eating my pockets when I was with him in his stall. He followed me around like he did for Jim the other day which was amazing (even though he was probably just looking for more treats). M'Stor and I had a battle over the hose when I was filling his and big Charlie's waters. He kept grabbing it and when he put it down I would splash his chest and he would grab it and splash me back. By the time that was done we were both soaked.

Chance doesn't look so apprehensive when I'm walking next to him now, and he's always nibbling at the air for treats or the leaves I usually hand him when I there. He stood and let me do his legs today when it came to NoFly. Every day I keep thinking of what it would be like to ride him, to have such power and wild freedom beneath me. He could go places. We could go places. I have to admit I got jealous when Jim put the halter on him and led him around easily. I asked him if it was hard to do and his answer was that Chance was a piece of cake.

Well, Jim has no trouble getting any horse to trust him. I wish I could lead Chance around like that.

Anyway, it was funny, because when I was mucking out the stalls I remembered what my friends had said they were going to do today: sleep in, go to the movies or watch TV. And there I was, shoveling horse poop at seven thirty in the morning. I now officially have my fifty hours I can complete for the summer, and I'm still coming to the ranch to deal with roaches and ants and the hot sun, to cope with non-cooperating hoses and sawdust and flakes of hay that break, to be stomped on (accidentally) or attacked (on purpose) and drained and robbed of my energy due to exhausting work. As I shoveled, I wondered briefly to myself, *why do I still come*?

Why?

Well, I quickly thought about why.

To hear Sweet Boy clang his bell for treats.

For the times Sedona eats perfectly and eagerly out of my hands.

To see myself reflected in Moosie's all-seeing eyes.

To have Ted nuzzle my arms.

For the moments when CharlieHorse lifts his head and holds it out to me.

To see Guess play with her water bucket until we're both soaked.

For Bella to tease me and let me feel like I'm winning something when I do her NoFly, to show me what natural beauty is.

To see Jani's ears flicker with understanding when I touch her nose.

For Heighten to hear my thoughts.

For Hudson to be my little brother, to play with me and rub his head against me and nip at my shoulders.

To see Mr. Steve Vai watch me carefully with liquid eyes when I stroke his forehead.

To feel Akira's sweetness and sassiness wash through me when I'm near her.

To see Mistah Lee limp with strength I could never possess when I take him for walks.

To hear RustyBob neigh innocently for his food, to whicker when I'm near him and look at me with trusting eyes.

For Little D to squeal playfully when I walk toward her.

To see Chance learn to trust me and the world.

For Bentley to innocently shove me into the fence as he tries to scratch his head against my sides.

For Suzie to snort with amusement and trot away happily when I come near her with the NoFly.

For Solo to pound the ground next to me when I don't pay enough attention to him.

To see Kiss giving me The Look when he wants treats.

To have Jericho greet me when a cheerful nudge and a loud neigh.

For Venture to remind me of the time when we rode together with just one look.

For John to stand proudly and teach me how to be a true leader.

To have big Charlie gently nibbling at my pockets when he knows there's food there.

For Min to snort and nip with dignity if I reach down to pet him and laugh at me when I'm not looking.

For my hose-battles and friendly romps with M'Stor.

To see the light in Rusty's eyes when I pat him.

To steadily show Tarzan I'm not there to hurt him.

And to feel Slayer's thoughts parallel with my own.

That's why I still go every day.

Jim and I talked about what's going on in Iran, about how the protests are still going on because of the rigged election. Those people want a say in how their lives are run.

I think it's sad, because while these horses dominate our every action at the ranch, there is a whole country a world away that doesn't get that kind of freedom.

Why is it like that?

Now that is a *why?* question to which I just can't find an answer.

June 24th, 2009

For these past few weeks, someone up there has mercifully been avoiding the heat switch and has allowed us to enjoy some beautiful June weather for Arizona. Today some stupid fool stumbled across the knob and flipped it up.

It was *hot*. Simply standing and doing nothing felt like a huge amount of work to do, let alone mucking out stalls (I had fans on me for that, luckily) and filling water and doing NoFly. M'Stor and I had our grand water hose war as usual and I happily let him drench me so I would stay cool. Jeans and thick socks in this weather are not working for me, but oh, well. I feel sorry for the horses, who have no air conditioning to which they can retreat!

I gave Rusty his de-worming medicine and Slayer kept on trying to pull me over to his stall. Chance banged his hooves on his stall door when I walked away after giving him leaves. I think he just wanted more food, but for a moment I pretended that he wanted me to be near him again. I think that maybe he's warming up a little more every day. Slowly, but steadily.

Today Dr. Rollins came with his two assistants to look at M'Stor's hooves. I walked the beautiful chestnut horse around and stood by his head to calm him while Jim and the other three talked business. I felt proud to be the one holding M'Stor, talking to him and leading him around.

When they went to look at Moosie I went off to do the lunch feeding (by myself!). Other than spilling Akira's grain and having to go back for more and, well, getting *way* too much hay, I think I did all right. The girls who come here every once in a while had put Akira and Mr. Steve Vai out in the arena and left them here so I went to bring them back so they could enjoy their lunches. Mr. Steve Vai panicked when he saw everyone by the tack room (Rob the farrier and his assistant were there by now, too, to do the horse shoes) and tried to bolt but I was able to hold him and calm him so he didn't run away. I went to get Akira, too, and after calmly approaching her and putting her back in her stall, one of Dr. Rollin's assistants asked me if I wanted a horse walking job.

That was pretty cool. I gave the assistant my number and she said she'd give it to the client of hers who needed a horse walker. We'll see if anything comes of it.

I was thinking today... if someone were to ask me what the biggest problem at the ranch was, I would answer with absolutely no hesitation: money. Or rather, the lack of money.

Today we were trying to think of ways we could fundraise for the ranch. The paintings done by the horses, obviously, are kind of working. We thought about riding lessons. Painted horseshoes. Writing books to sell (guess who thought of that one?). I am actually considering putting this log into a book so we can sell it for the horses. We need the money for food, horse-care supplies, but mostly medicine. Medicine eats up a lot of the money that comes in.

Well, we'll think of something. I like to think that the universe always looks after us.

June 25, 2009

My legs and arms are aching so much I can hardly walk or lift things. There's no good reason they should be like that, unless you count the fact that I'm up every morning by six so I can be out of my house as soon as possible to muck stalls and clean waters and feed and do NoFly...

I'm taking tomorrow off. I think I need a break.

But the thing is, when I left today and I knew I wouldn't see the horses for two days, I felt sad. Guilty, even. I love those horses so much.

It was much cooler today than it has been, which amounts to 90 or 95 for us, compared to 110. The sky was one big cloud but a little darker on the southeastern horizon. Like someone had taken a paintbrush and swirled it around until dark blue clouds sat there triumphantly. It was gorgeous. Heighten and Hudson kept looking up at the sky when they were in the arena. I think they liked it too.

Jim explained some of the background behind Iran's current situation to me while we were giving the horses breakfast. It's fascinating, really, the whole history behind a revolution. I just hope Jim is right when he says it's going to end soon. The tides are turning, he says. I believe him.

I was a little upset today because Chance was still a bit agitated with me while Sam could walk into his stall and he'd just stand there (if there was food involved, of course). Well, patience is the key. It's a part of the thread of trust that weaves us all together here. I've never been good with patience so I think it's about time I've learned it. Like when John and Solo were giving me a hard time yesterday when I was filling their water, I was as patient as I could be and today they were fine. Hmm. Progress? I think so.

When I was doing CharlieHorse's NoFly I found a huge boil-ly, massive *thing* (there are honestly no other words for it) on his underside. There were a ton of flies having a powwow there and when I figured out they were grouped around something that looked oddly like a tumor on his shaft I ran for Jim. He called the vet and the doc said it could be a form of skin cancer. Yuck. Jim and Sam looked at it while I did the waters. I figured it would be more appropriate for CharlieHorse if the men handled his problem. Well, I'm sure poor CharlieHorse could not have cared less. His eyes were downcast when I went in there to check on him later. He was probably humiliated. Ted was snickering at him the whole time.

Jim asked me for an opinion today, which was very neat, I think. He said some people were complaining that he put too much of his personal opinions on politics in his blogs, and that his language was a little rough, and he wanted to know what I thought of that. I snorted and told him that if people had a problem with what he wrote, then they could go read something else. He wondered aloud if that would affect donations. I said that people who snidely comment on his opinions obviously didn't give a damn about what he truly writes about – the kids – and they needed to go get lives. Jim laughed and said he agreed.

And this is very random... but as Jim and I stood in the breezeway talking a huge cockroach started making its way through the little hole where the door's lock goes in the tack room. I jumped back but not quick enough to miss the huge white round thing on its back. I shuddered when I realized the thing was an egg sac. Jim put some of the white powder (crushed shells) into the hole. Gross. Anyway...

Patience, patience, patience. I think I'm getting more of it every day. And that is what will make me acceptable in Chance's eyes someday. At least, that's what I hope.

June 27, 2009

I swear I melted a little bit today. If I thought Wednesday was bad...

Well, I kept cool by doing M'Stor's water since he usually grabs the hose to hose himself (and therefore me) off. I finally just grabbed the thing from him and hosed his entire body until he was sopping. He loved it.

Chance let me pet him today, too. Well, not really. But I got a finger or two on his nose before he lunged at me. I was able to get his NoFly over his eyes so I gave him a couple leaves and as he chewed them I reached out to him again. He moved uneasily and clipped his teeth together close to my hand. Put in my place, I drew back. I'm a little afraid, I'll admit. Horses like him are so powerful that if he makes a single movement and makes a snap a finger could literally be lost. But I tend to throw caution to the wind when it comes to this horse.

Speaking of powerful, Bentley nearly shoved me to the ground when he rubbed his head up against me. He loves scratching his head that way.

Ted has an abscess in his hoof. I think it's sort of like a pimple, and it hurts a lot. Poor Ted was limping around in his stall today.

Today Jim, Sam the Volunteer and I were trying to think up ways to make money. We talked about doing a maze in the pasture for Halloween, and maybe hay rides and pumpkin patches. I think we could do something like a fair as a fundraiser. It'd be fun.

Yesterday Jim wrote about me in his blog. Among many other things he said that I was now one of them since I volunteered so often for them in the mornings. I felt honored and happy and a little stunned. I didn't think I was helping all that much. It's such a good feeling, being part of something that matters, being part of a team. A team that can stand extreme heat and short funding and pretty much anything.

I noticed today that as I left, instead of saying, "Do you need anything from the grocery store?" as I always do, I asked, "Do we need anything?"

We.

That is such a beautiful word.

June 28, 2009

Today I took my camera with me (along with carrots and apples) to the ranch. I took tons of pictures and I'm going to make an album for Facebook so people will notice them and hopefully give us attention. We'll see how it goes.

Joy, Sam the Volunteer, and I were all there today so everything got done relatively quickly. When I filled the waters over by the field M'Stor wanted me to soak him several times as did Suzie. I went into T's stall to try and woo him a little but there was a woman making a ton of racket over next door so we didn't really make progress.

Chance was let out in the arena today and though he didn't really go wild, he followed me around as best he could from the sides of the gates, wanting leaves and treats. He ate almost contentedly out of my hand. Joy got to lead him out though, but that's okay. I'll lead him someday. Heck, I'm going to ride him someday. My heart's set on it.

Moosie did a couple of paintings and Ted's foot was doctored up a bit. And everything else was more or less normal. That is, as normal as our ranch can be.

I swear this heat is draining my appetite to write. I'm going to go make the Facebook album now.

June 29, 2009

Today I was the only volunteer so I was back to mucking stalls again. Oh, well.

Guess had an abscess in her foot today, like Ted does. Jim, Sam, and I went in and while I stayed near Guess's head, calming her, they worked heroically on her foot while she gave them quite the battle. At one point Guess wouldn't let them anywhere near her because of the pain, and Jim nearly gave up.

I felt so bad for him today. Just that morning as we exchanged our "Good-morning-how-are-you-good-how-are-you-fine-thanks," greeting, he had responded in a somewhat saddened tone, I thought. I asked him if everything was okay and he replied that money was just a little tight. Taking care of his 29 kids took a lot of funding.

God. I can't even imagine.

Well, a miracle that solved a little of the money problem was that we didn't have to call the doc for Guess. Sam went in after the abscess again and was able to get it punctured. Jim was relieved and grateful, and Guess felt loads better after they wrapped up her foot.

Today, after the waters were done and the meds were distributed to several of the horses the three of us sat for a good half hour, talking, while we waited to feed lunch. The subject of how many of the horses came to live at the ranch was brought up, and I have to admit we slammed people who tell Jim how we should run the ranch while doing nothing themselves to help us. (There I go again, saying we.) We talked about the people who overbreed their mares so they can save the afterbirth for drugstores, about slaughterhouses...

There are people in this world I will never understand.

Anyway...

I went up to Chance today and I was completely fearless. I don't know what it was, but I reached in to put NoFly over his eyes with more confidence than usual (he bolted upwards and I had to abandon that task). I was also able to touch his nose for a split second and give him his usual leaves. He paws at the bars on his stall if I don't give him food when I approach him.

It's odd; it was hotter today than it was yesterday and I had to work more than I did yesterday, but I was more tired than than I am now.

Hmm. Maybe I'm getting stronger.

Well, I'm going to the store today to get water and vinegar and pancake syrup for Moosie's "Mooseshakes". I'm going to see if I can get some people food, too, for Jim.

And one last thought... lately I've been singing the horses the song "Brothers Under the Sun," by Bryan Adams. It's such a good song. It applies to Jim and the horses so well.

June 30th, 2009

The doc came for CharlieHorse today.

He had three assistants with him, and with the four of them plus Jim and Sam crowded around in CharlieHorse's stall, I had to climb through the bars from the outside pen and watch from a distance. I felt like an overly worried mother hen and felt bad for poor CharlieHorse getting the tumor-like particles frozen off of his penis (everybody had a good laugh over what they were going to refer to it as; they finally decided on "his you-know") but CharlieHorse didn't seemed pained at all. After a while my palm was starting to hurt and when I looked down I realized I had been clenching the bar out of nervousness. Ted moved near me several times, as though he was trying to comfort me, but I was relieved when everybody went away to talk medical business (Jim made sure CharlieHorse got lots of hugs first) and I was left to take care of the "patient". I got to go in to his stall and wrap my arms around him and take his halter off and shower him with kisses.

I went with Jim to the hardware today and that was an adventure since he drives like a maniac! He drove well, but insanely. I'm one to talk, though. I drive pretty insanely, too. We got onto an interesting discussion about how our faith in humanity was diminishing but how horses were sometimes the only creatures we could have faith in. I'm starting to think we can talk about absolutely anything.

Chance, Little D, and RustyBob were all out in the arena today. Chance kept chasing Little D around and Little D, coy little girl that she was, kept shrieking at him when he got too close. I got a good video of that beautiful palomino horse running. He came right to Joy when it was time to go because he was so tired. I have to admit I was jealous. I wanted to be the one leading that horse.

July 2, 2009

Something amazing happened today with one of the horses here. Now, let me tell you about this one particular horse that I've never really dealt with at the ranch. Tarzan is blind in his left eye and since the day I started volunteering at Tierra Madre he didn't want me anywhere near him, and for a good reason, too. This horse was dropped off four or five years ago and the woman who owned him told Jim he had been blinded in a trailer accident nine years ago. But here's the interesting thing: since that day, T has apparently gone in and out of trailers like it was no big deal at all. If he really had been blinded in a trailer accident, Jim says he would have never gone near one again. But T did have an awful reaction to another object: the way he responded to rakes told Jim that somebody had hit him with a rake and blinded him that way. And it had to have been recently, not nine years ago.

The long story short is that T must have known some absolutely horrific abuse sometime in his life. Through Jim's patience and devotion Tarzan has come to trust him and him only, but he is still very nervous around everybody else. He's not violent, like Chance; he'll just run away if something frightens him.

Usually after I do Rusty and Slayer's NoFly, I go up to his pen and chat for a little bit, just so he can get to know me and recognize my voice. (Jim has always done his NoFly, not me.) I always had to take care to stay away from his blind side so he doesn't spook. But today when I went up to his huge pen, something felt different. There seemed to be less of the tension in the air, tension that T always emitted when I was nearby. So I crept toward him. He backed up once but didn't move again as I froze, talking soothingly, telling him what was around him and what I wanted to do. After a minute I walked toward him again, showing him my hands, and, when he did nothing, gently rested my fingers on his muzzle.

He stood.

No reaction whatsoever.

The horse that has probably been more abused than any of the other horses here let me, almost a complete stranger, touch him.

It's for these moments I wake up early. It's for these moments, the ones I can never properly explain, the ones that fill me with emotions that cannot be described, for which I seem to live.

And another incredible thing happened today. When I do the NoFly on the other side of the ranch, Chance always bangs his hooves against the bars of his stall because he knows I always give him food so I can get past him in one piece. His stall is right next to Little D's and RustyBob's, and because RustyBob has no door on his stall I always have to go through Little D's door to get to the side-opening between their stalls – but that means I have to walk right next to Chance.

Anyway, today I thought he needed to learn a little bit of patience. So instead of walking past RustyBob and Little D to get to him like I usually do, I went into RustyBob's stall first rather than last (and as a side note, that horse is the sweetest little roly-poly on the face of the earth) then went over to Little D and spent time with her before I even looked at Chance. When I did finally get to him, I was able to spray his legs with the NoFly and after I gave him a couple of leaves, I showed him the back of my hand. He didn't bite or look at me angrily; he nibbled it, looking for more food. I flipped it over slowly and rested it on his nose, then drew it back. Repeat three or four times. Chance didn't bite, or snap. He just nibbled with his lips and he only did that out of curiosity. The hatred and the uneasiness seemed to ebb away from his eyes.

I'll repeat what I've said several times in this journal already. To get any horse, a prey animal with instincts to flee at the very smell of danger, to trust a human predator is an unbelievable feat. But to have a horse that has already been abused open up to a person and trust what they can't see... that is a miracle.

Take CharlieHorse, for example. (He's doing better, by the way; he didn't really want me to touch him today but that's because I think he was tired.) If Jim hadn't taken him from the horrid people trying to get rid of him, CharlieHorse would have literally ended up as bear bait. He didn't care for me much when we first met, but now he lifts his head and turns to me when I walk into his stall. Now he lets me put NoFly over his eyes and rubs his head against my chest when he wants to be scratched.

The Moose is a miracle within itself, too. Every time he looks at me he just sees me to the core. I saw nothing but kindness in his eyes today. Nothing but affection from the horse who can barely walk due to Cushings disease and laminitis. Nothing but bravery.

I am so humbled by these incredible animals. Every single one of them is a teacher for me, and I'm doing my best to learn. Even Kiss, who ripped my shirt today, is teaching me patience. John seemed to go over and have a talk with the horse after he had upset me. John is the wisest leader I know.

They all are wiser than I might ever be.

July 3, 2009

Today after I finished feeding and mucking out the barn stalls, I did the NoFly as usual. (Jim says he loves that I have taken over that particular job.) All the horses did well for me, even Guess and Mr. Steve Vai who don't really like having their NoFly done. When I got to Hudson, my little brother, he rubbed his head against me so forcefully I was almost knocked over. But I gave him a good long scratch as I rested my forehead against his nose and he blinked lazily, loving the attention. His eyes followed me when I went on to the next horse, wanting me to come back.

When I got to Chance he didn't bang so much on the bars of his stall, and as I did Little D's NoFly he watched with his ears perked up, looking attentive. I took extra care to hug and kiss RustyBob and Little D not only because RustyBob and Little D are the sweethearts of the ranch, but so that Chance could see how kindly I treated them. I gave him his leaves as usual and when I sprayed his legs his ears didn't go back – a very good sign.

Oh, and Kiss and I made up. We had a fight yesterday after he ripped my shirt and I got mad at him, and when I apologized he put his head down and let me stroke his forehead. I could feel his apology in the energy he was releasing. I think we're good now.

But the real triumph of today was Tarzan.

When I was walking up to start with Rusty's NoFly, Jim, who was emptying his water, nodded to Tarzan and said, "I think you could do him now."

I looked around. Sally, Sam's wife, was watering her plants about a hundred feet away, up at their trailer that stays on Jim's property. A woman was talking loudly to her kids over in the house across the way. Mike was prowling the area with his collar jingling. And the hose was running.

"Uh, Jim, I think he'd rather have you do it..."

"No," he insisted, "you can."

So I went in. Tarzan looked over at me, ears twitching as he tried to make out what all the commotion was. As instructed, I moved sideways up to T and showed him my left hand. Several times he threw his head up and nervously backed away, walking quickly over to different corners of the pen, trying to see everything with his good eye.

"Jim, when I tried this yesterday it was dead silent. I don't think this is going to work – "

"He'll let you do it," he said with certainty. He had shut the hose off and was watching the attempt. "Go on – grab his flymask, right under his chin, with confidence."

I was incredulous but I carefully reached under T's chin and put my hand on the flymask, and kept it there for a moment or two. Then, when he didn't move, I sprayed some of the liquid on my hands and carefully rubbed the liquid on his muzzle. Overwhelmed, I sprayed his legs then paused before I sprayed his flanks again with the liquid. When I was done I gently stroked his neck for a minute or two, whispering to him.

And T stood there. And he let me do it.

"Well *done*, sweet thing," Jim said, beaming, as I climbed out of Tarzan's pen. I was ecstatic, and I still am. T let me do his NoFly. He trusted me. And Jim... he had known all along I was capable of doing it, even if I didn't know myself. In those brief moments he hadn't given up on me, just like he had never given up on T.

Tarzan came to the ranch four or five years ago but apparently, it was just in the last year he has really learned to trust. Jim has patience beyond anything I have ever seen; he said today that if it takes five years to heal a horse, then it will take five years. It's all in the horse's time, never ours. We can't do anything with trust except earn it.

And he's right. I'm floating right now and I'll be floating the rest of the day if not for the rest of my life. Tarzan trusted me. He trusted me.

July 4th, 2009

It's Independence Day.

That was my first thought when I woke up this morning. Today, the 4th of July, is the day to celebrate independence. We cherish and delight in our freedom so much that today, I took a moment to look around at the ranch and savor the liberty that the horses have, too.

See, not all horses are as lucky as the ones at Tierra Madre Horse Sanctuary. There are places where the horses are expected to stand in their stalls all day long, ridden occasionally, and then shoved back inside their pens while they are desperate to run or hear a kind word or, in some cases, escape a harsh blow. Well, that's not how it is at this ranch. The horses have it so well, and for that I am grateful.

Today Sam the Volunteer was here so I didn't have much to do. I did the NoFly as usual and mixed some more up for tomorrow. Jim, I learned, is a songwriter like I am, and he played me a few of his songs when everything was done. They were pretty good, and his voice is unlike anyone else's out there. It is straight from the soul; I could tell that he has poured himself into his work. Someday I'd like to play the guitar like he does.

There is not one day that goes by at the ranch where nothing short of incredible occurs. Whether it is a horse galloping through the arena or standing unusually still for me to do NoFly when they usually run away or one of the kids raising his head and penetrating me with all-seeing eyes, magic happens every day.

Tarzan let me do his NoFly again. I climbed into his big pen and, just as he did yesterday, he stood a little anxiously but he stood still. Jim said that it was routine that made him comfortable, so I made sure to put my hand on his flymask so he knew what I was doing. I stood patting him for a while after that, pride for T swelling inside of me.

Today when I went to Chance, he seemed much calmer with me than usual. There were a few girls were here today grooming horses, and Sam was filling waters right up next to him so Chance was pretty agitated from all the noise. When I walked up to him, though, his ears pricked forward slightly and the tension in the air seemed to drop a little bit. I gave him hay from my hands then threw a bunch in his feed trough.

Now, whenever anyone puts food in Chance's bucket he dives right for it. Before he had arrived at the ranch, he apparently had only been fed every three or four days at the place where he had lived. So whenever he is fed here at Tierra Madre, he eats every bite out of his trough for fear of someone taking it away or because he's worried he won't get fed again soon enough. Today, though, he glanced at the food that I had placed in his feeder, and then turned back to me. And he put his head through the bars again and started nibbling at the air.

He wanted me to feed him.

Me.

I stood there for several more minutes, giving him more hay and leaves, and I did something I had avoided doing for as long as I've known that beautiful horse since it tended to make him nervous: I looked straight into his eyes.

I saw no anger, no confusion, nothing upsetting within them. He just looked at me, something like a challenge reflected in his eyes, as though he expected me to grab a branch and start beating him with it. When I did nothing but speak to him softly, his ears went up again, one of them flickering back and forth with my words. He was listening to me.

Sam asked if I would take over filling his water so he could move on with his tasks (standing waiting for water buckets to fills is tedious), so as I stood there with the hose I talked to Chance like I would talk to a normal person. And he watched me, occasionally dipping his head down to sniff the ground for hay, but always raising his eyes to me in something close to wonder. I got closer to him and saw his eyelashes were wet from water or sweat, or maybe a little of both. For a moment I imagined that he had been crying, that he had, for a moment, shown that he was vulnerable, that he was trying his hardest to learn to trust again. And in that instant I wanted to cry with him, too.

From the moment I saw Chance I knew there was something incredibly special about him. After everything was done for the morning and I was driving away, I looked over (he is closest to the gate) and saw him eating his lunch contentedly. I wanted to park my car right then and there and run back to him.

I told Sam the Volunteer that I wanted to ride him. He laughed hysterically.

"Well, first you have to pat him without him ripping your hand off," he said. "He doesn't let anyone other than Jim touch him for more than a split second, let alone let someone put a saddle on him."

"I know," I said. "But I am going to ride that horse."

"That would be suicide."

"I'm going to ride him," I repeated. I couldn't explain myself, couldn't explain what I felt, other than to add, "Someday."

Sam smiled supportively even as he shook his head. But whenever I look at Chance and feel the tension in the air evaporate slowly, day by day, I always imagine what it would be like for him and me to go places. I always imagine being so mentally connected that there are no barriers between our minds, so that together we can heal the wounds that no one else can see. I'll ride him someday. I have my heart set on it.

It's Independence Day. Here is for all of those horses who are as wild and free as our forefathers were, and for the ones, Chance and Tarzan especially, who are learning to be independent once again.

July 5, 2009

Well, Sam the Volunteer pulled a no-show today so I had to do some of the mucking before I did NoFly. Jim was going to let me ride Akira today but there was too much to be done and everything was out of whack anyway. Poor Heighten was sweaty and acting up this morning and Suzie almost coliced the other day and she's still recovering... I have to admit I was bitterly disappointed but I kept my mouth shut.

But disappointment will be short-lived, I think. I've gotten so used to being disappointed throughout my life that I've learned to accept when things don't turn out how everyone promised they would. Like when Sam the Volunteer didn't show today when he said he would. I shrugged and told Jim it was okay but he shook his head, insisting that it wasn't. I know I'll always accept the way situations play out when I can't do anything about them, but at the same time, I'm going to try to distinguish the people who will promise things only to not follow through and the ones that will promise and stick to their vows.

Jim is one of those who promises and means it.

I'll ride tomorrow.

I had to work a little harder to get to Tarzan today, but he stood and let me do his NoFly once I had reached his head and could grab his flymask. He's coming along. Chance was a little agitated today because there was a sweet girl here that he's unfamiliar with, but he took his leaves and watched me go when I left after his NoFly was done. Progress is being made, and in that regard, there will never be a disappointment. I am sure of that.

July 6, 2009

I have had a great awakening. In other words, a powerful fact has crept into my mind and it will not go away no matter what:

I am incredibly ignorant when it comes to horses.

This morning I got to ride Akira, the sweet but tough-as-nails paint horse Jim uses for lessons. And underneath the pure joy of being able to truly ride again was the difficulty of trying to do everything right.

My mind this morning was a mess. "Okay, heels down, legs straight, elbows in, head high, shoulders square, pull the reins in, pull them harder when she doesn't walk, turn and shift weight when I want to turn here, bump her side with my leg there, look where I want to go, focus so she will, too...."

"Because that's what riding is really all about," said Jim today. It's about having fun, about having the rider and horse's minds molding together and becoming one. Flawless riding in the show ring is possible because of control and barely-there signals, but here at the ranch riding is a little more personal. I hope I'll ride like a champion someday but for now, just feeling the weight of a happy horse beneath me and flying around the arena at a trot is enough. (Jim wouldn't let me trot until I had mastered the "go-there" technique, where I focus on points around the arena and make Akira go to them, at a walk.)

My legs felt like water when I dismounted but I went around doing NoFly anyway, filled with the familiar happiness only riding can bring. When I came to Chance I gave him some hay and his leaves as usual and – here's the incredible thing – he stood for me. He shifted a little bit and followed me very carefully with his eyes but he let me spray the liquid all over him without moving all over the place as he usually does. I still can't go into his stall but he was much less nervous today, so maybe I will be able to soon.

When I came to Tarzan, he, too, stayed in one place. I walked carefully around his pen as I always do before stepping over to him sideways with my left hand out, and he didn't move an inch the whole time. He didn't flinch or shift his weight or anything as I held onto his flymask and sprayed him with the repellant. I stood there for a minute or two after I was done, stroking his neck.

Pride, unbridled, absolute pride for T, nearly swept me off my feet. I was floating the rest of the day. I was so proud of T for having so much faith when it had been beaten out of him before, for trusting me with his life as far as he's concerned.

It feels easier to trust in myself now, now that I've seen these abused and brave horses look at me through worried eyes before lowering their defenses and letting me reach out to them. If they can trust me, *I* can trust me.

Solo, Kiss, and Ted got their shoes done today, and after Rob had left Jim and Sam and I sat talking about fundraising. How to raise money for the ranch is one of the biggest topics that we dig into (the others including the horses, events on the news, or recent events in horseracing or showing). We were thinking about pulling off a fair that would have people coming from all around to play games, eat food, and, of course, see the horses. We'll see what we can do.

July 7, 2009

Is it July seventh already? Where is the summer going?

Well, anyway, when I got to the ranch all the feeding was done, so I mucked the barn and did NoFly as per usual. Chance stood wonderfully but Tarzan was a little fidgety, but in the end he stood while I put the liquid over his muzzle and sprayed it on his legs. I patted his neck and gave him a big kiss before leaving. I noticed that he seems to be all right whenever I'm talking to him outside of his pen. Before, if I were on his blind side, he would jump and run to the end of his pen whenever he heard me coming. But now he just turns his head to make doubly sure it's me, then twitches his shoulders in something close to a shrug and carries on.

Patience + time = progress. Oh, and add some trust into that equation, too.

A bookkeeper named Sam (too many Sams!) came to talk to Jim and Sally today. I stood in the tack room door listening to most of the conversation but it wasn't too interesting.

I have a list of things to get at the store today when I go into work at the grocery store. I won't be going to the ranch tomorrow and that thought made me quite sad when I was walking to my car to leave. I have to say, this ranch has fueled my obsession for horses rather than quenched it. I'm reading everything I can get my hands on and watching races, shows, you name it. I'm still against any type of control that isn't necessary (dressage is maybe okay) or events that can potentially hurt the horse (i.e. barrel racing), but there are times when I imagine being in a show ring or riding a racehorse to victory...

I've fallen too far to get back up again, I think, or risen too much to go back down, whichever sounds better. But I'm enjoying life much more down/up here than I would if I were stuck in reality.

July 9, 2009

It wasn't so hot today, thankfully. That, or maybe I'm just getting used to it.

A couple of updates...

Jim got a sprinkler for the horses. When he turns it on it goes from side to side slowly, so M'Stor and the horses out in the field can get as wet as they please. I had more fun with it than the horses did, I think. I kept running through it and laughing so much M'Stor looked at me as if I'd gone insane and Min let out a long snort from his and Charlie's pen at the start of the "hallway". But they were amused.

Chance was really uneasy as I tried to get through Little D's door but after I held the back of my hand to him and talked soothingly for a minute or so he calmed down. Because I never talk about him I think it needs to be said that I've officially fallen head over heels in love with his neighbor RustyBob. He is the cutest, sweetest little thing on four legs. He whickers when I come near or when I'm bringing him food and his nose – the cutest nose on the face of the earth as far as I'm concerned – twitches happily. Last week I remember brushing mud from his face and he just stood there, savoring the brush strokes, and now whenever I reach for his face he holds it out to me proudly. He is my little love. I just hope that Chance can see how I throw my arms around RustyBob and how happy that makes him.

I let Akira and Mr. Steve Vai out into the arena today, and when they were done galloping and playing around, CharlieHorse got a turn. That little old horse just rolled like his life depended on it, and it made my whole day, just watching him shake himself happily and trot around like a new foal. He's a sweetheart.

Tarzan seemed to have much more confidence in me today when I stepped into his pen to do his NoFly. He stood quietly as I patted him and even let me give him a kiss when we were done. And later, when I came back to say goodbye, he ate a few treats out of my hands. He was a little tentative to step near me, but he did eventually. And he did something amazing as I turned away: he whinnied his thanks.

This is a horse that's as silent as the grave. I had never heard a sound from him before and yet there he was, neighing softly, as though a low rumble was coming from his throat. I stood there, speechless, before Slayer nibbled at my back pocket and pushed me back into reality.

T whinnied to me. Now that was incredible.

I did something I had never really done before today: I went to each individual stall and said goodbye to all of the horses before I left. Most of them were eating, but I managed to kiss RustyBob's nose a couple times and give my little brother Hudson a brief head scratch (he loves those). Those horses have worked miracles on me. They really have.

July 10, 2009

I led Chance out to the arena today.

Granted, I was nervous – no, scared – no, I'd say half thrilled and half absolutely terrified; he was jumping around with his ears pinned to his head and snapping at me every now and then and multiple times I saw my life flash before my eyes... but I led him.

And Jim said I did a good job. He said Chance made everyone nervous, and not to worry. I just hope someday I can be just as fearless with horses as he is. Either way, when I went back to get one very happy RustyBob I felt a little better. That sweet boy is the love of my life.

I only stayed two hours because I have work. But I stuck around to do everyone's NoFly. Tarzan was even calmer with me, and John and Guess even let me do their faces.

When I arrived in the morning, Jim told me that he saw something "behind my eyes," when I told him I was doing well. After resisting his concern for a while, I gave in and told him about some of the stresses life has thrown at me lately. I wasn't sure if I felt better or worse when I left. I'm still not sure, overall, if it was a wise thing to do, but I think that if I can't trust Jim, this man who has healed bones and hearts, someone who understands life a little more than the rest of us do, I can't trust anyone. And anyway, a little weight is gone from my chest.

July 12, 2009

Today I got to ride Akira again. We did well, Jim said; we did some corner exercises that focused on weight shifting rather than using reins. My legs hurt but I had fun. Again I was astounded at Jim's ability to read me like a book; he said I looked like I wanted to say something when I, indeed, had been wondering when I would be able to lope.

It was so hot today. To complicate things, the NoFly spray bottle was not working so I had to use my hands after I had ridden for an hour or so. I could barely walk to my car when eleven o'clock rolled around. Not that we are concerned about time at the ranch. Volunteering is over when everything is done.

Oh, and Mistah Lee and I went for a walk today. He stopped to talk to Chance for a few minutes and I stood watching them silently, wishing I knew how to communicate to Chance so the anger would melt from his face. Mistah Lee sniffed him and he sniffed back, beautiful face solemn and curious.

We'll get there someday, Chance. I know we will.

July 14, 2009

Today I almost passed out at least twice, I'm sure of it. It's about 115 by lunchtime, and that's in the shade. It was so hot that I had to sit down every once in a while, feeling a little ashamed even as I did so since Jim and Sam seemed fine.

Let's see... it was a bit of an emotional day for me. I broke down and cried to Jim for a little while after he told me he knew something was wrong. The horses helped me, too; as I mucked out Ted's stall he was more forceful in his nuzzling. I swear whenever I come to the ranch and am sad, nobody there lets me leave without having made me feel at least a little better.

I did the NoFly for everybody and helped with the waters. Chance's ears were pricked up most of the time. Tarzan stood perfectly still and let me kiss his neck.

I'm so exhausted, too exhausted to write. I'm just glad that everyone there understands.

July 16, 2009

Today wasn't nearly as hot as other days, but it was still very, very warm. But the heat wasn't so much of an issue as something else that happened today. Dr. Rollins came for John and Mr. Steve Vai. John has an abscess (a very deep one) and Mr. Steve Vai has – to our horror – what we discovered in Little D just the other day: laminitis.

When Little D's laminitis was discovered several days ago, I really didn't understand the seriousness of it, didn't think about writing it down. But now that it's been explained as the number two killer of all horses, I'm concerned. Little D's condition, however, is nothing compared to Mr. Steve Vai's. I'm scared for him. I hope that sweet, shy, artistic baby boy will be okay.

I did most of the waters after I mucked out the barn and did the NoFly; time went very slowly but it was worth it as always. When I was doing Tarzan's NoFly he was much calmer and more willing to let me pat him; his muzzle still trembles when I touch it but he is doing so much better. Now, if I talk to him as I approach, he doesn't freak out if I walk up between his and Slayer's pen on his blind side.

Hmm... I noticed that these log entries are getting shorter and shorter. When I work there are always these beautiful little moments I could go on about forever in writing, but I either forget them or am too tired to write about them when I get home now.

Maybe cutting back will help me a little bit. I already have my hundred hours, anyway.

July 18, 2009

Well, Sam the Volunteer didn't show up again today as I had hoped. I was pretty proud of myself today though; today I was ridiculously fast. I put together the morning feed (most of it), helped do the actual feeding, mucked three stalls, did all the NoFly, and did the entire field side water-wise (that's about eleven or twelve huge things of water) in about two hours.

I gave Tarzan some treats today. He didn't come get them out of my hand, so I left them on the ground near him. He wants to trust me, I know it. He just can't do it yet. But he's progressing. I told him today he's one of the bravest horses I know. And he is. He spooked a little bit today when I did his NoFly but he stood still for me after I calmed him, trembling slightly, but trusting me to do my job correctly.

Good, T.

I had the weirdest feeling today as I was filling John's water, a feeling that I was completely, utterly alone in the world with no one but the horses surrounding me. I felt like I was the only two-legged on the planet, and it was my job, my duty, to care for the horses because no one else would. It was strange... and for someone who has wanted nothing more than to be alone in the world for a good two and a half years, I'm not sure I liked it very much.

Sam led Chance to the arena today and that horse was, in Sam's words, "the perfect gentleman." And he was. Chance walked quietly to the arena and stood patiently as Sam undid his halter, then trotted off, waiting until Sam got out of the arena to go wild. My heart burned with jealousy. Oh, someday I hope Chance will do that for me... though Sam did say he was surprised.

July 19, 2009

When I saw Sam the Volunteer's car this morning I was insanely happy because him being at the ranch meant less work for me. So I only did the NoFly. Then I followed Jim and Sam around as they put bleach and water on the horses' hooves so bacteria wouldn't get inside and cause abscesses. The heat finally got to me, though, and I blacked out for a minute or two. Jim shut me in the house (air conditioned!) until I was better.

Tarzan ate right out of my hands today. He was a bit nervous, but he did it. And Chance took some leaves as usual. Oh, and everybody in the field (except Jericho and Venture, who wouldn't move) got treats today as well as everyone from Min and Charlie to T.

I always write first thing when I walk in, so I'm always exhausted. I can't think of what else to write for now, other than the fact that I can't wait until this heat goes away. 120 degrees is not working for me and it's not working for the horses either. From colic to laminitis, we've really got to watch out for those kids until September.

July 20, 2009

Mr. Steve Vai got his feet done today. Jim and Sam gallantly sawed some of the hoof off his front feet and fit him into the most adorable little booties so his feet would stay cushioned (I joked that Vai was sporting sketchers). His laminitis is getting worse; Little D has her little feet wrapped up like he does but it's Mr. Steve Vai that everyone is worried about. I'm sure he'll be fine, but for now we have to take extra care of his feet.

By the way, laminitis is a hoof disease. It strikes horses like cancer strikes humans, and if not treated correctly, it's fatal. See, the coffin bone – which is the nearest bone to the hooves in both front feet – begins to rotate and sink so that there is danger of it crashing through the front hooves. Needless to say, it is excruciatingly painful for the horse. It is also impossible for them to walk, let alone stand. And if horses cannot stand on their own feet, they can't fend for themselves. Not to mention if their bones start falling apart, chances of survival are zilch. I'm hoping those two horses will be all right.

I did the entire morning feed by myself. Then I mucked out the barn and did the NoFly. When I was doing little Rusty's I noticed he seemed a little short of breath and was pretty fidgety. His eyes were agitated, and he was gazing at the ground in something close to desperation. I almost started crying right there and then, looking at my baby struggling to keep himself upright. I ran for Jim and he came to check him out. It turns out that Rusty's fine but a little heat exhausted. We got him hosed down, and I think it might have helped a little bit.

Why can't the heat leave these horses alone?

Tarzan was perfect for me today. When I left, I told him that there were times I didn't know why I came here so much, to work and exhaust myself in the hot sun, but when I looked at him, I remembered. And I knew he understood. I knew it.

July 22, 2009

I stopped by the ranch around five o'clock this afternoon to check on Jim and the horses. Apparently Solo coliced last night and I had to make sure he was okay. I talked to Jim for a while – poor guy, he only got about an hour of sleep last night – and he told me all was fine.

I had to park outside the gate because it was locked, so I went down the line of stalls that begins with Guess and ends with Chance towards the little pathway that led to the gate, where my car was parked. I said goodbye to each of the horses, from Guess and Bella and Jani to Heighten and Hudson, to poor Mr. Steve Vai and little Akira and Mistah Lee. Then I went back between

RustyBob and Little D (it was so cute, RustyBob kept whickering for me when I left) before I got to Chance.

I gave him a couple handfuls of leaves and talked to him gently; his ears were back and he tossed his head a little bit so I turned to go. As I started away from his stall, headed toward the path, out of the corner of my eye I saw him following me from inside his pen.

I was astonished. I turned around, halfway towards the path, to see Chance at the corner of his pen, ears forward, eyes bright and attentive, looking at me.

I swear heaven and earth moved as we stood there, facing each other, understanding for each other running through both of us. And I moved forward again with my hand outstretched. He sniffed it carefully and his ears stayed perked forward, but I pulled it back, somehow knowing that Chance would trust me more if I patted him on his time. And sure enough, as I walked away again, I looked back every few steps to see that beautiful horse standing still, eyes on me, watching me go.

Watching me go. Me.

The day we met he pinned his ears back and glared and snorted at me and lunged at me if I got too close.

And now...

Beyond words.

That is where I'm at right now.

July 26, 2009

Today there was a festival at the ranch. Well, that's what it felt like, anyway.

In addition to Jim and Sam, there was Sam the Volunteer and his friend Patricia and Joy's sister Christy. By the time I got there, all the stalls were mucked and Sam the Volunteer and Patricia were starting on the waters.

I went on a walk with Mistah Lee then brushed Little D all over. That girl loves to love and be loved. She put her head against my arm and held it there when I brushed her face, nibbling me gently in near gratitude for showing her attention. Laminitis is costing her her happiness, and it's important she gets as much love as she can receive. RustyBob, of course, whickered at me until I went over to say hello.

Christy was brushing Akira and she said she had never seen Chance so calm with anyone else besides Jim or Sam. Apparently he took a snap at her when she tried to get through RustyBob's door earlier.

"He's just used to me," I told her but my heart was swelling. I told her and Patricia both that Chance was my favorite and was amused by their stunned expressions. Patricia had said all the horses were nice except "that yellow one in the corner."

I love every horse in that place so much; they're more like my close friends now than anything else. But every time I look at

Chance I somehow see a piece of me reflected in his eyes. I want to understand his every thought and I want him to know mine.

Call me crazy, but it's almost like we've both been waiting for someone to share our secrets with, but neither of us is quite ready yet. But it will happen. Chance has as many as what he stands for: chances.

July 27, 2009

It's hard to believe that July is going to be over in four days. It seems like only yesterday I was thinking I had almost two months of summer left to go.

In less than a month, I'm not going to be able to come to the ranch in the mornings like I've been doing. I'm going to miss that. The ranch has been a sanctuary for me as much as the horses.

Anyway, Charlie, Jani, and Hudson got their shoes done today. As far as what I did goes, I worked pretty hard today, I think. I helped feed, brought Sweet Boy and Sedona in from the arena (they go out every morning) mucked the barn, did the NoFly, did all the waters on the field side, and helped fill the ones on the other side of the ranch. And between all of that I spent time with RustyBob, gave Chance his usual leaves (and walked through RustyBob's door without Chance rushing at me!), talked to T for a while, sprayed down M'Stor with the hose, got in a fight with Solo, soothed Rusty when the clanging of the farrier's tools made him nervous (he nailed me in the elbow with a hoof as he panicked; he was instantly forgiven as he is my baby), tried to convince Kiss I wasn't going to intimidate him like the rest of the herd does, gave Suzie Q her bran mash and stood with her while she ate it, let Min out of the "cage" part of his stall, gave Jani a good neck scratch, bullied Hudson into returning to his stall, pampered Little D because she needs all the love we can give her, convinced John to let me do his NoFly, made up with Solo, helped return Jericho and Venture to the field when they had had their run in the arena, and hung out with my knight in shining armor, Slayer, for a while.

I never realized how much I do during a day until I try to write it all down. But I love every minute of it.

I'll have to stop by the ranch every morning before I head off to school when it begins again. I don't know how I'm going to survive any other way.

July 29, 2009

I'm so glad I went to the ranch today.

For reasons irrelevant to the ranch, I was upset and rather sad as I worked this morning, and it doesn't help that I sprained my ankle last Sunday and it's getting worse. But as usual, the horses and Jim helped me feel better.

Ted gave me horse hugs as I cleaned his stall. John and Solo messed around and made me laugh. Suze was a perfect angel when I gave her her bran mash. RustyBob whickered when I came to do his NoFly and rubbed his face against me. Kiss stood still and let me throw my arms around him and scratch his cheek to get the dirt off it. And when I sat down to rest my foot the first time (I had to rest a couple of times today) Jim got an icepack out from his freezer and wrapped it around my ankle like I was his own daughter, and he told me not to get up until it felt better. For a few moments there I had the chance to be spoiled, and I loved it.

Little D and Mr. Steve Vai got their hooves looked at and X-Rayed; Dr. Rollins is going to call Jim tonight and tell them if their coffin bones have rotated or not. Jim, Sam, and I all had a good rant about the weather. Apparently this July is the hottest July here in history, and Jim said that the weather was hurting his kids and that's why he couldn't stand it. I don't blame him. This heat is causing laminitis and colic attacks and heavy breathing and other hoof issues and salty backs and utter misery for anyone who has to be outside.

I'm going to go wrap my foot up now. I hope it heals soon... I don't want it to be so bad that I have to be away from the horses for too long.

August 2, 2009

August is here!

Well, Sam the Volunteer was here so I did the NoFly and that's just about it, besides the usual feeding. It was great; today Chance wasn't so bothered with getting the NoFly, and even though Sam the Volunteer was filling waters on Tarzan's blind side, that brave horse let me spray his legs and put the liquid over his muzzle.

Oh, Bentley, Slayer, Kiss, and Suze all got baths today. That was fun – me, Jim, and Sam got baths, too. Rusty kept calling frantically for Slayer. He was so relieved when I brought his best friend home!

Mr. Steve Vai was lying down because of his sore legs and the heat. Sam the Volunteer moved Min's giant fan right in front of Vai's stall and put a couple of cartloads of shavings in his pen. Sam and Jim wrapped his feet again. I, exhausted and in pain beyond belief because of my ankle, sat under the tree by his stall and watched. The poor horse is a little more comfortable now, I think.

This is a bit off topic, but as I was sitting under that tree today, I kept thinking that I could stay there all day, that when school started I could even bring my homework there and be in the presence of my twenty-nine best friends. Except I think I'd sit under the tree next to Chance's stall.

It was funny, because today as I went along giving the horses bits of apples, I would bite pieces of apple off and give it to many eager, clipping lips. (Min, upon seeing I had apples, cornered me in his and Charlie's pen and I had to dart beneath the fence to avoid being attacked.) I would have never done something like that before; I would have thought it unhygienic. But nowadays, being clean and proper is not high on my to-do list. I come home smelling like horse poop. I work in the hot sun and sit with the other workers telling jokes and sharing stories afterward. I have no objection to biting food off and spitting it back out in my hands multiple times for the horses. They don't mind. They don't judge. I love those guys.

I'm more of an outdoors girl than I ever was. I think I'd live outside if I could.

August 3, 2009

My ankle has taken a turn for the worse, and so has Mr. Steve Vai. I can't pretend to understand what all is wrong but, basically, it's laminitis that is weakening him. And Jim said this morning that the shifting of bone in his front hooves could be fatal.

I keep telling myself that that sweet, innocent, special boy will be okay. He can't die... he just can't die.

This morning I put all the feed together by myself and distributed it. While walking around, I saw that there was a dead bird next to the trashcans that hold Mistah Lee's sweet feed. Jim said the bird had been drowning in Akira's water and he had gotten it out before it flapped around and died in Mistah Lee's stall.

Life is so unfair sometimes.

RustyBob tried to eat Little D's food, I yelled at him (I kissed his nose soon after and we made up), I mucked out Sweet Boy and Sedonie's stalls, and gave Suze her bran mash. And then I went home early, because of my foot. I literally cannot walk anywhere without fiery pain searing through my ankle and calf muscles.

But these are details. All things are just details to me now.

Mr. Steve Vai's life is in danger. I don't think I could bear going to the ranch every morning and not seeing his liquid eyes, not seeing him toss his slender neck and whinny for his food in anticipation of a good meal.

The doctor will be pulling up to the front gate an hour from now. I'm hoping with every fiber of my being that everything's going to be all right.

To the keeper of those horses' souls.... Don't take that horse.

Don't take that horse.

Please.

August 4, 2009

Somewhere, somewhere great and beautiful, two of Tierra Madre's horses are roaming, happy and free again as they should be.

By the time I had read the blog this morning and called Jim to confirm, by the time I was cursing my ankle that kept me from getting to the ranch to see the truth for myself, Mr. Steve Vai was gone.

And as if that weren't bad enough, as I read through the blog again and again to try and grasp what else I was reading, sobbing there at my computer, I realized that my baby Rusty had been put down, too.

Two of my best friends.

Gone.

Yesterday when the vet came to check out Mr. Steve Vai, that poor horse was pronounced doomed. His two front feet were in horrific shape: the coffin bones had shifted so much that they were in danger of pushing through to the bottom of his hoof, both hooves. Above that, the coffin bone had separated from his hoof wall in one leg. He was in terrible, terrible pain. Laminitis. It claimed the life of Dawn, Jim's favorite little mare, last year at this exact same time. And now it has taken the life of Mr. Steve Vai, one of the gentlest, most wondrous, trusting horses I have ever had the honor to know.

I have to admit I was somewhat prepared for this, knowing that his time was limited because of his condition. But the news of Rusty's death completely knocked the wind out of me.

Rusty, the horse that was two hundred and fifty pounds underweight when he first arrived at the ranch, has, no, had, been in bad shape for the last few weeks. His shoulder is – was – twisted and crooked, and his hooves were in bad shape. His spine had curved from something similar to scoliosis, and to get anywhere he has – had – to twist himself rapidly and stumble forward. He was constantly leaning on the fence in order to stand. And he would never lie down because, as Jim said in his blog this morning, Rusty knew he would never get back up.

So he was euthanized this morning, too.

And all I can think about was how, whenever I took his flymask off, Rusty would rub his head against my side gratefully, how he would lower his head to my hand and surrender his thoughts to me and let our emotions blend together. I can't stop thinking of all the times I would walk to his pen and feed him his special breakfast, how I would scratch the place between his ears and he would, for a moment, be content.

And at the same time I remember how sad he always seemed to be.

And Mr. Steve Vai! He never liked me putting NoFly on him, but after a week or two after I started volunteering there he began to trust me, began to thrust his nose in my palm and gaze at me with his beautiful eyes. I would put him out in the arena with Akira and he would gallop and buck and snort with the pure joy of being alive.

But then, the glow his eyes always held had vanished a week or so ago. He was suffering. Badly.

Well, he's happy now. He and my baby Rusty. I know that somewhere, Rusty and Mr. Steve Vai are running and playing like they never could here. And I feel selfish for wanting them back, for crying for them, because they deserve all the happiness our world couldn't offer them.

Today is a day for despair, and for triumph. Despair is inevitable, and we two-leggeds will mourn for two of our kindred spirits for a little while before we are able to move on. But the triumph is theirs. The triumph belongs to the horses, to the ones that have moved on, and to the ones who are left behind and rejoice for them.

We now have twenty-seven horses. I need to see the empty stalls before that fact sinks in. But for now, I'll mourn... and I'll try to celebrate because those two are so happy right now. I know it. I can feel it.

Good bye, Mr. Steve Vai.

Good bye, my baby Rusty.

I'll see you again someday.

And when that day comes, we'll run and we'll play and we'll all celebrate together. We'll celebrate because life is short, but in the midst of every ordeal we went through, we made the best of it.

August 11, 2009

I never realized how much those horses meant to me until we lost two of them.

It was weird to go there today in the morning; it was unnatural to be working amongst their empty stalls when I was half-expecting to hear Mr. Steve Vai whinny for his food or when I was automatically wanting to visit Rusty's stall so I could take his flymask off and he could rub his face up against me in gratitude.

My ankle, according to my doctor, had undergone a minor sprain, but I had to stay off of it for at least seven or eight days. This past week, however, I've been sneaking over to see Jim and the horses whenever I could. I couldn't work, and I couldn't really walk let alone stand, but I needed to see the empty stalls. I felt selfish for mourning two of my friends, for simply lying in my bed gazing at pictures I took of them ages ago while the rest of the world moved on. Most of all I couldn't stand the denial in my mind.

Slayer, Rusty's best friend, turned his head to study me the first time I stopped by one afternoon. Wordlessly, effortlessly, we stood looking at one another and communicating as emotions danced between our minds, and in a single movement Slayer turned and looked at Rusty's stall that lay empty next to him. I swear something in my heart cracked. I leaned up against him and rested my head against his neck.

"It'll be okay, Lex, really. Just cry now. You'll feel better, I promise."

"I can't, Slayer. I've cried so much already."

As we were speaking silently, Tarzan, from across the little path between his stall and Slayer's and Rusty's pens, walked up to the railing and put his nose against the gate, ears perked upwards and head held to my eye level. I walked toward him and slowly offered my hand to him in astonishment… and he took a step forward and nibbled it gently.

Tarzan.

And he did that every day I stopped by the ranch to say hi. Such trust, such utter bravery on his part… I was, and still am, speechless. I am still trying to put into words the courage he gave to me that day and every day since. This horse that had been abused beyond comprehension was seemingly reaching out to me, a mere two-legged that knew nothing about death and mourning and moving on. Tarzan gave me so much with that courageous gesture. And when I had smiled and wordlessly, tearfully thanked him, he contentedly went back to his grass, and Slayer stood patiently while I rested my head against him again, nuzzling the back of my neck until I kissed him and left.

Today was my first day back as a volunteer, and even after going to the ranch in the afternoons all last week when I could, everything took some getting used to. It was odd heading out to the field with only one bucket – John's – as I had always carried Rusty's on my other arm. And not seeing Mr. Steve Vai pawing at the ground and tossing his slender head in anticipation of his own grain caught me a bit off guard.

Luckily for me I had something, or someone, to help me take my mind off of Rusty and Mr. Steve Vai; a new volunteer about my age came today and she shadowed me the whole morning so she would get to know everybody. Her name is Abby, and the horses took to her pretty well. I watched their reactions carefully and when I saw that they were satisfied, I decided I could trust her.

It was wonderful, though, to tell her about my twenty-nine – twenty-seven – best friends. How they came here, what their personalities were like, games and antics they did. I told her about Rusty and Mr. Steve Vai as well. If Abby grew tired of hearing me go on about those two she didn't show it, but I think I would have been exasperated after long.

"Rusty used to lean right there, see? He couldn't really stand straight so he would always lean..."

"Oh, and whenever I came back through here with the grain I always had to give Mr. Steve Vai one more handful, along with Hudson. Those two were like brothers."

"Rusty hated his flymask, you know. He was always so grateful when I took it off."

"It was really funny to hear Mr. Steve Vai calling for Akira whenever I rode her; he really loved that little girl..."

Even with my constant dialogue about the horses we got along well; Abby helped me muck out the barn and followed me as I did the NoFly. We took Mistah Lee for a walk as we chatted. As we walked by Chance's stall she asked if I had a favorite horse. (She's taken to Charlie, I think, and I can tell that Charlie really likes her.) I smiled and nodded to Chance, saying, "Yes, and there he is," Abby looked surprised but I talked about him as we walked on, and I think in the end she understood why he's stolen a piece of me that no one could ever give back. And as we kept walking with Mistah Lee, Chance stood in the corner of his stall, eyes on us, watching us leave.

Oh, and we gave CharlieHorse a bath today, too. That boy is one of the most precious living creatures I've ever met. He did not like getting wet and he would twist around as Abby tried to hose him down, but he listened as I soothed him and rubbed his nose, his ears twitching and nostrils quivering. It wasn't too hot today since it was overcast, but it was still warm and I think the water felt good to him after a while. When I put him back in his stall he kind of shrugged and made a beeline for his grain bucket to see if anyone had filled it.

He's my sweetheart.

Just like Rusty was.

I fell asleep last night imagining Rusty running across a big prairie, hooves perfect and shoulder intact and back leg functioning and bedsores gone and spine straightened and a good hundred pounds back on him and his eyes bright and his head held high. And I swore I felt him pressing his head against my chest.

He's so happy now. He and Mr. Steve Vai are.

And that is something all of the horses knew the instant those two took their last breaths. The twenty-seven kids at the ranch knew that Rusty and Mr. Steve Vai would go on and that they would be at peace. And the horses didn't stop to mourn about it; they celebrated. They celebrated for their friends. And now I, too, am slowly beginning to celebrate. Mr. Steve Vai and my baby Rusty deserve it. They always will.

I got more than I bargained for when I first arrived at this ranch simply because of my senior project requirements. And I wouldn't trade what I've received here for anything else in the world.

August 13, 2009

When I was startled awake at 4 o'clock this morning due to the thunder and lightning, my first thought was of the horses. Some of them liked rain, some of them didn't, but I knew none of them liked the massive amounts of light and noise that came with it.

The sky was gray and the air seemed somewhat damp when I pulled up. The ground was absolutely disgusting. Mud, poop, and bits of hay mixed together everywhere in the stalls and in the field, and the rest of the ranch seemed permanently soggy. I gave Suze her bran mash as usual, mucked out the barn and did the NoFly, all while enjoying the blissfully cooler weather. I was so happy going from stall to stall, even if it meant sacrificing the cleanliness of my boots that sank in the muddy filth wherever I walked (not that they were clean to begin with).

Chance was at absolute peace today, too. I went in and out of his neighbor RustyBob's door without him reacting whatsoever. I sprayed NoFly on his legs and his face while he stood, head between the bars as he nibbled at the air for leaves. I think I gave him a quarter of a tree today. Sam led him out to the arena while I led RustyBob, and just before I left for the day, when we went to take both horses back to their stalls, Sam offered Chance's lead rope to me but I asked if he would lead him. I was still recovering from the last time I led Chance around.

Well, I'll do it someday. Sam said that I have to be confident and fearless otherwise the horse will sense it and freak out, and the last thing I want to do is make that horse afraid. And anyway, Chance is much, much calmer around Sam than he is with me by far.

Ted has a cold; he was coughing like crazy today and when I went in to muck his stall he put his head firmly between my shoulder and neck and refused to budge until I patted and kissed him soundly. He needs lots of love now that he's sick, so I gave him a good brushing before I did his NoFly. He seems to like that.

Oh, and Jim's stepdaughter and her two little kids came to visit today. The kids flocked towards me and followed me around as I showed them the horses. When we were next to Chance, I told them to draw an "imaginary line" on the ground and said that they couldn't cross that line because the horse would get mad if we did. They responded by pulling their fingers through the mud and making the line visible. The little girl, Macy, pointed to Mr. Steve Vai's stall and asked why it was empty. I said it was because the horse that had occupied it was sick and had to go away. Cooper, the little boy, loved feeding the horses; both kids laughed when the horses lowered their heads so they could pet them.

After they left, Doctor Rollins showed up to check on Moosie and Little D. I walked around taking – I kid you not – a hundred and forty pictures. I can't get enough of my friends in print. I talked to Slayer for a while then quietly walked over sat in Rusty's empty stall for a minute or two; Slayer stood there looking at me silently until I got up and patted him again.

I hope this weather lasts a couple more days. I've missed the cool air!

August 15, 2009

I got my wish: today, while hotter than Thursday, was much, much better. A little on the warm side, I think, but not so blazing hot.

Let's see... I did the morning feeding, mucked most of the barn, did the NoFly, and helped fill a couple waters. Jim's sister and stepdaughter and Macy and Cooper came again, too. I got Mike in the house (he barks at everyone he doesn't know) and the kids followed me around again. Macy and I fed everybody apples.

When I was mucking out Sedona's stall I saw Sam in Chance's pen. He had his hand out to the horse and as he seemed to be talking easily, Chance just stood there and nibbled at Sam's hand without fear.

I swear that my heart absolutely seared with jealousy. That is the horse that would nail anyone who came near him, the horse that had scared me half to death when I led him to the arena weeks ago, and here he was letting Sam actually stand in his stall and talk to him as his pen was cleaned.

I understood then.

Chance will not be nervous as long as I'm not, either.

As long as I don't startle him and talk to him gently and give him food and...

So I went confidently in and out of RustyBob's stall rather than just climbing through the fence as usual so I don't have to risk getting snapped at by Chance. And he didn't react at all. He just stood there and sniffed at the ground, raising his head every so often. But he did watch me when I was with Little D and again as I hugged and kissed RustyBob. As usual I gave him his leaves then sprayed his legs, and then I did something I haven't tried in a while: I sprayed my hands and briefly touched his nose, leaving a dab of NoFly on his face.

He just nibbled. I still can't do his whole face, but he wasn't throwing a fit after I put a few fingers on his nose for a moment or two.

And I know it was because I was fearless. At least, because I told myself I was.

Chance has come a long way in the time I've known him, or maybe I'm the one who has come a long way, instead. Honestly? I think it was both of us – both of us slowly, surely surrendering to each other.

August 17, 2009

One week from today I won't be doing the morning feeding.

One week from today I won't be bringing Sweet Boy and Sedona home from their playtime in the arena or feeding Suze her bran mash or mixing up NoFly. I'll be at school learning calculus and government and physics.

For kicks, I showed Jim my school binders this morning. I've decorated each one with pictures of all the horses at the ranch. He loved them. He didn't love the subjects I had written across them (Spanish, British Literature, etc.), saying he felt sorry for me.

It was funny, because today I learned how to mix up the electrolytes each horse gets in the afternoon. Apparently it's a proportion (four baking soda to three regular salt to one light salt) and I had to work out the math when we had twelve scoops of baking soda. It took a second for me to get back into my school mindset.

"Wait, so that's four scoops of regular salt after the twelve of baking soda?"

Jim laughed. "Calculus is gonna be hard for you, baby girl."

I tried to spend extra time with everybody today. While Moosie was getting his shoes done I was able to do Ted and CharlieHorse's NoFly as well as the whole field side (twelve horses). They're both doing much better. Ted's cough is just about gone, and CharlieHorse's summer sores have almost disappeared. Solo actually stood for about a second and a half as I snuck some NoFly onto his face, but tore off like a shot (as he always does) when I attempted to spray his legs. Suze was trying to scratch her neck on the fence so I helped her out, and she was pretty grateful, I think. After I scratched Kiss's neck, too, he nipped at my arm when I turned to leave, plainly demanding I stay.

Tarzan stood perfectly for me today; I actually took my hand off his flymask when I was done so I could pat him and kiss him for all it was worth. When Suze and Solo were getting new shoes, I snuck over to Chance to give him an apple (and of course I had to share with Little D and RustyBob, too). Then I held a very calm Solo (!) so Rob the farrier could trim his feet. We were all shocked at Solo's behavior today – he was absolutely wonderful. Normally he is what Jim and Sam affectionately refer to as a butthead.

Before I left Jim, Sam, and I sat talking under the breezeway. As usual Jim had a story or two to make us laugh, and then we started discussing the option of having other animals come to the ranch. Jim said we might be getting a pony mare soon. I said (and Sam seconded this) that we should get a pig. Jim laughed and said if it weren't for Mike he'd get a couple of chickens.

I may be able to visit the ranch in the afternoons but I'm really going to miss being there in the mornings. But I guess it won't be so bad going back to school.

August 19, 2009

Little D scared us today.

When I was doing her NoFly I noticed a little red spot on her left leg, near her ankle. I dabbed at it and I think my heart missed a beat – it was blood. But being as forgetful as I can be sometimes, I didn't think to mention it until Jim, Sam and I trotted out to her right before feeding time to work on her feet. Then and spoke up.

"I just remembered, Jim, when I was doing Little D's NoFly... well, I think she just nicked herself or something because I noticed a little bit of blood on her leg."

Jim stopped dead in his tracks. "Where on her leg?" he asked and I could hear panic in his tone. My heart jumped horribly and I remembered that Mr. Steve Vai had bled the morning before he was put down. I pointed to Little D's ankle and Jim looked at it, felt it, and concluded that it must have been a scratch because nothing felt off. Mr. Steve Vai had bled because the hoof wall had separated from his coffin bone, and Jim was concerned that the same thing might have happened to our little girl. But Little D was fine... it certainly scared us, though.

When a horse has laminitis, at least once a day his or her feet have to be wrapped up with suppression material (to support the sore parts of the hooves) and some liquid (I'm not quite sure what it's called) that helps with the healing. Little D has been doing far better than poor Mr. Steve Vai was. Her coffin bones haven't rotated much, but she's still in pain. When required to stand on her left leg earlier (her worst one), I could hear her breathing in and out in almost a death rattle. And as I stood in the midst of 110-degree weather, her uneven breathing sent chills down my spine. She was so brave, quietly standing there and trusting Jim and Sam to do their business and letting me stroke her neck and kiss her nose gently. She was in terrible pain a lot of the time but she stood, breathing in and out in that quicker-than-normal way, but not making a sound otherwise. RustyBob would not take his eyes off her the whole time. I realized just how much that horse loved Little D when he shuffled over quietly and stuck his head through the bars to touch noses with her. Little D, of course, being the demure little girl she is, refused to acknowledge him at first.

"Little D? Little D, I wish I could help you, Little D. Are you doing okay, Little D? I hope you are. Are you, Little D?"

"Well, my feet hurt a bunch, RustyBob," I heard Little D silently, patiently reply, "but I think those guys know what they're doing."

Jim called Doctor Rollins in the middle of it all to confirm that the bulbs of her feet needed to have more air, so Sam cut the wraps accordingly, Little D was hugged and kissed for all it was worth, then the three of us left her to RustyBob's care and protection. Mistah Lee, of course, who is secretly in love with Akira, glanced over at Little D every now and then to make sure she was okay, and even Chance put his head over his stall bars to check in on her.

I think she's going to be fine. It'll take a while, but she seems to be doing a tiny bit better.

Suze, on the other hand, was tubed a couple nights ago. She was sweating and pawing at the ground Monday evening and Jim took no chances. She's doing better now, though; we tried putting vinegar in her bran mash this morning since that helps with post-colic complications but she absolutely refused to touch it. I had to make a new one for her without the vinegar.

I also mucked out Sweet Boy and Sedonie's stalls and brought them in from the arena, did Moosie's stall, and then Abby arrived so she was able to do Ted and CharlieHorse's stalls.

Oh, speaking of CharlieHorse, when I was doing my part of the morning feeding (which is giving grain to the horses in the line of stalls), that precious boy trotted right up to his feed bucket and waited patiently until I got back from giving Ted his grain. He has never done that before since he doesn't get the grain the other horses get in the morning. I learned a while ago that this is because he had digestive problems a long time ago, and even though he's fine now it's always been a habit not to feed him grain at certain times of the day.

But my baby boy just waltzed right up there and looked at me expectantly, like I had always fed him along with the other horses and it was his turn to get a handful of grain.

"Oh, CharlieHorse, look at you! Baby boy, you're not supposed to get this grain right now."

"But I want it."

"You get this in the afternoons, with your supplements, remember?"

"But I want it."

"And how come you're suddenly coming up to your feed bucket, like this? I'm sorry but you don't get this grain right now, baby boy."

"But I want it."

I sighed.

"Please?"

And he looked at me with puppy-dog eyes (though here I guess it would be "foal-eyes" or something) and my heart melted. And he got a very small handful.

I told this to Solo today when I broke down from his constant staring and gave him the rest of Suze's bran mash after she was finished: when I was born, the doctors must have stamped "SUCKER" on my forehead, and only horses can read and understand it. They have expertly nestled themselves deep into my heart. They all have their own ways to tell me what they want, and their individual personalities make me give in to them so easily.

Like Jericho. A lot of the time he'll hold his head up high when I'm doing his NoFly so I can barely reach it, but after I just managed to get the liquid on his face today and was walking away, fuming, he trotted after me and started rubbing his face against my shoulder. I think he just wanted a free scratch, but it melted my irritation in a heartbeat.

Chance let me put NoFly on his nose again today. I am now able to spray his legs without fear of him charging at me from over the railing. I still don't go in his stall; he stands and lets me do it from the outside instead. After his legs I put some of the liquid on my hands and briefly swept a few fingers over his muzzle. He just nibbled. That's all he really does now. When I'm opening RustyBob's door and he thrusts his head between the bars to intercept my hands, he just looks for food. Before he used to bite. And his ears still go back, almost automatically, but they flicker forwards when I talk to him – and I talk to him more than I talk to anyone else on the ranch – and they are always, always facing front when I walk away and he's looking after me.

Every horse on that ranch has made my heart bigger, much bigger, than it had been before. But Chance has stolen it completely. Do I dare dream that maybe, just maybe, his heart is getting bigger, too?

August 21, 2009

We may be getting another horse soon! He's eleven years old and he's fresh from the racetrack. The poor guy apparently has been raced three times in the last eighteen days and the last time he was on the track he just stopped completely. He's lost the will to race, and I don't blame him.

But we all know what happens to racers that won't race that fall into the wrong hands.

Auction.

Luckily for us and for the horse whose name is Coloreado (?) his trainer or owner or someone called Jim up and asked if Tierra Madre could take him. I hope the universe sends him our way.

Anyway, when I got there the morning feeding had been done, so I mucked out the barn and gave Suze her bran mash but she wasn't in to it very much today; she's in heat and all she wants to do is be around John. Solo kept on giving me the eye so I let him have a few bites of the leftover mash. I was doing the NoFly by the time Abby came.

While I did Chance's NoFly today I noticed that while his ears were automatically pinned back every now and then, the rage was gone from his eyes. Now when I go through RustyBob's stall door he nibbles at my fingers, and I can even turn my back for a moment or two as I walk and turn to close the door. I was able to spray Chance's legs and chest because of how he was positioned, and that horse stood quietly, not twisting his head around to see what was going on or, better yet, not charging at me from behind the bars. I talked to him just as I would talk to any of the other horses as I do their NoFly ("Okay, let's do your legs. See, we'll spray so there are NO flies for Chance. And now there are NO flies for Chance. Good for Chance!") And since I was able to dab a few drops of NoFly on his nose, I reached out and stroked the top of it. Chance, his face somewhat sideways through the bars, only lifted his head in an attempt to nibble at my fingers.

He let me pat him. Not just a split second, hesitant brush of fingers, but an actual pat.

I floated the rest of the day.

Little D is doing a bit better. She didn't really want to stand on her left foot this morning but that little girl is very tolerant and so, so brave. I gave her half an apple (the other half was split between Chance and RustyBob) and she bit off from the pieces so delicately and chewed them like only a lady can.

I love that angel.

Speaking of angels, I turned our little paint mare Akira out in the arena as a sweet volunteer, Helen, was giving Mistah Lee a walk. I joined her half-way through the walk and we both laughed as Akira kept on running back in forth in front of the bars nearest to Mistah Lee, and Mistah Lee kept whinnying to her. I told Helen about their love affair, and how Mr. Steve Vai had been in love with Ms. Akira, too.

"And Heighten and Jani flirt every now and then, too, and Suze has a really special place in John's heart," I told Helen, "but I think the real lovers of the ranch are Akira and Mistah Lee."

It's cute the way these horses pair up or blend into groups. Everyone has a best friend or a sort of clique they belong in. John and Solo. Sedonie and Sweet Boy. Heighten and Hudson. Charlie and Min. Guess and Bella. Jericho and Venture. Ted and CharlieHorse. RustyBob and Little D. A while ago, Slayer and my baby Rusty.

Abby mentioned that it's easier to believe in love once you've seen the way horses love and care for one another. And she's right. Here everyone is a friend (or a worthy rival) and everyone, four-leggeds and two-leggeds alike, get along.

Three days before school. How am I going to explain to my twenty-seven friends that someone else is going to do their NoFly in the mornings from now on?

August 23, 2009

M'Stor and I had a good talk today.

I was watching the water fill up in the trough next to "the hallway which is the long space between John's gang's pasture and the other pens that house Charlie, Min, M'Stor, Slayer, and Tarzan. Since there were buckets lying around I turned one of them upside down between Slayer and M'Stor's pens and sat down next to them. Slayer gave me horse kisses then kept picking at his leftover hay, but M'Stor stuck his head through the bars and shoved his nose into my hands. He is always demanding whenever I'm around him – ears flickered back, snorting, pawing at the ground if he doesn't get his way – but I played with him for a bit anyway.

"You know," I told him as he nibbled at my shirt hem, "I think I'd rather be here, working in the hot sun with you, then go back to school tomorrow."

M'Stor continued to nip at me. He knew I just needed to keep talking.

"Mostly everyone there... they just don't get it," I said and whatever "it" I was referring to I'll never know. "Maybe I could run away. You'd let me stay in your house, wouldn't you? You wouldn't tell."

M'Stor snorted at this.

"Or I could take one of you guys and we'd ride away. Right off into the sunset, just like in the movies. And we'd go someplace where we could do whatever we want, whenever we want, and we would be free."

"You could do that, Lex," I heard M'Stor say, humoring me, "You could do it if you wanted to."

But we both knew that it wouldn't happen. One thing I've learned from the ranch is that running from problems doesn't solve them.

And school isn't a problem... just a dilemma, something that's getting in the way of me seeing my best friends every day. Either way, I'm not looking forward to it like I usually do.

When I went in to do RustyBob's NoFly, there were a few moments I spent pressing my forehead against his and wrapping my arms around his neck while he stood perfectly still. He let me close my eyes and lean up against him while I stood and wished the summer didn't have to end. So much was said during those moments, and neither of us made a sound. I realized, not for the first time, that these horses know what I'm thinking and feeling without me having to say a word.

Jim and Sam worked on building a stall right next to Guess while Sam the Volunteer mucked out stalls and did the waters. I did the morning feeding (CharlieHorse got a handful of grain again; that boy knows that he has a special place in my heart), gave Suze her bran mash, brought horses in and out of the arena, took wraps off of Little D, did the NoFly, and gave Mistah Lee his walk. We need another stall now, because a ranch friend named Suzanne wants to bring two of her horses over here for a few days (Cocoa and Sissy, they're called, and they actually used to live at the ranch).

Also, we're going to be getting the ex-racer! Coloreado will hopefully be coming to the ranch in a few days. He's going to live where Rusty used to live, next to M'Stor and behind Slayer. I can't wait to meet him, to see what his personality will be like, to see him transform from an over-worked racer to a happy and beloved member of the Tierra Madre family. Jim said that's he's going to get a new name and I'm with him on that one; "Coloreado" is just an odd name to pronounce. He's thinking about dubbing the racer "Iron Man". I like it. I've already decided his nickname could then be Steele.

When I did Chance's NoFly, he nibbled at my hands – again! – and let me rub his face with my fingers briefly. My hands stayed on the top of his muzzle for a good five seconds, a record for both of us. He's so, so much better than he was three months ago! I was almost crying with utter pride for him. Just seeing him relax around me and letting me through RustyBob's door or giving him water without him getting nervous has filled me with a happiness nothing can take away, not even the fact that this is my last day of freedom.

I suppose that now would be the perfect time to write my reflection on this summer, my reflection on these horses and their lives and how they have been completely intertwined with mine. But the only reflection I could properly describe is the one I see gazing back at me when I'm looking into their eyes.

There are no words for what I have learned in these past three months. I've been taught more about friendship and recovery and love and dignity and bravery and loss and life than I could ever write down. I drove through the ranch's gates that first day expecting to put in my hundred hours and take care of horses and learn a bit about how they are looked after while fulfilling my school assignment, but I've been given much more than that. I've been given an education no classroom could ever provide.

Life goes on. The morning after Mr. Steve Vai and Rusty died, the sun rose and everyone else woke up and went about their days. And tomorrow, when the sun rises again and I drive to school instead of to the ranch, this crazy adventure we call life will have kept on moving.

Before I left I went around, touching everyone's noses, whispering my thoughts to those horses as they whispered theirs to me. Somehow I needed to tell them that I wasn't gone for good, that I would be by for a moment or two every week if I could but that they wouldn't see me in the mornings for a while. I finally stopped by Tarzan's pen where he stood eating his hay.

"You know, something, T?" I asked and he raised his head, listening. "There were times when I first started here when I forgot why I worked so hard in the hot sun. I could have chosen a senior project that didn't involve me working outside all the time. And I forgot why I came here, T. I forgot."

T's ear twitched and he took a step closer to me. Three months ago he would never have done that.

"But I'd look at you," I whispered. "I'd look at you, T. And I'd look around at everyone here that has ever been hit, or beaten, or yelled at. I watched them snorting and rearing up and playing and living again. And you know what, T? I remembered."

It was déjà vu, telling him this. He's heard it before and now, I hope, he's starting to believe it. But he silently stood as we looked at each other; then, as though we were one creature, he stretched out his neck at the same time I held out my hand, and he sniffed at my fingers for a few seconds before going back to his hay.

And before I walked back to my car, I turned around and looked back at Rusty's empty stall. My baby is living proof that life, indeed, will go on.

The summer ends, just as it should.

Just as it should.

Autumn

August 25, 2009

Oh, Little D.

My strong, beautiful, poor Little D.

Her coffin bone has rotated seven degrees in her left foot in ten days. This last week or so she has been quieter, almost in a biting-her-lip sort of way, out of pure bravery and acceptance of her disease, keeping her pain to herself and going about life as well as she can. When I stopped by after school today to give everyone a carrot or two, I passed by her stall to talk to her for a bit. And I could see it in her eyes.

She's in agony.

But she loves the attention. That little girl needs to be loved and lives to give her love to someone she know won't shatter her trust. Lucky for her, she found Jim. He's been doing everything in his power to make her feel better, physically and emotionally, and in return she has given her heart completely over to him.

But we may be losing her. If her bone rotates any more she's doomed.

I have to admit my first thought, when I heard this from Jim's own lips today, was one of selfishness. *Not Little D*, I kept thinking as I walked up and down next to the stalls. *Not that little girl, too. Not Mr. Steve Vai and my baby Rusty and Little D...*

But I've learned something from these last few weeks.

Life is not set in stone. Things happen that no one can predict, or have a say in, or stop altogether. Death is one of those things, and we can't prevent it, nor, I have learned, let it take the only thing we have when the creatures we love have hell to pay: faith.

Little D's a strong and precious girl and the least she deserves is hope. My fingers are crossed and my mind is set: I will not give up on that little girl, not even if the worst happens. From now until the day either or us dies I'm going to have faith in something I cannot see: the fact that no matter what happens, she's going to be okay.

She doesn't deserve selfishness.

And if this is time for her to go, I'll have faith for her and her well-being until the end.

August 27, 2009

The Iron Man is here!

Since school started I've stopped by to see everyone every afternoon, to give them carrots and to pat and hug and kiss them and to tell them how much I've missed them in the mornings. Seeing the horses in the afternoons is not the same as getting down and dirty with them in the mornings, being able to go into their stalls and put NoFly on their faces and muck their stalls. Who knew I'd miss that?

Anyway, yesterday when I came by, Jim had two seconds to inform me that Iron Man had arrived before I was off and running, getting my school shoes dirty but not caring. And there in my baby Rusty's old stall stood quite possibly one of the most beautiful horses I've ever laid eyes on.

He's a racer, or I should say an ex-racer, so he has a broad back and long, long legs. He's such a dark bay he's almost black, and his eyes, so much like poor Mr. Steve Vai's, are liquid brown and innocently wondrous. Jim said that when he arrived, he was in near shock from not seeing a racetrack and being near cacti and dirt and trees and the sky. He wasn't sure what carrots and treats were, Jim said, and he was confused about sleeping under the stars. Iron Man was much calmer today than he was yesterday. I think he's getting used to not being shuffled from race to race and standing in a stall all day long until he's wanted. He nibbled at my hands and my hair and my sleeve and everything else he could get at for five or ten minutes – completely staining my uniform shirt – while I laughed and told him how happy I was to meet him.

Iron Man is such a sweet and curious boy, so much like his neighbor and my knight in shining armor, Slayer. Those two are grand old friends already. Even Tarzan, from across the little pathway, seems to hang around his front gate so he can talk to them.

And get this: T doesn't move away anymore when I walk up between the pens. Good, T.

Little D seems to be standing her ground. She's going to be x-rayed in a few days and until then we're all holding our breath. But I've spent time with her every afternoon this week, patting her and kissing her nose and telling her how much I love her. I could see in her eyes that she's accepted whatever fate the universe throws her way. She's still standing, strong and sure.

She's one of the bravest little mares in the world.

And Chance…

His ears only flicker back now when he's nibbling at my hand, and several times now he has let me rub his nose. I still can't touch his forehead simply because he's uncomfortable with it, but that's okay. Everything is all in his time.

And when I leave to go back to the gate where my car is parked outside, that boy watches me go from the corner of his stall, ears forward, eyes bright. "You're gonna leave? Well, okay, then. I'll see you later, maybe. I mean, you'll come back, right? And maybe give me some of those leaves again?"

"Of course I will. I'll be back, I promise. I love you, Chance."

"Do you? Do you really?"

"Yes, baby boy. I really do."

If this ranch could work wonders on my brother Chance so that he is beginning to trust again, so that his hatred of the world is beginning to ebb away, Iron Man's going to be living life like no other horse before long. I'm so, so happy for both of them.

August 28, 2009

It's odd going to the ranch during the afternoon feeding time rather than being there in the morning. There's less work to do in the afternoons but the mornings are so much cooler that it makes all the work (filling waters, mucking stalls, feeding, NoFly, meds) easier to do. Sam's not there for the afternoon feeding (no one is, actually) so Jim was thrilled to have a volunteer there, I think.

When I got to the ranch and had walked down the stall row and Mike had come running to greet me, Jim had already finished giving Suze her second bran mash (she gets two a day) and was just starting on the grain. Every kid gets grain with their electrolytes (the salts that make them thirsty so they drink water) and their minerals mixed with reddish salt.

When we went to give the kids in the field their alfalfa hay, none of them wanted it. They sniffed and rotated around to other piles and sniffed again, and Jim swore and wondered aloud what was wrong with it. He took it back and dumped the seemingly uneatable hay next to the poop pile and as he got new hay, I inspected a particular brown thing that was sticking out of the end of one of the piles. It was scaly, smashed, and disgusting.

"What is this?" I called over to Jim. "I don't know what that's doing there but whatever it is, I wouldn't eat it, either."

Jim came over and we worked it out of the hay. He turned it over with his boot. It was the carcass of a dead snake.

"Urgh," Jim said. "No wonder no one wanted to eat that hay."

No wonder, indeed.

When I walked around to say goodbye to the horses on the field side, I snuck a few treats past John's gang (all happily eating their snake-free alfalfa) and gave a few to M'Stor, Slayer, T, and Iron Man. Iron Man inhaled the treats I brought him yet he took them so gently from my hand. He's such a sweetheart. I'm so happy he came here to be with us. Every time I see him trotting around in his pen and playing with Slayer occasionally and looking around at the world through beautiful liquid eyes, this crazy world seems a little less hopeless.

I went into Slayer's pen for a bit to play around then ventured into Tarzan's. And you know what that horse did? He walked toward me. He actually closed the distance between us, stopping a foot or so away from my outstretched hand. And he stood there while I went and grabbed his flymask, just as he's used to, and rubbed my hands over his nose like I was putting liquid on his face. He stood as I patted and kissed him, telling him how proud I was of him, how brave he was, how much I loved him. He whinnied very softly when I left, ears flickering toward me as I softly called goodbye.

I've realized that I often talk about certain horses rather than all of them. Well, here's an update on the rest of the kids:

John, Solo, Suze, Venture, Jericho, Bentley, and Kiss – the gang – are doing well. Suze, of course, had a rough night a week or so ago when she had a minor colic attack and had to be tubed, but she's all right now. Most importantly, she's still the Queen Bee of the joint and John's main girl. John himself is still the boss, calm and sure as ever. Venture and Jericho, Venture especially, have to get baths once every week or two because when they sweat, it dries on their backs and leaves salt that irritates their skin. That happens to a lot of the horses around here, but for those boys it's particularly bad. They take it all in stride, though. Solo is Solo; in other words, he's still a lovable bully that runs the place when John's busy and makes fun of me when I'm not looking. Bentley is just one content little boy. He's happy to get his face rubbed, happy to get his food (except for the snake-infested hay from this afternoon, of course), and happy to be part of the group. I actually hid behind him when Kiss started walking toward me and aiming bites at me earlier. Kiss is still the low-man on the totem pole so whenever people come near him he gives them "love bites" to try to assume position. Love bites are what horses give to each other when they're playing; they don't hurt for a half-a-ton animal but for us scrawny two-leggeds, they can leave a mark. But he's Kiss, and I love him still. Maybe when he nipped me today he was remembering I never had the chance to give him a carrot two days ago.

Charlie and Min, the Odd Couple, are still good. Min always gets so excited over his food and being let out of his pen and lets out these adorable little whinnies to express his delight, nostrils quivering and everything. When he wants food and someone is over by the Bermuda grass, he'll stare at whoever is there intently until he doesn't seem like a miniature horse anymore due to the extremity of his gazes. And he always gets whatever he wants. Charlie, his best friend, is a bit like B: happy to be living life just the way it is and always living like a gentleman. One thing I learned about him that I don't think I wrote down is that never, under any circumstance, can anyone put a halter on him and tie the end of the lead rope to anything. He'll freak out. Charlie must have had a horrible experience that involved someone tying him to a fence and beating him. But he's happy now, as long as we steer clear of lead ropes attached to posts.

M'Stor, Slayer, T, and the Iron Man are all fine, of course. M'Stor, Slayer, and the Iron Man all seem to be getting along and Tarzan trots up to the fence to get involved in the hang-outs sometimes, too.

Sweet Boy and Sedonie always go out in the arena in the morning, and they are happy as long as they're together. When I left them today they were cleaning the muck off each other's backs contentedly. And they both love their treats. They live for their treats.

The Moose is The Moose: always stable, always wise and fearless and utterly humble. My strength through and through. Ted's cough is completely gone now; he still likes to nuzzle me and nibble at whatever part of me is available and give as much love as he can muster. And CharlieHorse is still my sweetheart. He is precious and always wondering quietly to himself about the meaning of life, so it seems. And every time he holds his nose out for me to stroke he teaches me about what he's come up with, tells me briefly about his thoughts and ideas.

Guess and Bella and Jani are the Girls, with a capital G. Guess is the clique's beautiful leader and Bella and Jani are still the sweethearts with their own minds, Bella perhaps a bit more so than Jani, who likes to be left alone. Hudson and Heighten are both stable and reliable as ever. They are so close and love to play. Heighten, of course, is in charge over on the stabled side of the ranch, while Hudson continues to happily be what we call a Galoot.

Little Miss Akira Jones and Mistah Lee are still secretly in love. Mistah Lee gets his walks whenever I'm there, and he always limps along with such a graceful elegance. When he came to the ranch he could barely stand due to the severe arthritis in his hip, and now he walks like a champ. Akira is the sassy little girl that still gets excited over her hay and whinnies when I bring Mistah Lee home. I'm still in love with that angel. She's an excellent teacher, too, when it comes to riding. I believe she's taught me more about riding than my old instructor ever did.

Little D still seems content; I went into her pen to rub her forehead and pick bits of hay from her mane and she really soaked in the attention. That little girl nibbled at my ankles like she used to and looked a bit upset when I had to go. Her feet are still really bothering her; she still can't walk that well. But she's a sweetheart and a strong one at that, and I know she's doing better now.

RustyBob, my little love, always whickers when I'm near him; his adorable little cow nose always twitches happily when I lean my face up against his and kiss his forehead. Knowing that he is always so thrilled to see me makes my day. And we could stay like that, forehead to forehead, for hours. RustyBob has always been my little cheer team, the horse that always looks me right in the eye and joyfully chirps up, "Go Lex, go! You can do it, I know you can!"

And Chance. Oh, how he is still my brother. Proud, stubborn, confused and lost sometimes, but still looking toward the horizon with blazing, determined eyes.

One last thing I've forgotten until now:

When I first went up to the Iron Man to say hello, I noticed something gray hanging from the railing all the way at the end of the pen, where the hose is. I trotted down and looked at it, and my heart twinged.

It was Rusty's flymask.

I bit my lip and blinked back tears as I held it close to me for a moment, imagining my baby rubbing his head against me and putting his nose in my hand. Then I heard a soft neigh, and I turned to see the Iron Man walking up to me curiously.

I laughed out loud, tears gone, and put the flymask back. And as I turned to pat that amazing horse, as the Iron Man began to nibble at my fingers, real, true happiness washed through me. From where, I'll never know. But either way, I think Rusty would have liked that.

August 30, 2009

When I got to the ranch this morning (yay weekend!), everything but half of the NoFly was done. Waters, stalls, meds, everything. Joy and her friend Brianna were there before me and had done mostly everything. I was stunned. I had arrived early because for some reason I had a feeling Sam the Volunteer wouldn't be there. (And he wasn't.) So I finished up the NoFly on the field side, and that was about it. I did the Iron Man's for the first time; he was a bit nervous and kept moving around a bit, but he was fine.

The girls had kept as far away from Chance as possible, so Sam and I went to clean his stall, fill his water, and do his NoFly. Sam put a pile of alfalfa in for Chance and while that horse dove into it, Sam mucked his stall while I filled his water. I was astonished when Sam took the NoFly bottle and walked right up to Chance – right in his stall! – and started to spray him.

"Come on now, a big bully horse like you, scared of fly spray?" Sam said in his gentle way when Chance started walking in circles to avoid the spray, ears pinned to his head in irritation. I stood in something very close to awe, amazed that Chance wasn't leaping at him. When Sam left I sat next to the stall, watching Chance eat and marveling at the simple courage a two-legged must have in order to go into the stall of a nearly wild animal and work calmly, let alone walk up to him and spray his face with fly spray. I'd done NoFly for Chance out of his stall thousands of times, but going in there...

I wondered if I'd ever be brave enough to do that, too.

Only one way to find out, I thought and I got up. I walked over to Chance's door and opened it. That horse kept eating contentedly, ears flickering my way but not moving otherwise. So I stepped inside the stall.

And stood there.

I felt like every one of my senses was sharpened; something like an electric current was flowing through me as I stood with my hand was on the door handle, ready to bolt and duck should he charge at me. But he didn't even raise his head. He saw me, but he kept eating.

So I backed out quietly and closed the door. I was nervous, and I didn't want to irritate him. One step at a time, I decided as I walked away. And that wasn't too bad of a start.

I hung out with RustyBob for a bit, then I went and I sat next to T's stall, facing Slayer and the Iron Man. The three of us talked silently for ten or fifteen minutes before Jim and Sam came back from the store where they had to get a car part for Jim's truck. Then I brought Kiss into the arena as Joy and Brianna left then went back to get Bentley so he could join Kiss. Other than running into Solo and Suze on the way, which caused B to panic so that he crushed my foot, (I've still got a bruise) that went well.

I mentioned Rusty's flymask to Jim, and he said it was going to go in the Hall of Fame. The Hall of Fame is a single bar hanging between the breezeway and Sedonie's stall with fly masks, halters, and lead ropes hanging off of it. They are from horses that had lived at the ranch in the past that, at one point or another, had to be returned to what Jim refers to as "The Great Herd." Dawnie's flymask is there, too, as are the items of horses that I had never known. Little Bird Sing Pretty. Winston. Mr. Bernie Rivers. Horses that were part of the Tierra Madre family and, like Mr. Steve Vai and little Rusty, had moved on.

So Jim hung Mr. Steve Vai's halter on the bar and I went to get my baby Rusty's flymask. I held it close to me as I walked down the hallway to bring it to where it belonged. John and M'Stor sniffed it out of curiosity then turned away, but I didn't want to part with it. In the end I kissed it, draped it over the bar next to Dawnie's and forced myself to walk away.

When I was leaving for the day, Chance and RustyBob were tearing around in the arena like fire. I stood watching them run together for a while before I got into my car. When I drove through the gate and turned back to latch it, I stood for another moment or two just gazing out at two of my best friends galloping and rearing and rolling and snorting for all it was worth.

I won't be here tomorrow morning, I thought to myself. And then I realized that now I know I can't look at it that way. I'll be here other days. I'll be here when I can.

But in this moment, *this* one, this is now and the best there is.

And as I locked the gate and turned my car onto the dirt road, I held that single thought as close to me as I had held Rusty's flymask earlier, smiling slightly as I drove away.

September 3, 2009

Slayer's a bit depressed, I think. Ever since Iron Man came to the ranch and moved in next to him, I think Slayer's been a little jealous of all the attention the new kid has been getting. Jim even wrote about Slayer's new, sad attitude in the blog this morning. So when I stopped by after school today I went to observe the situation myself.

It can be very hard to determine how a horse is feeling and what he or she is thinking; it has a lot to do with the energy they emit and the hidden emotions behind their eyes, emotions only horse whisperers (or horse whisperers in training, if you're counting me) can observe. But I could see it in Slayer's eyes instantly. He hadn't received as much attention as his neighbor and was very hurt.

So I stayed with him for a while, scrubbing salt off his back and talking to him gently. He didn't face me; he was watching Jim and the feed cart as all horses will do during feeding time, but he stood with his ears flickering back toward me every now and again, telling me he was listening and that he was grateful. The grieved shine in his eyes faded a bit as he lowered his head to nibble at my uniform skirt every now and then and I laughed in amusement. He put his muzzle to my hand before I left, and let me kiss his nose and throw my arms around his neck and tell him he was still my knight in shining armor.

When I stepped over to say a quick hello to Iron Man, Slayer's ears didn't go back. Instead, he trotted over to his feed bucket where Jim had finally placed his grain and electrolyte mix, eyes bright and ears fixed forward.

In the brief moment I got with him before he attacked his food, I was able to rub Iron Man's neck and he put his nose against my shoulder, lips quivering against my skin. That boy is one of the sweetest horses I've met and by far one of the most beautiful. His eyes are so much like poor Mr. Steve Vai's were: so bright and artistic and curious. Every time I look into them I see such an innocent wonder, like that of a child's, and I swear whatever wounds I carry deep inside of me in that moment mend with just one glance.

Chance would not let me anywhere near him today, but I think that was because he was hungry and was trying to figure out why I didn't have food for him. Yesterday when I went to say hello he snapped half-heartedly at my hand when I offered it to him. I was more surprised than I was afraid.

"Chance," I said softly and his ears immediately went back. "That wasn't necessary, my brother. It's just me."

"Well, you startled me! I forgot it was you for a second, seeing that you went and ditched me in the mornings and all. That's not my fault!"

"I know it's not, Chance, but it isn't mine, either. Right now I have to work around my schedule. I'm coming here when I can."

"Fine, whatever. Do you have food for me, or what?"

"No, but Jim's coming soon."

And Chance flattened his ears and turned away. But I smiled.

I told him long ago that he would have every right to keep his barriers up until he was comfortable with letting them down. Just as Jim did when Chance first arrived at the ranch, I told him to not lower his defenses until he was ready, and that if he needs to rush at me or snap his teeth together and pin his ears back to feel safe every now and again, that's fine with me. I hope he knows that.

It's all on his time.

September 4, 2009

Today when I stopped by after school to say hello to everyone, the kids were all eating lunch and weren't too interested in me. Everyone but Little D.

As I was walking back to my car she was standing silently next to her pile of hay, looking off absentmindedly into the distance while everyone else around her chowed down. I blew a kiss to her as she was too far away for me to reach, then proceeded to walk back toward the gate and to my car.

But something pulled me back. When I turned around on the little pathway and glanced back down the row of horses, everyone – Chance, RustyBob, Mistah Lee and the rest of them – had their heads down as they consumed their meals. But Little D's head was raised, and she was looking right at me.

And that's all it took.

I ran back to her and climbed through the bars of her stall door and threw my arms around her. And for the next ten minutes or so I rubbed her neck and kissed her nose and patted her beautiful little face and told her how precious she was. She blinked happily as I murmured encouragement, looking off into the distance but gently pushing her nose to my hand if I stopped patting her. In those moments that little girl needed to hear that she was brave, that she was strong and courageous and patient and that she was loved beyond anything else in the world. She needed to hear that she was going to be all right and make it through laminitis no matter what. And I held back none of it.

"You're a fighter," I told her as she closed her eyes and soaked in the attention with utter contentment, "and you're going to be just fine. Keep fighting, Little D. Don't give up, don't give in. Not now, not ever."

"I'm trying, Lex, I really am. But it's hard sometimes."

"I know it is, angel. But every day you refuse to give in you'll be one day closer to being healed for good. And that's what we want for you, Little D. That's what you deserve."

Three or four days ago, Dr. Rollins came to x-ray her and Jim, shaking his head and rubbing his eyes as he told me how the appointment had gone, said he feared the worst. Jim said the doc was going to call back later that evening and if Little D's results showed that her coffin bones had rotated any further... well, that would be it for her. No question. One more degree of rotation in either leg and they would have to do the right thing by letting her join the Great Herd.

Jim resigned himself to the fact that he was going to hear bad news, and I, remembering my promise to be strong for Little D no matter what, prepared to hear that she was going to die, that it was her time, that she was suffering too much and she was going to have to be euthanized. Laminitis had killed Mr. Steve Vai. Now it was going to take our little angel away from us.

But when the doctor called Jim that day after I had left, he said, voice thick with astonishment, that Little D had clung onto life with every ounce of strength she could muster.

She hadn't rotated. Not one bit. Not a single degree.

Recovery will be a long, painful road for our Diamond, and for Jim, too, as he's going to be paying for medical expenses and continuing to take care of her as he always has. But if Little D is the mare I've seen her to be, she's going to pull through.

She'll do it with her head held high.

When I had given her one last pat and told her I loved her and started to head back to my car, Little D turned from the spot in the distance she had been gazing at to look after me. I turned around again and our eyes met for a moment or two before she shook her head and finally lowered her head to eat the Bermuda grass sitting in front of her.

And the next moment was incredible, because I felt her inner strength wash through me as I understood that if the time for her to leave us really was approaching, she was not going to go out without a fight.

You show us all, Little D. Don't give up and don't give in.

Not now, not ever.

September 6, 2009

It's always interesting to see the horses' reactions whenever I come in the mornings to work with them after being away all week. Today when I showed up at 7:30, I got some funny looks before everyone settled back into summer mode.

Good, everybody.

After I gave Suze her bran mash I did the NoFly, and that took me almost an hour and a half because I took care to spend as much time with everyone as I could. Sweet Boy and Sedona get their NoFly when they're brought in from the arena, so I moved to Moosie and Ted who were eating and flicked their ears back out of politeness but were more interested in picking up bits of hay from their stall floors.

So I hung out with CharlieHorse, who nuzzled me and let me baby him for a while. When I left he glanced over his shoulder, shrugged, and went back to his thinking. My little baby boy. He knows he's got a lock on my heart and that there is no key.

Guess, as per usual, didn't like getting liquid all over her face so we played for a bit, me running one way, her running another, and me finally meeting her at her water bucket where she stood innocently, ears twitching and laughter in her eyes. She's got a mind of her own, and I love her for that.

When I moved onto Bella, I realized with a small start that I have never really spent a lot of time with her in the past or even patted her more than was necessary when I did her NoFly. I felt tremendously guilty. So I stayed with her for a long time, rubbing her neck and massaging her nose and forehead. She stood still and watched me as I talked to her. And when I looked in her eyes and saw happiness there, I knew my previous lack of attention was forgiven.

Bella is one of the most beautiful mares at the ranch – probably in the whole world, as far as I'm concerned. The girls are all breathtaking in their own ways, but just looking at Bella really knocks the wind out of me. During those moments I spent with her today, I felt strangely reassured, as though she was convincing me that everyone deserved forgiveness, that there was true beauty still left in the world. She is an angel. A pure, unbridled, absolute and loving angel. I'm so glad I spent time with her today, and I think she was, too. She walked me to her gate when I had to leave and gently shoved her nose through the bars in farewell when I walked on to Jani.

Jani, who's been worked hard all her life and likes to keep to herself now that she's retired, doesn't let people in unless she trusts them with all of her heart and soul. And I think she's letting down her walls bit by bit. I scratched her neck when her NoFly was done and I got her to dance (when the right spot on her neck is scratched she raises her head and moves it back and forth and it's adorable). And when I left she glanced back at me and lowered her head in something very much like a nod, then turned away as I walked over to Heighten.

Heighten was looking off into the distance at something beyond the Tierra Madre gates. I thought he was playing with me like usual, but when he did not turn around or even look at me after a moment or two, I walked over and followed his gaze to see what had held his attention for a good three or four minutes. He was looking over at the riding place that was about a hundred feet away from our fences.

There, in that place, a bunch of girls and their women instructors saddle their horses every morning and go ridding in their arena. From what I've seen, their idea of riding includes tight cinches, painful bits, and rough martingales. Their ridding, from the sounds of crops that I hear every now and then and the glimpses I see of each horse collected beyond reason, seems to be a lot like the riding I had learned before I found this ranch: riding that focuses on stomping the spirit out of the horse and forcing him to respond to correct leg movements and rein fixtures that are calculated in ridiculous ways.

Heighten stood there with all of his attention focused on this sight, eyes blazing sadly and filled with one question: *why?*

"I know," I murmured quietly as the two of us stood there gazing at the girls going around and around on their horses. "I wish I understood, too." After a while it became almost painful for me to watch, so I put NoFly on Heighten's legs and face, patted him, and moved on to my little brother.

Hudson looked out at the riding place in curiosity, too, but he had none of Heighten's utter confusion and disgusted wonderment at the sight of the girls having such strict control over their horses. As I went into his stall, he trotted right up to me and began eating my shirt happily, chewing and nuzzling and rubbing his face against mine until I tacked him, half frustrated, half overjoyed to see my little brother in such a good mood. And all of the horses in that row were in wonderful moods, even Little D, and especially RustyBob who was overjoyed that I merely existed and was there to pat him and love him as always. Akira followed me to her gate after we were done and Mistah Lee whinnied when I entered his stall and Cocoa, a horse from a friend down the road who's staying with us for a while, let me pick thorny burrs from her coat that she had somehow picked up from laying on the ground. She's a cute little bay mare with white hairs already starting to take over the dark color and she has a dark, fuzzy mane and big black eyes. As she's not a Tierra Madre horse, I'm trying not to get too attached because soon she'll be going home. But it's hard not to like her.

And Chance.

My Chance.

Sam the Volunteer was emptying waters all around us and Chance had nearly nailed him several times when he tried to walk through RustyBob's door. Chance pinned his ears to his head and snapped at him with rage in his eyes when Sam (the Volunteer) got anywhere near him, just as he does to people he's not familiar with. I thought this was odd, as Sam the Volunteer is always at the ranch Saturdays and Sundays and had been there as long as I have, and surely Chance would be used to him by now.

"He just doesn't like me," Sam laughed as we stood outside of Chance's stall, me with the NoFly in my hand, Sam with the hose and cart next to him, as Chance snarled and snorted and banged his hooves on his gate. Sam offered his hand to him vertically – a trick Jim had taught both of us when it came to calming horses that had been spooked – to no avail.

"He just gets nervous," I said and I set down the NoFly and Sam snatched his hand back before it was ripped off. "Here, let me get him some leaves. That usually makes him happy."

"He doesn't deserve leaves!" said Sam with a snort. "That demon is only happy when he's got a human in front of him to take bites out of!"

He was joking, but in an instant my temper flared up.

"That's not true," I said quietly and, right on cue, Chance took the leaves from my hand calmly. His ears perked forwards and some of the hatred drained from his eyes within seconds. He stopped banging with his hooves as he munched his leaves, nibbling contentedly at my fingers for more.

"Oh, he likes *you*," Sam huffed and he walked away to finish the waters. I don't mind Sam the Volunteer, and he is usually fun to talk to, but I couldn't help but notice that Chance really calmed down when he went away.

The two of us, horse and two-legged, rested there for a moment or so while the tension left the air, the NoFly bottle abandoned on the ground.

Chance gazed at me with his ears forward and his eyes full of something I couldn't exactly make out. Maybe it was scrutiny.

And then I heard him speak to me.

"Okay."

It was only that thought, that idea, and I understood it to be permission or perhaps that's just what I wanted it to be. But either way, as I reached out and slowly rested my palm against the warm skin of his nose, I knew I had interpreted the emotions dancing between us perfectly.

I swear time itself froze in the amount of immeasurable moments that we stood in silence, my hand on his face, fingers touching his nose gently, his ears flickering back out of habit and his eyes never leaving mine. His nostrils quivered and I spoke to him without words, simply by focusing on being fearless, by soaking in the realization that here I was, my hand on the wildest horse at the ranch, and there he stood with the light of trust slowly beginning to shine in his eyes. I knew Chance could see through any barrier I might have chosen to construct there and then, and in the seconds, minutes, hours (or so it seemed) we spent standing and simply looking at one another, I felt the ones I had built long ago come crashing down.

Someone behind me stomped a hoof, then the sound of another horse whinnying loudly and the gush of water from Sam's hose and every other sound that time had struck dumb hit us both as I lowered my hand from his face and the world kept on turning.

And Chance didn't move an inch as I picked up the spray bottle and began to do his NoFly, he continuing to watch me carefully, cautiously, and me sweeping the remains of my barriers from my mind as time began again.

September 7, 2009

My last entry was getting ridiculously long; I didn't go to the ranch today but I wanted to finish writing about everything else that happened yesterday.

When I walked over to the field side to do the NoFly, Jericho trotted right over to me happily and thrust his nose into my face. I was surprised, and then overjoyed, since that big gray horse never shows too much emotion to me. And then he turned around and shoved his lovely behind at me in an attempt to get me to scratch it. Of course, I gave in.

Min was led on a walk yesterday, too. And I'm telling you, there was nothing so incredible as seeing that little horse bucking and rearing and trotting around and tossing his head like there was no tomorrow. He has laminitis, just like the Moose and Little D, and his back legs have always bothered him, but he's not in extreme danger since his laminitis is chronic rather than acute. There's a slim chance he ever will be.

Charlie, Min's best friend, stood smack at the fence and watched as Jim led Min around in lines and circles and glared at me and Sam as we stood there laughing at our cute little terrorist. He whinnied loudly if Jim took Min too far from their home.

When I did the NoFly for all of the horses, two things stood out to me (other than my encounter with Chance). One: Iron Man has really taken to getting his NoFly. He was nervous the first time I attempted to put my wet hands over his face but now he stands quietly and allows me to do it as long as I talk to him and put my hands on his sides so he knows where I am. And Solo... well, Solo has always been a bit of a bully, so it was rather funny yesterday to see him quake with uncertainty and bolt to the other side of the field when I jokingly sprayed his side with the NoFly. He's a crazy boy. As second-in-command of the horse herd in the field, he's always scaring away somebody and trotting around like he's the king of the world. But then he comes right to the fence when I walk over with treats, his ears forward and expression innocent. I tell him he's responsible for the gray hairs I'm already starting to find weaved in with the rest of my dark blonde hues. He tells me to shut up and give him his treats then laughs when I turn around.

Mistah Lee and I went on a walk before I went home. He was happy to see me, whinnying when I got the halter that hung from the tree next to his stall and walking right to me so I could put it on him. Every time anyone walks near him, it is an unwritten Tierra Madre requirement to yell his name in triumph before saying anything else to him. So whenever I walk into his stall with his halter I always say, "Mistah Lee!" loudly before taking his flymask off and adding, "Okay, Mistah Lee. Let's go see the world. You wanna go see the world, Mistah Lee?" And his halter would go on and I would open the gate and Akira would whinny goodbye and all the horses in the shed row would come to their gates to watch our grand entrance into the world and off we would go.

Every time. I just realized what a ritual it has become.

Halfway through our walk today, as we stood in the little wash area right against the gate to the ranch, Mistah Lee ate bits and pieces off of Mother Nature's plate and I stood beside him, stroking his mane and began to sing one of my favorite songs to him.

for you are my brother ... my brother, under the sun.

I looked back at Chance at this last line. And there he was at the corner of his stall, eyes on me as he watched my every move and chewed on his hay.

We are the same, just the same, you and I.

September 15, 2009

Yesterday I stopped by after school to say hello, and I was glad I did.

Little D is loads better. Well, she's not as well as she should be yet, but her eyes are brighter and she moves around more and she screams at RustyBob again if he steals her food and it's enough to tell me that she's improving. It's great to see her acting like herself again.

I went around to say hello to everyone on the field side, and I swear Iron Man and Slayer stood fighting over me. Slayer is never really aggressive, but when Iron Man thrust his beautiful head over the bars today to shove his nose to my face, Slayer's ears went back and he chased him away faster than anything so that he could have me all to himself. I compromised by stepping far enough away in two places so each horse could talk to me on their own for a bit. Slayer snorted and pawed at the ground when Iron Man got attention first.

"You boys gotta get over this," I told Iron Man as the horse stood, looking at me with liquid eyes and nuzzling my hands happily. "You and Slayer are friends now. There's no need to fight over anything."

"Sorry, Lex. It's just that I'm real happy to see you. I kinda like attention now that people care about who I am rather than how much I make."

I love that boy so much. He's so gentle and so sure of himself at the same time. There's no way he'll ever be known to me by his racer name (Coloreado) as it doesn't seem to suit his gentle personality. He's an unbridled, wondrous, content little sweetheart.

But my special boy will always be Slayer.

"My knight in shining armor," I murmured to him when I finally walked over, to his relief, to give him my attention. And he nibbled my school uniform shirt collar in utter contentment as I told him I loved him.

"Okay, Lex," he said. "I knew that, I really did." But he doesn't get the attention he deserves now that I have to split my time with Iron Man, and I know it bothers him slightly. When Rusty lived next to him, Slayer almost encouraged me to spend time with that boy; Rusty was his special friend. But now that Rusty is a part of the Great Herd and a handsome, young, curious horse has come to live in his stall, Slayer's been a bit uneasy.

And he probably misses his friend, too.

It's hard to believe it has been more than a month since Rusty's and Mr. Steve Vai's deaths. At times it feels like that horrid day was part of a dream, at others I swear it was only yesterday I was sitting at home with a sprained ankle, reading Jim's blog and crying as I realized that two of my best friends were gone.

Slayer helped me move on then. Well, I have to help him now. Slayer has always been able to read my mind and when I left him today, I think he understood that I will never let him down. I love him as much as he loves me. I hope he knows that, too.

Whenever I park outside the gate I go through the row of horses that starts with Guess to get to my car when I leave. I always end with Chance as he's closest to the gate. And whenever I leave, I always spend a few extra minutes with him.

"None of that," I told him softly when I walked up to him and he threw his head over the bars with his ears pinned to his skull. But his eyes weren't flashing. His action had been purely out of habit. "It's just me, Chance. Just me."

"Oh," came his response. Pause. "Can I have some leaves?"

The breeze tossed the tree branches around as I picked some leaves off of them. It was a beautiful sound, those whispers of the wind that I heard, combing through the limbs of the plants and all the manes and tails of the horses. My hair flew behind me and Chance's mane flew toward me, the wind waving them together in unison.

"Do you hear that?" I whispered, looking toward the direction the wind was coming from. Chance snorted, took his leaves, then raised his head over the bars and eyed me carefully. I smiled and offered a hand to him. He sniffed and nibbled it once or twice, then turned his head to face the same direction I was looking toward.

We stood there, Chance and I, listening to what I think no one else could hear, for a long time. He turned to let me pat his nose once in farewell and watched me walk to my car before turning to face the wind again while I drove away.

September 18, 2009

One reason I'm glad it's Friday is because I knew I would get to hang out at the ranch after school a little more than usual. I did, and it was great.

Jim and I went around giving the horses their electrolytes and grain and alfalfa grass. I told him about school and he told me about everything going on at the ranch. Several days ago, he said, ten to fifteen senior citizens had stopped by for an hour or so to tour the place. I would have loved to talk about the horses with them, to tell the seniors the horses' stories and teach them about their personalities, but I was in school. Apparently Tarzan (Tarzan!) came right up to the fence of his pen to say hello. I would have given anything to see that.

When I went to put Min in MinHouse (everything of his is accented with "Min" in front of it; we call his belongings "MinWater," and "MinDoor," and "MinBucket,") that little demon literally chased me out of his stall, ears pinned and jaws clipping together, me yelping with surprise, Jim laughing hysterically.

"He's back!" he laughed as I walked back to him, shaking bits of hay out of my hair. "Osama *Min* Laden is back and in full power, sweet thing! Let me see your arm, there. Are you alright?"

And suddenly I was laughing, too. That's one thing I absolutely love about Jim. He turns everything into a funny or meaningful story I can hold and cherish. And that's how I saw MinAdventure today. A hilarious episode that's still making me laugh.

Good, Min.

I took several pictures of Iron Man as I don't have any of him, and after Jim mentioned that one of his favorite things in the world was to walk down the row of stalls and see all of his kids with their heads down, enjoying their food, I stood on Heighten's stall bars and took a group shot. It turned out pretty well, I think.

Jim said that several volunteers were going to be there with me, him and Sam tomorrow. Two women, Sam the volunteer, and a man named Trent that I don't know and am already not eager to meet. Apparently he was sentenced to a hundred hours of community service for hitting a horse while giving him a bath. The instant Jim mentioned this my inner alarm went off, and I was stunned to hear that Jim had allowed Trent to carry out his service at the ranch. Jim must have seen the disbelief in my eyes (he sees everything in my eyes) because he quickly said that Trent was, indeed, a very "in your face" sort of man and very opinionated but an okay guy just the same. Well, I'll hold my judgment till tomorrow. One second of seeing Chance's reaction to his presence will tell me whether or not I can trust him.

September 19, 2009

Trent showed up when I was doing Mistah Lee's NoFly.

He was on his cell phone, talking loudly. He waved at me as he walked by the shed of horses on his way to the breezeway and the tack room. I hardly watched him; I was looking at Chance as Trent walked by his stall to see what the horse's reaction would be to this stranger's presence. His ears went back but went up again as Trent strolled on by. Hmm.

By the time I reached Little D, Trent had shown up with the cart and rake to muck RustyBob's stall. "Hi, there," I said when he walked through the door.

"Hey," he replied. "How are – don't you mess with me, you little bastard!" This was directed at Chance, who had thrown his head over the bars with his ears pinned against his skull and hatred in his eyes. Furious outrage exploded inside of me. Opinionated this man might be, but no one called Chance names like that.

"You must be Trent," I said, trying to keep the disdain out of my voice.

"So you've heard of me!" Trent answered, sounding cheerful. "What, Jim's telling the story already?"

"He just mentioned you were going to be working with us for a while," I said as politely as I could. "I'm Alexis."

"Nice to meet you, Alexis. Alexis. That's a pretty name. And what's a pretty girl doing here working knee-deep in horse shit?"

My patience evaporated instantly. Had he been anywhere near my age, I might have thrown a punch or two at that comment, but instead I settled for scowling. "I like horses," was all I said. He changed the subject.

I was surprised about how well he took to mucking out the stalls. I had figured, as a horse trainer in the racing business, that he wouldn't be used to getting too dirty, but he seemed fine with mucking. As we talked (or, rather, as he talked and I listened), he cleaned out RustyBob's pen in a matter of minutes. Not that he was thrilled about it.

"I'm telling you what," he said to me, "I don't mind doing shit like this, but I've been fucked over by this whole horse accident thing."

"Horse accident?"

"Well, I was washing one of my big eighteen handers this one morning, and the big guy stepped on my fuckin' foot and you gotta know what that feels like, right? It ain't fuckin' fun. But as I shoved him away I accidently hit the bastard in the eye..."

As he talked I glanced over at Chance. He was watching Trent carefully, eyes glistening strangely.

" ...and a bunch of people saw it and screamed horse abuse and blah blah blah . . . and here I am now mucking horse shit. But that's okay, huh, big guy?" he asked RustyBob, turning to the horse who was sniffling him innocently. "At least I've got this beautiful woman to talk to. And you, old cow nose."

He had shouldered the rake and was heading toward Chance's stall as he spoke.

"Uh, be careful of that one," I said quickly as Trent put one leg up on Chance's railings and as I saw my brother paw at the ground, ears already laid back. "He doesn't like strangers."

"What, that yellow asshole?" snorted Trent. "I've heard about him, alright. He won't do anything to me when we've had a session or two." And to my horror, he swung over the top bars of Chance's stall and climbed right in. Chance threw his head up and charged, and Trent, caught off guard, hurriedly leapt back over into RustyBob's stall, swearing loudly.

"I ain't scared of you, you fucking bastard," he yelled at Chance, whose nostrils were flared and whose eyes were flashing dangerously. "You'll learn before long! Just know I ain't scared of you!"

"He's not a bastard," I snapped and Trent froze with one leg up over the bar.

"What'd you say?" he demanded and Chance glanced at me with his ears flickering my way. I repeated what I had said. Funny how I'm nervous with certain horses sometimes but I'm fearless when it comes to humans.

"Well," Trent said hesitantly, seeing my furious expression. "I call my own horses that sometimes. I don't mean it."

I glared at him.

"You like him, don't you? Well, he's a beautiful animal, isn't he?"

"He is," I said, happy to agree with him on something. "Beautiful and proud."

I kept an eye on Trent the whole time I was there, mostly so I could make an escape if he came my way. He seems like an okay guy but his encounter with my favorite horse at the ranch really made me angry. Seeing Chance so agitated and vulnerable, even for a few moments, struck a part of me that I can't explain too well in words. All I know is that anyone Chance has a problem with is someone I don't care to trust.

"What's wrong, baby girl?"

I jumped. I had been standing by the tack room wiping a few fly masks off and looking at Trent emptying waters in the distance. Jim had snuck up behind me. I realized he had seen me watching Trent uneasily.

"Nothing," I said quickly.

Jim wasn't fooled. "You look like you have a problem."

"I don't have a problem," I answered and he looked at me with that piercing gaze of his, that simple, questioning stare that breaks down whatever walls I've constructed. I quickly looked away and changed the subject to CharlieHorse, who has a problem with his right front leg now.

I'm going to keep my distance with Trent. Before I left he tracked me down and asked if he could call me Lexi and, as I hate being called that, I said I'd be fine with Lex, my nickname. "Ooh, what about sexy Lexi or something? Ever get called that?" he asked jokingly. Hudson snorted then as though in irritation and I wanted to snort, too. Jerk.

"Don't worry about me!" called Trent cheerfully as I began to walk away. "That's just me, that's just who I am. I'll give you shit if you can take it."

I turned around and faced him with my head thrown up just as I knew Chance's would have been had he been facing this man who hadn't yet learned his place.

"Bring it," I said flatly and as Trent laughed I glanced back at Chance, who was drinking from his water bucket, and I felt as though I had spoken for the two of us.

September 20, 2009

I think Trent realized we hadn't gotten off on the right foot yesterday because he really toned himself down. He's from a racing world, a different world than ours, so he can't resist giving Jim advice about anything and everything, which is irritating sometimes, and he certainly talks a lot about the racing itself. But he's not so bad. Anyway, I can live with him.

Today he fired questions about myself at me whenever I was within ten feet of him. I know he was trying to be friendly, but I answered somewhat hesitantly. I got good at swiftly changing the subject and asking Trent about Iron Man. Trent had raced against him and had known him for years. He told me about all different kinds of racing and complications horses often get on the racetrack, which were interesting to hear about.

As I said, I think I can live with him. He calls Chance "The Yellow Horse" (in my presence, anyway) and as I find that a courteous term, my anger from yesterday is starting to evaporate.

There was also Lynn, a really sweet woman, volunteering today. Between her and Trent and Sam, the mucking and watering and the NoFly were all done in almost two hours. Jim was in and out of stores, getting supplies, so I worked on CharlieHorse. My poor baby boy banged his knee on the fence or something and his whole right front leg is swollen from the knee down. His arthritis is bad down there, too, so it could also be from that. Anyway, we're trying hydrotherapy on him, to see if it will loosen up the muscles in his leg, so I got his halter and walked him out to the nearest hose and sprayed water on his knee for fifteen minutes. CharlieHorse stood patiently for the most part, shifting a little every now and then, sometimes twisting around to see what was behind him, but otherwise letting the rush of water heal his leg. Every time he started to fidget I sang snippets of a lullaby to him, and his ears strained to catch what I was singing, and he'd stop trying to walk away.

I love my little old sweetheart so much. I hope he's going to be all right, and I'm sure he will be, but this morning I certainly thought otherwise. When I was coming around from giving Ted his scoops of grain, I saw CharlieHorse lying on his side in his stall, unmoving. I swear my heart stopped beating.

I bolted around to the other side of the stall, where his door was, yelling for Jim, and looked inside only to see CharlieHorse sniffing contentedly at the ground where he was laying. Jim came running and after a few seconds' inspection, we both realized that CharlieHorse was fine; he was just resting his sore leg.

But still. I never want to be scared like that again. That was absolutely horrible.

With nothing else to do after CharlieHorse had been given hydrotherapy, I brushed down Little D and RustyBob then scrubbed salt off of Iron Man and Slayer. I attempted to brush M'Stor but he kept on moving away and trying to play instead.

Little D loved the attention. She arched her neck proudly as I brushed her and put her nose to my face when I kissed her goodbye. She's improving so much now; she walks to her food trough in the mornings and screams at RustyBob if he thrusts his head through the bars to steal her hay. She's winning her battle, the battle so many horses have lost.

The reason I had to brush RustyBob down today was because as I was grooming Little D, he stood gazing at me with bright eyes, his adorable cow nose twitching, whickering for all it was worth. And I can't turn away from that loving little face. Not for anything.

Slayer snatched one of the brushes from my hands the instant I stepped into his stall and played with it as I brushed his beautiful coat with another. Iron Man poked his head through the bars to watch me work and hear me sing, and he looked overjoyed as I slipped through the railings into his stall to groom him as well.

"You've probably had this done to you thousands of times," I told him as I started brushing the salt from his coat. Slayer handed me the brush he had taken, and I started scraping bits of loose hair from the Iron Man's coat. The two boys touched noses as I stood between them, and we all chatted for a while. I was so glad to see them getting along.

I gave Mistah Lee a walk today, too, and I swear he covered the distance between his stall and the entrance gate in ten seconds. Looking at him now, you could hardly tell that his hip had ever been broken and/or had been badly arthritic at one point. By looking into his eyes, you would hardly guess that when he first came to Tierra Madre, he had been waiting and desperately hoping for death to come relieve him soon. Now he thrives. Now he is happy.

Good, Mistah Lee.

I'm trying something new with Chance. I'm giving him a few pieces of hay and while his head is still through the bars as he's eating them, I'm reaching up and rubbing the white star on his forehead. Three months ago if I had attempted to do that I would have gotten my hand ripped off. But now he munches his food and lets me pat his head, not just his nose, if only for a second or two.

I'm not like Trent, I realized. I don't go marching into Chance's stall waving my arms around like there's no tomorrow and demanding respect I haven't even begun to earn. I'm not like Jim, either, who fearlessly gains trust through gentle discipline and unyielding courage.

I'm just me.

I wait patiently to earn Chance's trust. I don't go into his stall because I know he's not ready for me to go in there and that I'm not ready, either. I don't have any expectations as to what he should do or how he should treat me. All I can give to him as I wait is unconditional love.

Several weeks ago on a Sunday morning, Sam the Volunteer's friend had come to help us. She had liked all the horses except for Chance as she, like most people who come to the ranch, viewed Chance as a violent, angry, "bad" horse who enjoyed hurting people. When I laughed and told her that I loved him more than anyone else, she had looked absolutely astonished. "You do?" she had asked incredulously. "Why?"

I couldn't tell her then. But I think I could tell her now.

Chance and I are the same.

We've both been abused in the past. We both don't know who to trust for fear of getting hurt again. I think we are both gentle at heart, but our automatic defense mechanism is to lash out at anybody who gets too close and to keep those barriers up so no one can cross them and see what we really are.

And as to what we both really are? We don't know yet.

But we're learning. At least, I know I am.

If there's one lesson I've learned at this ranch, it's the fact that one soul can heal another. I don't know how much I've helped Chance's heart to recover from his wounds, but I do know that bit by bit, he is healing mine.

September 24, 2009

Today is my birthday, and I have come to a conclusion: I don't know whether or not I like being eighteen. Now that I'm an official able-bodied citizen in the eyes of the rest of the world, I feel like a little more responsibility has settled onto my shoulders. And when the whole world is looking at me with their expectations higher than what I am able to aim for, the weight can be a little difficult to bear.

But there is one thing of which I am completely sure: no matter how old I get, I can still come back to Tierra Madre, where both two-leggeds and four-leggeds give me unconditional love and strength no matter what I do or think or say.

And speaking of four-leggeds that are composed of unconditional strength, I have to talk about Little D.

If there is anyone on this planet that has proven herself to be a true warrior, it's that little girl. There is such bravery within her eyes, such grace and courage in the way she turns her head and gazes right through to my soul that I want to cry sometimes when I look at her. As Jim tells her and us every day, she's fighting the battle of her life and she's winning.

She's winning.

My mind was so overloaded with thoughts, both good and bad, that I drove up to the ranch around seven tonight, just wanting to be in the company of my good friends and to check up on Jim. I intended to stay ten or fifteen minutes. I ended up talking to Jim for an hour and a half. And there is one story he told me, a story about something that had happened earlier this morning, that made my appreciation of my intuition – and that of the horses – skyrocket.

Let me say this: I knew there was something about Trent I couldn't trust.

I knew it.

Jim's tone of voice was something like forcefully casual when he told me that he had kicked Trent out of the ranch earlier that morning. Instantly I asked why and he hesitated before telling me.

Trent hit Chance.

He hit him.

I knew that Trent was an asshole the moment I saw him. And so did Chance. I knew it. We knew it. I'll never doubt my instinct or his ever again.

Apparently Trent had been talking on his cell phone as he headed toward RustyBob's stall with the poop cart, intending to muck it out. (The instant Jim mentioned this I knew where the story was going.) Jim, who had been in Akira's stall, saw Trent obliviously chatting on the phone and walk into RustyBob's stall with his back to the horse who despised him...

Long story short: Chance nailed him in the back, ripping into his skin so that Trent had to get a tetanus shot afterward. And Trent, in a fit of fury, whipped around and struck Chance in the shoulder/chest area with all the strength he could muster.

The moment I heard that, I seriously almost leapt out the couch I was sitting on, enraged.

"Trent did *not*," I breathed even though, for obvious reasons, I was not surprised.

"He did."

No one can ever let their guard down around Chance, but the thing is, I know that he doesn't just strike out at people for no reason. He'll snap out at a two-legged passing by when he's nervous, or if he senses something about them he doesn't like. Maybe he would have attacked me (he's done it once before, anyway), but at least I would have known that it was my fault. And anyway, I know better than to act in a way around Chance that would get myself nearly killed.

But to turn around and hit him? To strike a beautiful, incredible animal when he's done nothing but defend himself against what he views as terrifying danger?

Unforgivable.

I was beside myself. I had so many thoughts and rants spring to my mind and I couldn't say them all at once, so I sat silently in anger as Jim continued to say that Trent had called back later in the afternoon to ask for a second chance. He really needed the hours of community service, Jim said, and Trent would be willing to stay away from Chance as long as he got his hours in.

I shrugged at this, and Jim continued to say that maybe what Trent needed was redemption and forgiveness.

"You don't like it, I know," he told me. "It's hard, but sometimes we gotta do it, sweet thing."

And I told him exactly how I knew that forgiving a person who has done something wrong is difficult, and, well, I'll never forget the absolutely stunned look on his face. He looked as though my awful past was a story like Tarzan's, or Charlie's or Sweet Boy's or Mistah Lee's, a story that so awful that to hear all of it at once was beyond overwhelming.

"So maybe you're right," I said finally when I was done. I was almost in tears. "I had to learn to forgive once, Jim. I can do it again."

Both of us were silent for a minute or two.

"Sweet angel," he said suddenly. I looked at him, and he was gazing at me with something in his eyes I haven't seen in a long time: pride. "You're a brave little girl, you know that?"

Little D's shining face came to my mind just then. I remembered all the times Jim had called *her* his brave little girl, and at the realization that I was at the same standard as her, tears rushed into my eyes and I had to blink to keep from crying.

"It doesn't matter how old you are now," Jim went on, "there's just an innocence to you that I don't see anymore. No matter what you've been through it's still there. And it's a breath of fresh air, baby girl. It really is."

It was silent for another moment, then he added, "And I'm sorry that I don't have a present for you on your birthday."

"What are you talking about?" I was able to say. "You just gave it to me."

And in all honesty, it was the best present I've received in a long, long time.

Later on, as I accompanied Jim on the nine o'clock "walk around", I heard my mother drive up to the gate, calling for me. Since I had left my phone in my car, I had a feeling that I would have to skip the goodbyes for the horses and hurry to let her know I was okay. Before I started heading toward the gate, I turned back and called, "Jim?"

"Yeah?"

"Thank you."

There was complete understanding in the silence that followed as his smile lit his whole face. "Happy birthday, sweetheart."

As I was hurrying over to the gate, not paying too much attention to where I was, I realized that when I was running beside Chance's stall he was running beside me.

He had been the first thing I'd seen in this new, nighttime Tierra Madre. Chance had been there at the corner of his pen, almost as though he was just waiting for me to show up. He took my breath away then, and as I was leaving, even though I was in a hurry, I had to stop and gaze at him for another moment. In the moonlight, his palomino coat glowed in a ghostly, magnificent way. He moved with such a flawless grace, as though he was floating on the moonlight itself. We stopped, me right beside his pen, he in that corner that had wordlessly become out meeting place.

"Bye, Chance," I whispered and I held a hand out to him. He put his head through the bars and stood still as I put my hand on his nose briefly. "God," I breathed after a moment or two, "how on earth could anyone hit you?"

His light brown eyes were glistening in the dark, and I gave him one last, brief pat on the nose before I quickly walked over to the gate where my mother was still waiting.

Chance watched me leave as he stood in his corner under the night sky, giving me the impression that though the area in which I disappeared was pitch black, he could still see me. Before I turned away from him the last time I swear I saw something shift behind his eyes.

And right before I climbed through the gate, I heard it. Chance was whinnying quietly, calling me. And as I turned back for a moment to see him gazing at me intently, in silence I heard what he meant to say:

"Hey, Lex? Happy birthday."

I cried all the way home.

September 26, 2009

I got to the ranch around eight today and discovered that Joy and her boyfriend were there and mostly everything was done. So I gave Suze her bran mash, put Solo out in the arena with John, and did the NoFly on the field side.

Solo would hardly let me get Suze through the gate, but once Suze had finished and was back in the field and I went to put the halter on him he stood perfectly, walked, in Sam's words, "like a perfect gentleman," and stood quietly as I took the halter off and exited the arena. I love that little bully. He has a really good sense of humor, I think.

When I went up to Bentley to do his NoFly, his eyes reflected the calmest and loving energy I've ever seen within them before. I was thrilled, because B hardly ever shows me emotion, and I did his NoFly slowly so I could hang out with him more.

Enter Trent.

He came walking up the "driveway" as I was with B, and called out a cheery, "Hi, there, Lex!" as he went by us. Even though I felt fiery anger rush through me at the sight of him, a rage I hadn't felt in years, I automatically answered back, "Hey, how are you?"

And B snapped at me. I don't think I've ever seen him so pissed off. I jumped out of the way just in time for him to only get my hair caught in his teeth. Trent didn't see, as he was walking to the barn with his back to us, and I was glad. I was completely caught off guard.

"What was that?" I asked Bentley who stood, staring at me with his eyes simmering. At my hurt tone, they softened a little and he stood quietly, ears twitching. I was so bewildered by his sudden attack that I stood, speechless, for a moment or two.

Maybe he wanted the attention all to himself. Or maybe he just didn't want me talking to Trent.

I still don't know...

Rob the farrier came and the Iron Man, M'Stor, and Bella got their shoes done. Jim was at the store when they arrived, and Sam was doing CharlieHorse's hydrotherapy, so I went to get the Iron Man and lead him to the work area and stood with him for a bit as he got his new shoes. I could go on forever about his innocent wonder, how happy and curious he was as I stood there with him.

For the first few hours today, I had a sickening, burning nervousness in my stomach that I knew was making the horses anxious, too. Chance laid his ears back and tossed his head a few times when I went to do his NoFly (Joy and her boyfriend had stayed far away from him). But I went in to groom Little D and as she stood silently, not rocking back and forth on her hurt feet, just standing bravely and surely as any horse could, the anxiety drained away. I sung to her and as she basked in the attention happily, RustyBob stood right smack against the fence, as close to me as he could possibly get, with his ears perked in my directions and his eyes wide and his adorable cow nose twitching. He stood riveted to my voice as though there was nothing else in the whole world that was more fascinating. After I was done brushing Little D I had to go in and throw my arms around him and kiss him, too. And as always, he was thrilled that I even took a few steps closer to him.

Good, RustyBob. Good, Little D.

I went to leave through RustyBob's gate, where Chance was, and as I was about to reach for the door handle I heard an angry yell in the distance. Me and Chance and RustyBob and Little D and Mistah Lee and Akira all looked around to see Trent shouting at Mike, who had not stopped barking at him since the moment he came to the ranch. At the sound of Trent's voice Chance threw his head up again, ears pinned to his skull, eyes flashing. He clipped his teeth together when I offered him my hand, and stood glaring at me as I smiled at him sadly.

"I know," I said quietly. "I don't like him, either."

Chance snorted, eyes blazing. "Good."

"But we gotta work around this right now, okay?" I told him. "We both have to go through things we don't want to. But we can't run from them, can we? We have to go right through them. We have to forgive."

At I talked, Chance's eyes slowly grew softer and his ears flicked forward again. I laughed out loud and offered him my hand. He did nothing, so I reached up and rubbed his nose for a long time. He stood and watched me, ears flicking forward then going back then forward again.

"You showed Trent, though, didn't you?" I said suddenly, starting to laugh. "You nailed him when he didn't show you respect, huh? You taught him who itancan was!"

Chance turned his face sideways as though he wanted nibble my fingers, but he took a very light snap at my hand as I drew them away. At first I thought I had startled him, but then I saw the light in his eyes. He was playing.

"Are you gonna show me, now?" I asked him as he nibbled at my fingers. "Are you the boss of this herd, Chance?"

"Why, yes, Lex. Yes, I am."

"I don't think so, baby boy."

I reached up to pat him again and he moved his head out of my reach. I laughed as he pinned his ears back in mock anger, and I knew he was joking around because his eyes were shining gently. He thrust his head through the bars, looking at me the way Suze does when I catch her stealing the running hose from the water trough and tossing it on the ground. He looked so different from the horse I had first laid eyes on, the one who had pinned his ears back and snarled and pounded his hooves on the gate and lashed out at me if I got anywhere near him, and that simple fact made my heart soar.

When I left him he gazed after me, head perfectly balanced over the bars, then he did something he had never done before. I looked back about ten steps away to see him nibbling at the spare bits of hay around his stall door. He raised his head when he noticed me looking back at him, flicked one ear in my direction, then returned to his food.

I think Chance trusted that I would come back eventually. He wasn't concerned as to when he would see me again, he knew that I would find a way to spend time with him no matter what. And if that is what he really thought, then that is absolutely incredible. I had felt the shift in his thoughts toward me the night of my birthday, the shift from me being "that one girl who pets me a lot and isn't scared of me," in his eyes to "that girl called Alexis, or Lex, or whatever, and she may not be so bad."

Slowly, surely, we're getting there. It's all on his time.

I helped give Moosie a haircut today. And let me tell you, only the Moose would stand perfectly still for hours on end without a halter while his coat was being shaved. See, Moose has Cushings disease (as well as chronic laminitis – not acute like Mr. Steve Vai's had been) and as a side effect of those, his hair grows like crazy. If it isn't cut every month, it's dangerous for his body temperature if it's too hot outside.

Jim showed me how to angle the razor to cut his long hair, and while I observed Moosie stood patiently, even as Jim cut the hair around his ears and eyes. "He's such a handsome horse," I mentioned, pointing out the three or four different types of brown and tan around his eyes and nose and stomach.

"He is. He's the Moose," Jim said. At Tierra Madre, that is only one way to describe the incredibility of our medicine man, just by stating that he's the Moose. "I'm sure he was one stunning colt, all those years ago."

He was silent for a moment as he continued shaving, then mentioned, "I have a hard time imagining you as a foal, Moosie."

I silently agreed. As I did Moose turned his head to give me one long, piercing gaze, and he spoke soundlessly.

"Yes, I was young once, Lex. And things were very different during that time."

I've never questioned my ability to interpret horses' actions and energy, nor thought it odd that I usually can guess what they are thinking, but as Moosie spoke to me then, I realized for the first time that he had never shown me those emotions that I could read and study. And he had just done it. Just then.

So after Jim had left and I stood shaving his long coat off, I asked him hopefully, silently, "What were you saying before, Moosie? How was everything different when you were a just a foal?"

I couldn't read an answer to that particular question. But Moose flicked one ear back in my direction and let out a long breath with his eyes, full and profound, focused straight ahead.

"I'm old now," was his response. "But I was a foal once. As were you."

"I still am a foal, Moosie."

"At heart you are, Lex. But now you're grown just like me."

I thought about this as I kept shaving his coat.

"You haven't seen all that exists in this world," Moosie went on, his thoughts emerging in my mind as he turned to look at me, "but though you're not a foal anymore I know that you've been through a little more than anyone should have to endure."

"I think you're right about that. Does that make me brave, Moosie? Brave like you?"

Moosie looked back at me again, eyes unblinking. There was an infinite amount of gentleness in his eyes.

"We are all as brave as we can be, and need to be, in the circumstances we are in." The words – what he meant to say to me – were so clear. "From the battles you have fought I would say that you have a great amount of courage within that barricaded heart of yours, Lex."

Trent was walking toward us at that point, water bottle in hand. Moose raised his head slightly and looked up at him, one ear flickering toward him politely, one turned toward me and all of the new emotions that had welled up inside of me. As Trent stood resting and chattering, I didn't feel any nervous tension coming from the Moose and after a moment or two of just standing next to the medicine man of Tierra Madre Horse Sanctuary, I wasn't anxious at all.

And I made him a promise, right there, right in that moment: no matter what else I had to face in my life, I was going to be brave through it all. Even if the world comes crashing down someday I'll stand among the wreckage with my head high. Just like him. Just like the Moose.

Well, I'll come as close to his strength as I can possibly get.

Moose has the surest, quietest inner confidence of any creature I have ever met in my life. His courage is enough to get me through anything, and if he believes I'm brave, well, then there is nothing I can't do.

Oh, Moosie.

What on earth would I do without you?

September 28, 2009

Oh, God, I spoke too soon.

Why is life like this? *Why*?

Moose is dead. When Jim went to feed him this morning he wouldn't get up. He died in his sleep.

My hands are shaking so much I can hardly write. I'm crying so hard I can hardly breathe.

Why the Moose?

Why Moosie?

September 29, 2009

Was he trying to tell me something?

As I stood with him three days ago, as we truly talked for what I realize now was the first and last time, was he trying to tell me goodbye?

Did he know his time was coming? Was he trying to pass on enough courage to get me through his death? Did he even call me brave at all?

There are so many questions tumbling around in my head now, questions that I'll never get answers for. All of those times the Moose was there, standing in his stall, I could have climbed in and asked him anything, I could have received answers. I could have spent more time with him. I could have told him how he had affected my every emotion just by looking at me. I could have told him everything.

But I didn't.

And now he's gone.

Yesterday when I opened Jim's blog up in the morning to read about the most current news of the ranch – just as I do every morning whether I'm headed there or not – I was paralyzed when I read the title of the newest entry, written in all capitals: "MOOSE IS DEAD." I couldn't breathe, I couldn't think – all that echoed within my mind were the words Moose . . . dead . . . dead . . .

And in an instant I was crying. And to make matters worse, as I scrolled down later on to see what Jim had posted before, I read about how Guess had coliced during the night and that she had a slim chance of survival.

Moose was Jim's best friend. Guess is Jim's best girl.

God in heaven.

When I stopped by after school yesterday to check on Jim, he said Guess had pulled through after being tubed and given four bags of liquid to make sure her intestines hadn't been twisted. She's doing fine now, but yesterday that fact was a small comfort to Jim. He had mentioned in his blog that he'd called Moose for breakfast several times and when Moose hadn't stirred he had gone into the stall with utter dread...

I cried all through my drive to school this morning and had to leave first hour so I could sit in silence outside; just imagining Jim calling Moose over and over again and his horse never getting up was agonizing to me. And Jim had told me how he had seen Mike lying in Moose's stall, curled up next to his head as Moose died... well, it was a rough day for everyone at the ranch.

Especially Jim.

So. What do I do now?

I had counted on the Moose to keep me on my feet, to remind me of my promise to him. I had counted on the fact that he would be there to either nod his head in approval when I did something good or stare at me, reproaching, if I should have acted differently or with better intentions. I had counted on him to stand between Trent and me when I got nervous.

But you know what I'm thinking now?

A year or two ago I would have never felt pain like this. Why? Because I would have been too scared to love anyone like I loved

Moose, like I love any of the horses at the ranch. Because I would have been too afraid of being hurt the way I was the last time I trusted someone.

Moose helped me through that, just like Mr. Steve Vai and my baby Rusty did. Now, I would rather feel this pain of losing someone I care about than never care for anyone at all.

We all fall every now and then. We feel pain. But we hold our heads up through it all. Just like the Moose did.

I know that now. And there is someone else who I think might be learning that same lesson, too.

Chance.

My brother Chance.

When I was walking to my car yesterday, headed to the little pathway that leads to the gate where I had parked outside, I walked past everybody in the shed row, hardly speaking to anyone as I was so overwhelmed with grief I could hardly speak. When I started to walk past Chance's stall, he raised his head slightly but otherwise didn't follow me to the corner closest to the gate as he usually does. I stopped outside his stall door and looked at him wearily. I waited for him to bang on the fence for his leaves, or push his head through the bars and nibble at the air or lay his ears back in confusion.

Nothing.

Chance did nothing. And when I say nothing, I mean that his ears were perked forward, his eyes didn't flash, his head didn't spring up. He hardly even looked at me. He lifted his eyes to mine when I moved to make sure he saw me, and when he continued to stay utterly still, eyes on me, I reached in and rubbed his nose. And he stood silently, watching me with something very, very close to sadness in his eyes, upper lip twitching occasionally to lightly graze my palm.

"Chance," I murmured quietly as I blinked back tears, "do you think I'm brave?"

Chance gazed at me as he started to turn his head to nibble my fingers. Even though my vision was blurred slightly I remember being taken aback by his eyes, not only by how beautiful they were, but by the gentleness they held within their light brown color.

"Here's a better question," I amended as I drew my hand back from his face, "do you think I *can* be brave?"

Maybe I interpreted his next action and his energy wrongly, but I could have sworn that Chance could sense my promise to Moose right there and then. He raised his head over the bars with his ears flickering back once or twice, and studied me carefully for a moment or two.

"You doubted that you ever were?" was the answer I heard.

Maybe he thought it.

Maybe he didn't.

But either way, he wouldn't have thought it four months ago. He wouldn't have even spoken to me four months ago, he wouldn't have opened himself up like that. I'm nearly in tears just thinking of him now. He's coming along, slowly, but surely.

Yesterday when I went driving around after dinner, I couldn't help but look up at the sky for a bit. There was something about its openness, its utter confidence in the fact that it lay within no boundaries, that absolutely struck me.

And then it hit me. Of course the sky is more beautiful now. Moosie is up there guiding it.

Yesterday I was miserable because of Tierra Madre's loss. Today I'll try to be joyful because of the Great Herd's gain. I'll be happy for the wisest, gentlest, most courageous, most loving spirit that I've ever encountered on Earth. I'll be happy because I opened my soul to him, and as he gained his eternal freedom in the Great Herd, I gained another stitch that is slowly repairing the gaping wound on my heart.

I'll be brave.

I'll never forget my promise, Moosie.

Never.

October 3, 2009

I now have another horse to worry about, besides Chance, when it comes to my physical safety and well-being: Min.

Min is now The Min. He is back to his normal, happy self after a long period of being unable to walk very well due to his hooves and back leg, and unfortunately for we two-leggeds, a happy Min is a mischievous, biting little demonic Min, miniature horse he may be.

Today when I went in to do his NoFly I was expecting him to nip at me and stomp his little hooves on the ground in irritation. Instead as I approached him, he stopping eating (!), turned his head toward me with his ears pinned back, and then, with all of the dignity in the world running through him, he charged.

Actually, I didn't see him charge. I had turned and bolted toward the nearest gate out of pure instinct, and just as he reached me with his teeth bared I dove out of the pen and rolled swiftly onto the ground. And yet I was laughing so hard I could hardly stand while Min stood at the fence with his little head poked between the bars, looking angelic.

"Seriously?" I asked him as I got up and sprayed him full in the face with the NoFly to protect my own dignity. "What did I ever do to you?"

Min blinked, ears perked and furry face expressionless. "I'm innocent."

I snorted at that. "Yeah, right. It's a good thing you're a miniature horse, Min. Otherwise you could have killed me."

I gave him some Bermuda grass later, as a truce. He took it happily and munched it like a good little boy eating everything on his dinner plate, and I had to laugh again at our little adventure, even though my arm is bruised and it was a bit of a scare in the moment. But I wish someone had caught it on tape. My dive out of the pen must have been epic.

Today for the entire time I was at the ranch, I was nervous. Or anxious. Well, I don't know what I was feeling. But whatever it was, it made my heart race so that I always felt that at any given time a horse could turn around and snap at me, or lift a leg and nail me when I wasn't looking. Trent wasn't at the ranch. In fact, I was the only volunteer, besides a fellow Foothills student, Bre, who's been coming here for far longer than I have and who comes on Saturday mornings now that the summer is over. The weather was beautiful and all the horses were in wonderful moods and yet I was so anxious the whole time. Every few minutes I'd look over my shoulder, or rotate to see everything around me like Tarzan does, and I wouldn't talk to the horses like I usually do out of fear of not hearing something that could be behind me.

And it wasn't until I left I realized why.

Moose.

He was the moral compass of the ranch. He kept things in balance, he kept things calm. And now he's gone.

Well, that's what I think it is, anyway.

John sensed my unease more than anyone else. Out of anyone in the ranch, it's King John that is the most like the Moose, from the way he carries himself to the noble energy I feel when I'm around him to the regal confidence in his eyes. So when I had finished his NoFly I hopefully reached up to pat his face, and he threw his head up in the air and started to walk away. Almost in tears, I tried to reach him again. He quietly moved from my hand and looked at me with a gentle but firm look in his eyes that spelled out a reprimand that couldn't have been clearer: "Will you knock that off? Stop trying to reassure me, Lex. Start by reassuring yourself."

So I headed toward Chance to do his NoFly, and as he was eating leftover hay in the corner of his stall, I couldn't reach him, either. And I stood outside of his pen for a good five minutes, trying to work up the courage to go inside.

I couldn't do it.

I wasn't brave.

Maybe it had something to do with my encounter with Min, maybe it was a higher power keeping me safe, but in the end I just could not go in to the stall. I haven't gone in there before (I don't count that one time I ventured in when he was eating), but for some reason I had thought I could do it today.

In the end Chance came to the gate so I could rub NoFly on his nose and spray his flanks and legs through the bars, but he lowered his head and nibbled at the loose hay on the ground even as I, angry at myself, tried to ask what I was doing wrong. After being ignored for several more minutes, I wailed, "Am I just weak, is that it?" and walked away feeling like a hopeless coward. It was only out of habit that I turned around to glance at him after I was twenty feet away or so.

His head was raised halfway and he was looking at me, but his ears were turned to the side and his eyes were incredulous, as though I'd offended him. I looked straight into them as he gazed at me for a brief moment or two, and with a start I was reminded of Moosie's piercing stares.

Chance flicked one ear in my direction and raised his head another few inches from the ground, eyes blazing, but not in an angry way. He said nothing, or maybe he did, and I just couldn't read it. But I knew exactly what he was telling me.

I can't doubt myself. Not around the horses. Not around born leaders like John, or brave warriors like Little D and Tarzan. Not around Chance.

And at the end of the day when I look back at all that I've accomplished, I have to realize that I did my best.

Maybe there's a difference between being brave and careless.

Maybe being fearless is more about understanding we can't do everything and less about refusing to see reason.

Maybe the bravest thing I can do right now as I struggle with my self-confidence, as I continue to struggle with the heartbreak that is dealing with the loss of a friend whose spirit reflected my own, is simply fight on.

October 7, 2009

Today I am asking questions. These are questions that I can't find answers to, questions that I've asked myself ever since I started volunteering at Tierra Madre, and they all rotate around one single word:

Why?

Why is it that sometimes, after so much progress, it feels like nothing has been accomplished?

Why does it take years to build trust and only seconds to shatter it?

Why must we all feel fear?

Why can't people keep promises they make?

Why do people drive Mercedes and eat prime rib every night when there are horses who risk homelessness every day due to lack of funds?

Why do people hurt others?

Why won't people do what they say they'll do?

Why does hopelessness strike at random times when all is seemingly well?

Why don't humans understand that they can make a difference?

October 10, 2009

Why *don't* humans understand that they can make a difference? Maybe people do understand, maybe that initial fire is there inside of them, or maybe they just can't figure out what to do with it. Maybe people know what they can do to help, but they just won't get up and make it happen.

I know that if I want something done right, I have to do it myself. I'm going to make a difference.

Well, I'm going to try.

The thing is, Bentley coliced a few days ago, just like John and Solo and Suze and Guess all have at one point or another. He scared us all, Jim especially. And when I went to help feed in the afternoon one of the two days he was sick, poor Bentley was in the arena rolling around, groaning in agony. Jim was on the phone with the vet, frantic, all the while desperately begging B to get up. When I had to leave B was struggling to his feet.

But he's fine now. The downer? The medical bill was outrageous.

So I decided to make coin bins and ask local store managers to put them next to their cashiers. At this point we'll take spare change and rumpled dollar bills happily.

For a long time I've never wanted to depend on anyone else out of fear they would let me down. I've done things myself rather than ask someone for help, but I have to ask for help now, for the ranch's sake. For the horses. We're doing everything we can to bring attention to us – November 28th, for example, we'll be having an open ranch. It'll be a day for people to come and meet the horses of our sanctuary and donate money for them. I'm so excited.

On our open ranch day, people will see Sweet Boy clanging his bell for treats. They'll see Sedona's face pop up over his stall in the hopes he'll get treats, too.

They'll watch John and Solo gallop around in the arena and they'll laugh at Min's dignity. They'll cheer for Little D as she limps toward her stall door and marvel at her strength, and they'll smile as Iron Man and Slayer fight for their attention.

They'll stand in awe as Tarzan walks right up to them.

These complete strangers will be amazed at Chance's wild beauty and fall in love with RustyBob, and they'll ask CharlieHorse their questions and chuckle when Guess chases Bella away from her food bucket. They'll see it all. They'll see every miracle that these horses create.

I can't wait.

Anyway, I stopped by in the morning to say hello (I'm not feeling well, but even though I decided to skip the morning volunteering over the past few days, I couldn't stay away). Lynn and Trent were there helping Jim and Sam. It was wonderful to see Lynn, as always, but Trent was so friendly towards me that I was a bit stunned. That burning nervousness I am all too familiar with crept inside me as he talked, so I instinctively kept trying to get away from him. As I made my excuses at once point and tried to walk over to the field to watch Jericho and Venture playing with a cone, Trent called after me.

"Now, Lexi, you gotta promise me something now, okay?"

I sighed deeply. "I don't make promises I won't keep, so that could be difficult. But we'll see."

"Well, just listen closely. When my hours of community service are up – " (and I will leave to the imagination exactly how many swear words were mixed in with this) "– you gotta come out and see my ranch, where all of my racehorses live in these great big stalls and they're gentle and sweet and they won't act up and cause hell like some of the ones around here."

Sam threw him a dirty look from where he was standing. He loves Chance as much as I do, and I'm sure I was glaring at Trent, too.

"Thank you," I said simply, "and I will definitely think about it."

"You should! You'd like it there, Lexi. It's a different world than the one y'all live in here."

"I'm sure it is," I said sweetly, and I turned on my heel and walked away.

Lynn was doing the NoFly for Tarzan when I approached my boys Slayer and Iron Man. Tarzan was moving around nervously and I stood watching Lynn's attempt to calm him down. I wanted to give her advice, to tell her how to get him to stand still and ease his anxiety. I wanted to offer to do it so I would save her the trouble (and be a bit of a show off, too, I think). The bossy, stubborn part inside of me fought in favor of doing just that as I stood there watching them. But for some reason, I held my tongue.

I thought of how Trent always tells Jim, "You could do it this way," or informs Sam, "Here, let *me* do that – " (and the looks on Jim and Sam's faces afterward). But more than that, I thought of the time Jim had insisted that I do Tarzan's NoFly instead of going in and doing it himself. It would have saved time and hassle had he done it. But he wanted me to learn.

Maybe I have to stop telling others what to do and how to do it, and just as I thought this, Lynn took another step toward Tarzan and he stood still. Slowly, surely, she held her hand out and took his flymask, and I remembered how T had allowed me to do the same thing all those months ago. And as I continued to watch, Lynn put the NoFly over his face as he stood like a champ.

I was so proud of both of them in that moment. I was not the person that should have been feeling pride, but it was just amazing to see that there are other people in this world that understand horses. And seeing Tarzan opening his heart up to another human being was a miracle to witness.

I'm glad I stayed silent.

Chance and RustyBob were led out to the arena as I was leaving. I kept my distance when Jim came through with Chance, knowing that at any second the horse could turn and charge. But seeing him walk even a short distance was a breathtaking sight as it always is. There is something about the way Chance just towers over Jim, something about his pure might and the power I see in every muscle that pushes him forward and something about the way he tosses his head and flashes his eyes that takes my breath away. I ended up staying an extra few minutes just to watch him gallop around in the arena like the wild and untamed horse he is.

I'm going to ride him.

But only when he lets me. When he's ready. When I'm ready. Somehow, someway, I will ride him.

October 14, 2009

Jericho is dead.

Colic.

Moose must have wanted him in the Great Herd badly. Why else would such a beautiful, precious boy have been taken away from Jim, from Venture, from all of us?

This isn't fair. This isn't right. Why do horrible people stay alive when all of the amazing creatures of the world are dying left and right?

First Mr. Steve Vai. And Rusty. And Moose. Now Jericho. My poor Jericho.

Who's next?

***

Every time Tierra Madre loses a horse, I think the same, selfish thing.

I should have...

I should have spent more time with him.

I should have told him how special he was, what me meant to me, what he taught me.

I should have let him nibble my forearm and shove his head to my face and trot away from me when I would come with the NoFly. I should have played with him more.

I'm going to be different around all of those horses now. I'm going to spend more time with each of them. They don't deserve for me to say a hello and give them a pat and walk away feeling as though I made a difference in their lives. No, they need my undivided attention for as long as they want me. Because they all have done more for me than I could ever repay.

I don't want to lose another horse and have these feelings come up again.

Anyway, I stopped by after school armed with carrots and apples and salts and vinegar and everything else I could possibly think of to donate (including Top Ramen and cookies for Jim). As I got out of my car and climbed through the gate, I looked out to the field at John's gang, and there was no blinding white coat among Solo, Suze, and Venture's bays and Kiss's chestnut and John and Bentley's blacks. No Jericho.

I was immediately overcome with that familiar, horrible finality that only hits me when I see an empty stall.

I tried not to cry as I walked through the pathway toward the line of stalls and saw that Chance was standing at our corner, looking right at me with shining eyes. And in that moment, he was all I needed to see. Comfort that I cannot describe washed through me at the mere sight of him, looking at me in such a breathtaking and regal way. I smiled my first real smile of the day.

"Hey, you," I murmured and one ear flicked toward me as he inclined his head as though he was nodding. I was reminded of the time I had watched him talk to Mistah Lee, when Chance had been composed of respect and utter nobility. His ears went back as I got closer, but they twisted forward again as I started to walk away. I felt his eyes on me as I moved, and suddenly I felt a lot better though logically I shouldn't have. Usually when I'm in a depression episode, when I know that someone is relying on me to be strong, I just crumble faster. But knowing that Chance was looking to me as though wondering how I would react to another death made me feel almost protected, maybe even needed.

How I love that horse.

I understand now why people have funerals, why people lay flowers down and light candles and pray for their dead loved ones. Seeing Venture, Jericho's best friend and partner in crime, seeing Jim, seeing the field filled with too many dark coats now that

Jericho's white was no longer there to keep it all in balance... all of that made me want to honor our poor dead family member. I wanted to reach out to those who missed him more than I did, to make a difference and help heal the new wounds.

But you know what was amazing? Jim was fine. He laughed and played with the remaining horses out in the field, he joked around with Min and John and everyone and cheerfully fed them their grain and supplements. He put his face close to Venture's and talked to him for a long time. When he came back for more grain, Venture seemed a bit more at peace.

It is incredible to me that people have the courage to move on like horses. Horses don't mourn for too long. They take each day as it comes, keeping things real and positive, knowing that whatever happens is for the best. And Jim seems to have learned how to do that, too.

So why can't I?

As I left I took a last look behind me as I always do, to see the horses in the shed row – Guess and Bella and Jani and Heighten and Hudson and Cocoa and Akira and Mistah Lee and Little D and RustyBob and Chance – all eating contentedly. And as always I had to do a double-take at Chance. It's impossible not to. He is too beautiful for words.

And I was struck by a horrible, paralyzing fear.

We've lost four horses since I started volunteering at the ranch. Out of the original twenty-nine, there are twenty-five left. Iron Man is a part of the family now, and he plus our visitor Cocoa makes twenty-seven. I don't know if I can handle losing another one.

But Chance.

If we lost Chance…

I can't write it. I can't even think it.

I'm hoping that no matter what happens, I'll be brave, just as I promised. But beyond anything else in the world I'm hoping for extra protection around all of the horses. Especially Chance.

Take good care of Jericho, Moosie. He'll need you.

And please help me be brave.

Help us all.

October 17, 2009

It was like old times today, but not.

Not one volunteer showed up today. No Trent (thank God), no Lynn, no Lori. Sam the Volunteer disappeared a long time ago. It was just me and Jim and Sam. And the horses. Just like it had been during the summer.

But no Jericho. No Moosie or Mr. Steve Vai. No Rusty in Iron Man's stall.

It was weird.

All the horses were a bit confused when I did the NoFly today. See, everyone has been so used to Lynn doing it for at least a month, so when it was back to me I swear they were all thinking, "Wait a minute...." It took ten minutes for me to get Tarzan to stay still. In the end I was able to, singing a lullaby and patiently taking steps toward him, but it stung a little bit.

I tried to spend more time with everybody. I want them to know me again, to like and understand me and to know that I'm one of them, not just a volunteer who, in Jim's words, shows up two or three times, take some pictures, proclaim themselves superior horsemen/women, then decide that working in the hot sun is too much for them and vanish. I want those horses to trust me completely.

So I went around, patting noses, rubbing foreheads, scratching necks, talking and laughing as if I were meeting everyone for the first time. Guess let me put the NoFly over her nose as she was eating. Bella looked at me with liquid eyes and followed me to the stall door. Jani danced when I scratched her neck. Heighten and I played our old chasing game. Hudson rubbed his face against me in typical Galoot fashion. Cocoa stood still as a statue for me as I sprayed her flanks. Akira flicked her ears back and eyed me wearily at first out of her old sassiness, but she dipped her head in acknowledgment when I left. Mistah Lee gazed at me happily and playfully threw his head up out of my reach. Little D thrived in her attention and put her nose to my hand before I left. RustyBob… RustyBob. I have to talk about him.

I have fallen more in love with that horse than I thought was possible; unbridled, unconditional, head-over-heels in love. He is the sweetest and one of the most incredible animals I have ever met.

No wonder he and Chance are friends.

Today when I went into his stall his nose twitched in utter joy and he gazed at me with devotion in his eyes. I threw my arms around him and buried my face in his mane for a long time. He stood utterly still, not looking for food or shifting impatiently like the other horses always do, just standing and contentedly lending his strength to me.

I realized how much I had never really spent time with him before, how I had always hurried through his NoFly to get to Chance. Little D always gets the utmost attention when I'm with her, and of course Chance gets more of my attention than all of the horses combined. But RustyBob, living in between them, oftentimes gets next to nothing. He stands there every time, day in and day out, looking at me with big eyes, just waiting for me to come back into his stall and love him a little extra, too. And I haven't.

But RustyBob has given me nothing but unconditional love since day one. No matter what I've done (or haven't done), he has always stood still for his NoFly when even Slayer or Ted would move away and held his head out to me when I needed comfort when all the other horse I would try to hug would want to graze.

As I stood there in his stall today, all of this flooding into my mind, I felt horrible.

Over and over I ran my fingers through his mane as he stood happily, silently telling him I was sorry. The thoughts weren't even out of my head before I knew I was forgiven. "I love you, my baby boy," I told him again and again. "You've always been there for me, RustyBob. Always."

And he nibbled at my shirt hem, almost shaking with the happiness of having me close to him. When I finally let go of him and studied his eyes, they were wide and shining with loyalty.

"I love you, Lex, I do," was his blissful reply, "I think you're the most special person in the whole wide world. Thanks for spending time with me, Lex. Thanks a lot. And I love you. Did I say that already? I love you."

Out of the corner of my eye I saw Chance looking at us in something close to wonder (or maybe it was disgust). When I turned to look at him with a big smile on my face, he laid his ears back and snorted.

But Chance stood still when I did his NoFly. I rubbed his nose and sprayed his legs and flanks and gave him some alfalfa when he banged on the lower bar of his stall door. RustyBob sniffed on the ground for food, occasionally looking up to watch, and he stuck his cow-nose through the bars to touch my hand as I gave him a little bit of alfalfa, too, before walking back toward the tack room. Chance, of course, watched me leave.

When I did the NoFly for the other side (taking care to spray Min from the outside of the fence) I looked automatically for Jericho's white coat when I was in the field before I remembered. John and Solo were out in the arena, and Suze had allowed Bentley and Kiss to come with her into John's "office" to finish off any food John had left. But Venture was eating all by himself in a corner on the opposite side of the corral. He was slowly picking hay out of one of the troughs as though he wasn't really hungry. He looked utterly, completely lost.

I think something in my heart shattered.

I almost started crying then and there, seeing him all alone. Jericho was his best friend. And as Jim said, it was a cruel, mindless crime for Jericho to have been taken away from Venture so heartlessly. Those two horses were always together. I honestly can't remember a time when they weren't within ten feet of each other.

I tried to talk to Venture, tried patting and kissing him, but other than holding his head briefly for me to do his NoFly, he ignored me. He didn't want attention unless it was from Jim. He wanted to be alone, and I, for one, could understand that. So I walked away, holding back tears that were for Venture and his tremendous loss.

It wasn't until later, after I had lamented about not being able to help that poor horse in any way, that I realized that I had helped Venture, just by leaving him alone.

Jim's taken to riding him bareback all throughout the ranch and up and down the street. Venture loves being ridden and he feels special because of Jim's undivided attention, and we all think that's the best thing for him right now.

As I walked to my car when it was time to go, I kept wondering what it would be like to ride Chance bareback, as though we were one being, just as Jim and Venture seem to be whenever they're together. RustyBob would do it in a heartbeat, but his back ankles are bad he can't really be ridden. Slayer, as much as he loves me, has a mind of his own and he would do his own thing no matter what. Same with Ted.

I wonder if Chance would let me ride him in a year or so, when he's ready. I wonder if he would listen to me like RustyBob does, like Venture listens to Jim.

At this point I'm starting to think that if colic can claim a horse's life in less than twelve hours, if I can rebuild Tarzan's trust with me in ten minutes, if RustyBob can forgive me and if brave warriors can die in their sleep and strong little mares can look death right in the eye and still pull through and if belligerent trainers can strike innocent and beautiful horses and if the love from these horses can keep me from falling back into a depression... anything is possible.

At this point, I've thrown my hands up.

We'll see what happens next.

October 19th, 2009

I went to see everyone today after school with a bag of carrots in my arms. Needless to say, I was the most popular person there. Whenever someone enters the gate with a big bag of treats, or apples, or carrots, it's like someone sends off an alarm so that everybody knows within a matter of instants. The shy horses become demanding. The quiet ones become domineering. The bossy horses become almost violent. It is not morally possible to give a carrot to one horse and not give one to another – the look of utter loathing that the neglected creature gives is one that nobody could possibly ignore. Overall, carrot/apple/treat giving is an epic ritual at Tierra Madre.

Here's the script: Enter me. Enter carrots.

Chance: "INCOMING!"

RustyBob: "Lex, it's you! Oh, boy, carrots, carrots, carrots!"

Little D: "Wait, did somebody say–?"

Mistah Lee: "Hey, Akira, look! We're gettin' carrots!"

Akira: "Carrots? For us? Yes!"

Cocoa: "No way! Hey, Hudson..."

Hudson: "Yo, Heighten, carrots! Check it out..."

Heighten: "Jani, Bella, Guess . . . hey, LADIES! Carrot time!"

By the time I visit Ted and CharlieHorse and go around to give Sweet Boy and Sedonie their beloved treats (they're nearest to the field side), Min is shooting piercing holes into my soul with his angelic look of longing and Charlie has whispered the news to either M'Stor or John, both of whom will scream the announcement to Solo, Suze, Bentley, Kiss, Venture, (I almost wrote Jericho's name) Slayer, Iron Man, and Tarzan.

It's a production and it's a chain reaction. And I love every part of it, from the snaps of irritation aimed in my direction when I seemingly don't give enough, to the mass stampedes toward me that send me scrambling through fences for my life, to the loving little nips I am given (usually by Slayer, Kiss, Ted, Guess, Hudson, Solo, and RustyBob) after they get their treats. I wear those bruises proudly.

And if there is ever a day when I don't feel wanted, or appreciated, or needed in any way, all I have to do is come to the ranch with carrots for that to change.

I was a bit surprised when I came to Iron Man and Slayer. Instead of them seeing the carrots, they each took a mouthful of my school uniform and started chewing. "Here are my best boys," I told them happily as I stood between them. Actually, I have two sets of best boys: those two, and Chance and RustyBob, but nobody needs to know that. "Didn't you see the carrots, guys?" And as I showed them the bag they instantly stopped nibbling at my skirt and shirt hem and thrust their noses at me, lips clapping in anticipation. Tarzan whinnied from across the way, and when I offered him a carrot he took it from my hands without any fear.

Good, everybody.

I love those guys.

October 24, 2009

People never know a horse until they've seen what he or she is like around children.

I took my sister, Riley, to Tierra Madre today, and because she's five she was scared of Mike at first, and it took her a while to warm up to everyone. But the horses were on their unbelievably best behavior, and Riley was dragging me around happily before long.

Slayer loved her. He followed her around as well as he could from his pen, making her laugh and giving her the courage to reach out and touch his nose. He gazed wonderingly into her little face and stood rock still when she was close to him. RustyBob was the same way. His eyes shone when he saw me coming and he whickered happily when I reached in to rub his nose. He shook all over with joy and he snorted and nibbled at my fingers happily, but when my little sister timidly held out a hand to him he stood still as a statue, looking at her curiously.

Chance, of course, would sooner allow Jim or Sam to saddle him than hold his head still for a complete stranger to pat. I told Riley, as I had told Jim's grandkids long ago, to draw an imaginary line between RustyBob's and Chance's stall doors, and not to cross it. Chance stood quietly, ears back, but he gazed at my sister with mild interest and turned away when we left and headed back toward the barn.

When I took my sister around again to say goodbye, I saw Trent leaving, walking down the pathway toward his car. He thrust his hand at Chance as though trying to prove something to an audience (Lynn and her daughter were right there with RustyBob) and I couldn't hear what he said in a triumphant tone but whatever he announced pissed Chance off. He threw his head up over the bars and lunged at Trent with his ears laid flat on his head and his teeth snapping. Trent dove out of the way just in time, and he swore quite loudly as he picked himself up off the ground. But he didn't stand and fight. He practically ran for his truck.

I pulled my sister from Little D, over to Lynn and her daughter.

"What just happened?" I asked, watching as Chance paced back and forth in his pen, eyes flashing. Lynn shook her head.

"Trent's just trying to pat him, I think. But Chance won't ever let him do it," she said sadly. "You know what I think? Trent is more about force, and power, whereas here we're more about trust and love."

"Yeah, and Chance knows that," I finished.

"Absolutely," Lynn said. "I just wish Trent could get his act together, you know?"

"I can't stand him," I told her. "He's from a racing world, remember. He doesn't fit in here at all."

"No, he doesn't."

Lynn and her daughter were giving RustyBob leaves from the tree, and when Chance saw me standing there, he pounded on the lower bar of his stall, looking at me expectantly. Riley and Lynn's little girl both jumped and took a few steps back. I smiled at my baby boy.

"Stay right here for a second, okay?" I told Riley, and I went to give Chance his share of leaves from the tree outside his stall. As I touched his nose briefly, with three people watching, I couldn't help but feel utterly uplifted. Chance would not let Trent anywhere near him but for me, his eyes would soften and he would willingly put his nose through the bars for me to touch.

"I thought you said no one could pat him!" my sister said, sounding as shocked as only a five year old could. Lynn, her daughter and I laughed.

"Chance is nervous around strangers; he just likes certain people near him," I answered, and I restrained myself from adding, *and I'm one of them.*

Jim gave my sister a little white stuffed horse before we left. Her eyes lit up and a big smile stretched across her face as she reached for it.

"What are you going to name her?" I asked her later, as we walked to my car.

Riley hugged the little horse to her happily. "Little D!"

Thank you, Tierra Madre.

October 31, 2009

Is it Halloween already? Wasn't it just yesterday I was learning all of the horses' names?

Today was the first day I actually brought a jacket with me to the ranch. The jeans and thick socks and boots I resented during the summer were suddenly appreciated very much, and I found myself working harder throughout the day just to try and warm up. The sun shone brighter after an hour or two, though, and then the weather was beautiful.

Bentley got his back done today. Jim thought that something was wrong with his withers since the poor horse doesn't have any muscle up there, and sure enough, when the chiropractor, Dr. Wood, pulled up today, it was confirmed that something had to be done.

So they put B between two stacks of hay and the doc stood above B on one of the stacks, pushing down on his withers to put it back into place. Lynn had left so Jim, Sam, and Trent held B while Doc gave orders. Sam and Trent would hold him up on one side and Jim would swing B's head around so the withers would be positioned correctly. They had to tranquilize B to make it happen, but in the end he did well and felt a lot better afterward.

Bentley was what stood out to me the most, but tons of other things happened, as always, in the four hours I was there. I hadn't spent so much time at the ranch in a long time, and I was so happy that I was there this whole morning.

I brought Sweet Boy and Sedonie back from the arena to their stalls then put John and Solo out. It was difficult to lead John in, because Solo got into his corner house and it pissed him off, I think, and it took me a few tries before he would follow me into the arena. But when I brought Solo out, all hell broke loose. John ran around in circles right next the gate and Solo threw his head up and pulled at the lead rope and tried to run with his best friend. Jim had to hold John back as I calmed Solo down and when I finally got him in, both horses took off and started bucking, rearing, galloping for all it was worth.

So that was some excitement.

Lynn got there sometime around then, and she took over the NoFly. Sam and Trent were doing stalls, so I got some brushes and started working on horses that needed mud scraped out of their coats. Ted was restless, and didn't want me anywhere near him, so I went to CharlieHorse. He stood rock-still and munched on his hay and thought to himself quietly as I groomed him. All of the horses' coats are so soft now. Their winter coats have grown in so most of them are much darker and they are absolutely beautiful.

I talked with Trent as I worked on my little brother Hudson. (His whole left side was coated in mud.) Jim and Sam both refer to Trent as "dickhead," and absolutely cannot stand his constant chattering, but for some reason, I had no problem with it today. Maybe the cooler weather didn't make me so crabby. Anyway, Trent told me about his ranch and I asked questions, genuinely interested. Hudson stood calmly next to me and pushed his nose against my shoulder whenever my nerves acted up, and eventually I was talking to him easily.

"I've got some girls working for me who are a bit like you," Trent said at some point as he mucked out Hudson's stall beside me. "They're all horse crazy, you know, and real patient with the animals, and they get their jobs done. But you're real cautious when it comes to people you don't know, aren't you? Like the Yellow Horse. But I guess that in this day and age that's a good thing."

I nodded in agreement. "It sucks how life has to be like that, though."

The Tierra Madre magic is finally starting to work on him, I think. This morning when he walked up as I was feeding the shed side of the ranch he actually got off of his phone (!) and asked me, "So what's going on, beautiful?" Poor Trent's had a rough week because he lost his grandfather several days ago. That's definitely the only reason I let him hug me right after I told him I was sorry for his loss. It was funny, because Chance had his eye on us, and after Trent had walked toward the barn to get the cart and rake, I looked back at that horse to see his ears back and his eyes on me uneasily. When I smiled, however, Chance's ears pricked forward again and he turned back to his food.

Anyway, although he's had a bad couple of days, Trent was working with the same cheery and yet rather pig-headed confidence he always has had, if not a little subdued.

Lynn said it best: "This place *does* something to you."

I hope Trent will go back to his ranch when his community services hours are up and treat his horses more like the precious creatures they are rather than as though they were bags of cash waiting to happen. Chance was uneasy around him today but didn't lunge at him, to my knowledge, anyway. But hey, it's a start.

Speaking of Chance, I have another experiment for him. I went up to him with the brush after I was done with Hudson, and I showed it to him and let him chew at it for several minutes.

"You may not like this," I told him as he nipped contentedly at the bristles. "Ted didn't want me to do it for him today. But some of the other horses live for it." And I raised the brush and gently brought it between his eyes, where his white star is, and brought it down his nose. His head was through the bars, so this was difficult, but he didn't react to it at all. I brushed his nose again several times, and other than nibbling at the brush when I brought it near his lips, he stood still and let me do it. His eyes were softer than I had seen them in a long time, lowered in almost a sleepy, content way, as though he were thinking, "Huh, this isn't so bad."

"That's great, baby boy. Someday I'll go in there and brush all of you. Would you like that?"

"I dunno. I guess. But don't do that for a while, okay?"

"Of course, Chance. This is perfect right now, just as it is."

I gave both CharlieHorse and Mistah Lee walks after that. CharlieHorse's leg is still arthritic so it needs daily exercise to keep it tightened up, but my little boy just wanted to go home after a few minutes. Mistah Lee, however, was the opposite. Back in June when I walked him he would barely make it in a circle around the ranch and he would be exhausted by the time we got back. Today, he pulled at his lead rope, walked so quickly around to several areas that I had to trot to keep up, whipped his head around to see everything and happily touched noses with every horse we met. We explored different areas and saw new things, and Mistah Lee loved it. He was so alive and happy today that I nearly danced back to his stall when it was time to take him home. His newly found wonder is a true miracle.

I had a scare later on, when the doc and Jim and Sam and Trent were working on Bentley and I was taking Ted out to the arena to get him away from the action. Ted was so thrilled to be out of his stall that he nearly leapt through his door and he pranced around as I opened the arena gate and let him in.

But then the halter I was using would not come off. The hook was stuck in the buckle, and Ted, dancing around and impatient to get loose, was not making my job easier. Then, without warning, he broke free of my grip and launched himself in one direction.

We were both in the arena and the gate was closed, but the halter was still on him and the rope was dangling dangerously between his two front legs. I swear my heart leapt straight into my throat. If horses trip over a rope at such a speed, a rope that is connected to a halter that is strapped around their face, they could easily break a leg or an ankle or snap something in their neck or worse. A neck injury would be easier to cure than a shattered leg. Well, actually, I take that back – a broken leg would be easier to handle because the only way to cure *that* would be to put the horse down.

So when Ted galloped away, lead rope swinging, utter terror swept through me and I cried out with all of the authority I could muster in that split second, "Ted, *whoa!*"

And he *froze.* He froze with one hoof in the air, his neck stretched out in halted eagerness to roll and play, and he looked back at me like a playground-bound child looking back at his mother who had yelled at him to stop. A huge, eleven hundred pound animal, standing utterly still for a scrawny, eighteen-year-old girl.

Heart pounding, I slowly stepped back over to him, putting a smile on my face, trying desperately to stay calm.

"Easy, there, baby boy!" I said as cheerfully as I could as I reached over and took the rope in my hands. My hands were trembling. "We gotta get this off first."

Eventually it came off, and with a word from me a very happy Ted sprinted away, shaking his mane. I watched him bolt around with my heart still thumping wildly. I am so, so thankful that he screeched to a halt when I told him to, otherwise we could have had a disaster on our hands. And it all would have been my fault.

Maybe these horses listen to me as much as I listen to them after all. Either way, I know that we understand each other, and if anything else were to be, today Ted could have been seriously injured.

November 5, 2009

A new horse has come to our ranch!

His name's Chester, and he's an elderly gelding with Cushings disease. His former owner (and I use that term loosely) apparently stopped caring for him, and a young woman named Ivy took him under her wing for several weeks until the owner decided to send poor Chester to the auction.

Auction.

And Ivy pleaded with him for more time to find Chester a home, and she found Jim Gath of the Tierra Madre Horse Sanctuary. And now Chester is at the ranch, safe, wanted, and happy.

I can't wait to meet him. I'm gonna go over right after school tomorrow and see him.

We're also getting three other horses next week. A brother and sister and a mustang that's never even been halter trained. Man, is that gonna be rough. But mustangs are my favorite kind of horse, and I can't wait.

On the downside, Tierra Madre is gonna have to scrape up the funds to support four more horses.

And we gotta continue to help find homes for the others, because if we don't...

Auction.

November 6, 2009

Chester is the biggest sweetheart I have ever met in my life. Today I stopped by for a visit after school and when I saw him standing with his face to the wall in Moosie's old stall, I have to admit my heart jumped a little. I was imagining Moosie standing there.

Chester's a chestnut gelding with a white blaze down his face and big brown eyes. His left eye was closed; we think there's some sort of infection going on in there. He is skinny, too skinny, and his coat is rumpled, but he is just the sweetest horse I've ever met. The horse had his nose in the corner of Moosie's stall (it will forever be

Moosie's stall to me, no one else's) but when he heard me talking to him, Chester flicked one ear my way, turned around slowly, and waddled right up to the fence where I stood. He put his nose to the rail where my hand was and let me rub his white blaze and tell him how happy I was that he was there. He blinked sleepily and stood there for a few minutes, decided that I was okay, and shuffled back over to his place where he had been dozing.

He's home now, saved from slaughter. I'm so, so happy for him.

The three horses that are coming in should be coming to us next Thursday. Oh, and speaking of them, here is something that has thrown me a bit off guard.

Jim and I were talking about finding a "Santa" for our open ranch day on the twenty-eighth, and for show he put on an old Santa hat he found on his chair. I laughed and asked, "Hey, Santa, can I have a horse?"

"What, is that all you want for Christmas?" Jim said and I nodded.

"I've asked for a horse every Christmas and birthday since I was five," I told him. "It won't happen, so I can't wait to move out so I can have one."

"We can get you a horse here," he said.

I stared at him for a moment or two, mind reeling, then responded in the only way I thought applied to the situation.

"That's really funny, Jim…"

"I mean it. You could have a horse." He was dead serious. "Heck, you might be able to have one of the three that are coming in next week."

I thought of the mustang that had never been halter-broken, and my heart positively soared.

"You're serious?"

"Absolutely."

I thought for a minute, and then I said, "If I had a horse, I'd get up at the same time you do, at like, 2:45 in the morning, to take care of it. I'd do anything."

"You can take care of all of these guys, then, and I'll sleep in," Jim said jokingly, and he picked up his guitar and started to play my favorite song of his. I gazed out the window, daydreaming, imagining having a horse a horse that would look up to me like the others look up to Jim, a horse I could take care of and learn from and ride and call my very own.

I'd give anything for something like that.

"How much does it cost to keep a horse here?" I asked and started calculating with the answers I got. Jim said he would be fine with him paying me for my volunteer work, so that I would earn the cost of boarding a horse rather than me taking on another paying job. But, like I had during the summer when he made the same offer for the first time, I fought him tooth and nail. I told him I couldn't accept money from him, and after a long battle he shook his head, threw up his hands, and said, "You're being ridiculous."

I shrugged.

"But I guess the thing is," he went on, "you have class."

"What's that supposed to mean?" I demanded.

"It's a good thing," he said, smiling, "It means you don't take the easy way out."

"Well, the easy way out usually leads to a road that sucks," I told him, and he laughed.

"You," he told me when I was leaving, "are an angel."

I shook my head. "No," I said and he just nodded in reply.

"Yes, yes you are. I know angels," he said.

I kept shaking my head, speechless.

"And you are one, baby girl."

I smiled weakly. "Maybe someday I'll believe you," was all I could say.

I walked back toward the gate, still dreaming about owning a horse. Chance pounded on the lower bar of his door as I passed his stall, and I gave him a few bits of alfalfa. RustyBob's sweet, hopeful eyes pierced through me so I ended up giving him some, too. I love them both, as I love every other Tierra Madre horse, but I kept thinking about owning one of my own, coming to the ranch before and after school so I could look after him or her and going on trail rides and spending time with my horse so that he or she would follow me around in utter trust, the way the Tierra Madre horses do for Jim...

I couldn't believe Jim would do something like that for me. My mind started spinning again.

"I don't get it," I said aloud.

I didn't get an answer from either Chance or RustyBob other than the sound of their happy chewing, and as I walked back to my car, I was convinced that maybe they understand something I didn't.

November 8, 2009

This is ridiculous. Out of the ten to fifteen places I went to today to ask if I could put coin bins by their checkout lines, two stores allowed me to put donation tubs by their registers. Two!

One of those stores was the Starbucks my older brother works at. The other was the place I worked at for over a year.

I am not trying to solicit people, I am not trying to take up space on countertops (three inches, the horror!), and I am not trying to run corporations out of business. I am trying to save twenty-eight freaking horses.

What is with people nowadays?

November 9, 2009

I wish I could write eulogies.

Because Little D deserves the most incredible one anyone could ever write.

Lately she's been lying down too much. She's been sore and the pain of laminitis is showing too clearly in her eyes, and when I came by the ranch today Jim told me sadly that he thought her time was coming.

I couldn't believe it.

She's fought so much. She's fought for her life since July, she's made it through heat and misery and exhaustion and discouragement and now this laminitis is going to take over? This battle is going to be lost? It's not right. It's not fair.

Before I left the ranch I went to see her.

"Oh, angel," I sobbed, crying and stroking her nose and looking into her pain-stricken eyes, "I'm sorry. I promised. I promised you that I'd have faith no matter what happens."

But Little D did nothing. She just looked over to where Jim was, waiting patiently for her food. I wiped my cheeks and gazed at her. She was suffering, God knew she was suffering… but through her agony I could see strength shining in her eyes. Pure, unbridled determination that nothing could ever take away.

Over and over I've tried to write how much this meant to me, again and again I've tried to describe the nobility and the grace and the bravery I saw in that dying little mare today… but I can't do it.

Her courage is indescribable. Indescribable.

Now is not the time for me to be selfish. If Little D must fly on tomorrow then I'm going to try to be happy for her. I'll know that her suffering will be gone and that she won't have to fight ever again. I'll try to be happy because that angel deserves every bit of joy she'll receive when she's a part of the Great Herd.

The doctor will come to x-ray her in the morning, and they'll act on the results they get. Jim said he may not wait until Wednesday to do what needs to be done if the results are what he thinks they will be.

I have to believe that whatever needs to happen will happen.

Little D is in someone else's hands.

November 10, 2009

Fly high, Little D.

You didn't deserve to live in this horrible world. Go on and light up the next.

Run with Moosie, and Mr. Steve Vai and my baby Rusty and Jericho. Run as fast as you can, and roll and buck and rear like you couldn't before.

I'll miss you, little angel.

***

After Jericho died, I wondered who would be the next to go.

I thought about CharlieHorse, one of our older horses. I thought about Heighten or Hudson rough-housing it too much in the arena one day. I thought about Mistah Lee and his bad hip. I thought about Min, another one of our laminitis-stricken horses.

I *never* thought it would be Little D.

I had always assumed she would pull through. I figured that if she had fought since July, she would be okay in the long run. And though lately she's been having a few bad days, yesterday, when Jim told me that he thought her time was up, it was a bit of a shock. I had hope for her until the very end.

And now she's gone.

Ever since the horrible day she started limping, ever since that day in mid-July when it was confirmed that she had laminitis (a mere week before Mr. Steve Vai was diagnosed, too), I've dreamed of her being cured for good. I've dreamed of us leading her out to the arena so she could run and play and toss her head and gallop across the pasture and roll and dance again. Every day I would imagine all of this and look forward to the day Little D would be released from her suffering.

Today when I read the news from Jim during class, I was heartbroken.

Little D would never have the chance to do any of that.

But you know what I realized? Right now, right now in the Great Herd, Little D is doing all of that. She's released from her suffering. And she's happy.

And for the first time since August when we lost Mr. Steve Vai and Rusty, I'm happy, too.

I cried yesterday when I realized that it really was Little D's time to die. I cried a little today, too, but later on, I wasn't sad. Now? I'm so happy for that little angel. I'm so happy that she's free.

When I stopped by the ranch today and saw her stall, I only paused to look at it for a minute or two. Chance and RustyBob watched me. RustyBob had actually moved into Little D's stall since their stalls are connected and they had left the door open. He was nibbling half-heartedly at her food. I reached in to Chance's stall and rubbed his nose. He blinked and studied me.

"There are those soft eyes," I whispered. "How's RustyBob doing?"

RustyBob looked up as I passed him, his eyes shining at the sight of me. I remembered with a pang how much he had loved Little D. I rubbed his nose and he looked at me with affection in his eyes, happily listening to me talk and nibbling at the Bermuda grass that lay in Little D's feeder. RustyBob is sad, too, but he knows what I have finally realized.

I could choose to be miserable because I've now lost five of my best friends. Or I could look at it in an unselfish, more positive way: I could recognize that those five horses are now a part of something much greater and more beautiful than anything here on Earth and count myself lucky for getting a chance to know them, if only for a short period of time.

The angels of Tierra Madre have taught me that the here and the now is all we have.

Back in August I realized that Little D would not give in without a fight. And she didn't. She fought, all right. And she chose the right time to surrender gracefully.

She's home now. She's at peace.

And so am I.

November 13, 2009

Sundance, Katie, and Holly are here! They are absolutely tiny – less than 15 hands each. But they are so sweet. Katie's a dark, creamy brown and her younger brother is Sundance, a caramel-colored gelding. Holly is the mustang, with a reddish brown tint in her coat. Jim calls them a box of chocolates.

The three of them are in the round pen, and they're happy as clams in there. I don't know them very well yet, and I'm looking forward to spending time with them.

The coin bins are doing pretty well as far as coin bins can go. This past week and a half we've raised seventy-five dollars!

November 15, 2009

There were so many people at the ranch today. Jim and Sam, of course, and Bre was walking around grooming the horses with a few others. Plus I met Nicole, a new worker. She's very nice; we were talking easily almost at once.

I helped Nicole muck out stalls and as I was doing this, I realized I hadn't mucked out a stall since August or September. But I fell back into it, helping her with Chester's (almost wrote Moosie's) Ted's, CharlieHorse's, and all the kids in the shed row. Chance and RustyBob were out in the arena so Jim and Sam could work on the fencing at the back of their stalls, so there were no problems there. I said goodbye to Cocoa today, too. She's leaving to go back home soon, and as I hadn't really gotten to know her, I took time to rub her nose and talk to her for a bit. She's a bit like Bella – very soft and sweet but when something pisses her off she can flare up easily. Either way, she's a sweetheart. I'll miss her.

I also did the waters on the field side, another task I hadn't done since August or September. All of the other volunteers (Trent and Lynn) usually took over those jobs, but I found myself enjoying doing the hard work. There is something I love about being with the horses, getting dirty and muddy and bruised due to playful nipping. Today I couldn't figure out why at first, but when one of the middle school girls wandering around would tap their fingers on the bars of the stalls and ask whoever was in the pen to walk over to them, and that horse would come to *me* instead, I'd remember.

The NoFly no longer needs to be done since it's getting colder, so that was one less thing to do. So I gave B his medicine in his sweet feed/bran mash and fussed over him as well as I could. He soaked in the attention like a sponge, happily eating his food and standing as I patted his neck and talked to him softly. Bentley is the biggest horse at the ranch (next to Charlie) and he's black as night, but he has the most tender, gentle spirit of any big horse I've met. He loves to be treated that way, not as though he were a Trojan War horse.

Chester is quickly nestling himself into the place in my heart that I'd once blocked off as well as I could, the place that Chance and Slayer and CharlieHorse and RustyBob and Ted and the others have wormed their ways into. He stands with his nose over the bars, looking expectantly and lovingly into the eyes of whoever is close to him, and it is impossible to not pat him and tell him how special he is once I see his soft eyes. There's nothing but innocence there, and it's wonderful to see.

I wandered into Little D's stall today when I was mucking. And not one trace of sadness washed over me.

I told her I'd have hope for her until the very end, and I did my best to keep that promise. She's gone now, but I realize now that it's not the end. I still love that angel. I still think of her every day. Every time I think about taking the easy way out of anything, I feel her determined eyes piercing through me. I'm not sad. Not at all. On the contrary, I keep thinking of the dream I had every day when she was alive, the dream of her running free again, painlessly and effortlessly, without the horrors of laminitis to hold her back, and I'm blissfully happy.

That dream has come true.

November 18, 2009

Tierra Madre has set up a new Adopt a Horse program! For fifty dollars a month, anyone in the country (or the world, for that matter) can support one of our thirty horses (John, Solo, Suze, Venture, Bentley, Kiss, Charlie, Min, M'Stor, Slayer, Iron Man, Tarzan, Sweet Boy, Sedona, Ted, CharlieHorse, Chester, Guess, Bella, Jani, Heighten, Hudson, Cocoa (she's still with us), Akira, Mistah Lee, RustyBob, Chance, Sundance, Katie, or Holly) and be sent from their horse a lock of mane, set of shoes, a biography, monthly updates, a big picture, and an adoption certificate.

This program was put together yesterday, and I thought long and hard about whether or not I wanted to "adopt" a horse. I realized that I could never ask Jim to give up one of the new kids for me, not after what he did to bring them home and financially supporting one of the thirty horses would be the only way to have a bit more involvement in his or her life. So in the end I decided to commit to giving $1.67 a day to the ranch, if only for a month or two.

And I don't think I need to tell you which horse I chose.

I told Jim to forget about giving me the lock of mane and the shoes, as that would not happen without someone getting hurt, and that I didn't need the biography or the picture or the monthly updates. All I have to do is climb through the gate to Tierra Madre to learn what I would otherwise not know. But Jim says that I am getting a free horse painting, because I am the first (and unfortunately, only) person to adopt a horse. I think everyone was a bit surprised that I chose the youngest and wildest (and most beautiful) horse at the ranch. But as there are not a lot of people out there who understand Chance like I do, that was expected.

On another note, I'm redoubling my efforts to raise money for this place. The coin bins are still up and running and I'm going to go around and put up flyers advertising our open ranch on the 28th. This Saturday, if my former managers at the grocery store I once worked at will let me, I'm going to set up a table outside of the store and talk to customers about Tierra Madre. I've contacted fundraising companies and I'm looking into local news stations. I will do whatever it takes to help keep the ranch running. Jim doesn't have time to raise as much money as the ranch needs. He does everything he possibly can, more than he can... but as he's said, there just aren't enough hours in the day for him. He gets approximately five hours of sleep a night – five! – and sometimes less. Day in and day out. I can't even begin to imagine what that's like.

So I'm going to do everything I can to keep the ranch together. Those horses have become a part of me, and to see them torn apart, to see them hauled away on trailers, never to be seen again... I couldn't bear it. John and Solo split up? Sweet Boy and Sedona separated? Charlie and Min placed in separate trucks headed in different directions? Tarzan shipped back to a world of despair? Akira and Mistah Lee broken apart? Jani forced to be ridden again? CharlieHorse hauled to Montana for bear bait? Ted and Bentley and Heighten and Slayer's backs broken again? Kiss and Suze forced back into the show ring? M'Stor and Hudson and Iron Man dragged back to the race track? Chester sent back to auction?

I'd die. I'd die with each and every one of them. And all of this is just one more piece of added stress that is settling on my mind.

Because lately I've been stressed out about too many things. School is insane, my family is demanding, too many people need me for help and advice and whatnot, and I'm still dealing with the same issues I've been fighting for three years, problems within that Moosie saw the moment his eyes met mine and the problems every other horse in this place can sense. But how could they not? They were once abused too.

There are times when I'm driving home from school when I wonder why I always stop by to see everyone at the ranch, even for a few minutes, why I put so much of my time and soul into this place. When I stay to help do the afternoon feeding even when I'm exhausted, sometimes I wonder why I don't just make excuses and go home and rest. I wonder why I don't sleep in on the weekends, I wonder why I spend my own money on carrots and apples and why I walk around getting horse slobber on my hands and my clothes and my hair and mud and poop and bits of hay on my school shoes. There are times when I seriously wonder if I've gone insane.

But I walk through that gate, and Chance is always waiting at our corner. And he lifts his head and he gazes at me.

And that's all it takes. That's all I need.

His ears still go back if I get too close, his eyes still flash out of habit and whenever I'm anxious or tired since he soaks that energy in until he, too, is nervous. But I see the way he looks at me, with something hidden behind the hurt in his eyes, as though he is just waiting for me to flourish and overturn the world. He looks at me and through all of the confusion and the anxiety in his eyes and in his soul, I get the smallest, wildest feeling that be believes in me. He wouldn't admit it. Not now.

But I swear, every time I'm near Chance, I feel as though there is nothing I can't do. He reminds me of the strength I've had for years but never known, strength that keeps me going even when I'm running on empty.

All I have to do is look at him. And I remember everything.

November 20, 2009

I went to drop off another fifty-five dollars at Tierra Madre today. Fifty-five dollars! All from the coin bins!

Jim and I talked about the open ranch. We need tons of posters and flyers, we need to price out all of the gifts that have been sent to us, and we need to get bags of carrots and water and donuts to sell. Akira is going to be the horse the kids can sit on to get their pictures taken with Santa, and Bre will be running that. We need someone to run the refreshment table, the gift table, and the horse paintings we hope to get done. And, of course, volunteers need to be walking around making sure the horses are all okay.

Everyone's a bit worried about Chance. He lunges and snaps and kicks at anyone that walks by him. I forgot to ask how we were going to warn the passerby about him, but I hope we can maybe rope the outside of his stall off, so people know not to get near him. I hope he'll be all right – I don't want him to be any more nervous than he can be now.

Before I left I made sure to offer him my hand and let him nibble at it for a while. As we stood there together, I remembered that I had "adopted" him through the Adopt a Horse program and, as that is probably the closest I'll ever get to owning him, my heart soared. Well, "owning him" is the wrong phrase.

I want to be Chance's sole caregiver, the one person he relies on and looks to for food, water, a clean stall, and unconditional love. I want him to trust me and know that I'm here to take care of him. Paying fifty dollars a month, however, is the closest I can get. And right now, it's all I really can give. And it makes me so happy.

Chance's ears pricked forward after a minute or so of our game, him nibbling at my fingers and occasionally pulling back, me reaching up to tickle his nose and tug at his lips. His eyes were so soft as he watched me, and one ear occasionally twitched as he listened to my voice.

I sang to him bits of his lullaby, parts of the song that must have been written for us: "I had a dream of the wide open prairie..."

He nipped at my hand playfully and I remembered, as I so often do, that first day I had met him when he had refused to let me anywhere near him. Now we can play games – with a gate between us, of course, but still. He's come so far. That within itself is a miracle no money can buy.

November 21, 2009

Well, today was my first day volunteering *away* from the ranch.

From ten to two, I sat outside of the grocery store at which I used to work, talking to people who were interested about our open ranch. I knew that walking up to people that were trying to get on their way would irritate them, so instead of ambushing unwilling customers, I waited patiently for them to come to me. My sign ("Help the Tierra Madre Horse Sanctuary save those who cannot speak for themselves") spoke for itself.

Many people walked right up to my table. Others would stroll on by, glance at, it, and back up a few steps in order to read everything. Some marched by, determinedly looking away from me, but I wasn't bothered. So many people were interested in the ranch that the four hours I was there went by pretty quickly.

"Saving horses, eh?" an elderly gentlemen would say, or a woman with cowboy boots on would ask, "Where are ya guys at?" or, "What's this open ranch about, on that flyer?" couples buying their Thanksgiving turkeys would say, or best of all, "Are you guys looking for volunteers?" from a woman who apparently worked with horses as well. And more often than not, people would take the flyers (I gave the little kids candy canes) and stuff a few bucks into one of the two coin bins I had with me. Soon I had to push down all of the cash in both bins in order to make way for more.

Several of my old coworkers came to keep me company on their breaks. Some of them took flyers. A few put five-dollar bills in the bins. And when I eventually had to break camp and take everything to my car, they wished Tierra Madre all the luck in the world. I couldn't stop smiling the entire way home. When I poured out all of the money and counted it, I realized, to my utter astonishment, that I had earned the ranch two hundred dollars.

Two hundred dollars. From dollar bills and fives and a ten and three twenties. From dimes and nickels and quarters and pennies. Two hundred dollars could buy new fencing, or cover farrier bills. Two hundred dollars could pay for medicine or help cover vet expenses. It could buy apples and carrots and treats and hay and buckets and hoses and rakes and carts and bran and oats and wood shavings and halters and lead ropes and anything else we might need.

Well, some of it.

I'm so glad I went out there today. I had no idea I could make such a difference. And when it got too hot, or when I got the occasional irritated look from a grumpy man passing by, I thought of those thirty horses waiting for me at Tierra Madre, and I felt better. They believed that I wasn't just wasting my time.

I can't wait to tell Jim.

***

I emailed Jim not too long ago:

Hey, Jim!

So the 10 - 2 thing at Bashas went really well today. A lot of people were really interested and they asked questions about the ranch. They wanted to know how many horses we had, how they had gotten there, how many people we had working there, etc. One woman taught special-needs kids how to ride and she thought she might like to bring them to the open ranch, and another asked if we were looking for volunteers. (Of course I told her yes.) People were so nice and ate up those flyers (I made fifty copies and most of them are gone). The downside of today is that I forgot to ask about donuts and stuff, but I'm going there tomorrow to empty the coin bins at the registers (I do that every three days) so I can ask them then.

I won't be able to make it tomorrow, but you will definitely see me Monday after school. If you e-mail me what you want on those posters, too, I can make time for that and have those done as soon as possible.

Talk to you later – hope everyone is great over there!

Alexis

Oh, and by the way . . . I saved the best for last.

In those four hours I was there, we raised two hundred dollars from the coin bins I had put on that table.

I'm still in shock.

November 24, 2009

Yesterday I brought with me to the ranch another thirty-three dollars from the coin bins, and a twenty-five dollar donation from a friend in Florida in addition to the two hundred from Saturday. And a woman donated five hundred dollars the other day and Tierra Madre has started a Hay for the Holidays program that has raised over two hundred so far.

We're in business, now.

On the downside, yesterday Jim told me that he had let our worker Nicole go. Apparently she had called in twenty minutes before she was supposed to show up to say she had a convention to go to or something, and as she had been working for pay, she was told to not come back. Another worker, one I hadn't gotten to meet, is being fired today, too, because she hasn't been doing a good job with any of the work. (I learned all of this yesterday.)

Ah, well. I hope we find some good workers soon.

Four more days until the open ranch. I'm going to make some posters tonight and look at pricings of things we might need.

November 25, 2009

If such a thing were possible, I'm more excited about the open ranch than I ever was before.

We're going to have enough people to operate the merchandise and food "booths", including Brandi, a new worker who Jim is happy about. So Jim said my job will be to walk around and lead tours. I'll tell people the horses' stories and talk about their personalities and answer questions. I can't wait to tell people about these thirty angels. It'll be wonderful to see new people getting to know the horses and watching as the horses work their magic.

I finally asked about Chance, and Jim said that he was, indeed, going to rope him off. We all are concerned as to how he'll react to so many people, so that's why we're going to make sure no one risks life and limb by innocently standing next to his stall. If there's one thing that I'm not looking forward to on Saturday, it's the fact that I will probably not see those big soft eyes all day. However, Chance has been in wonderful moods lately, and he hasn't done anything drastic in a long time. Maybe he'll surprise us. Knowing Chance, I'm sure he will.

This afternoon I helped feed everyone their grain and talked about preparation plans with Jim. I've already made four posters, two that say "Open Ranch" with an arrow pointing in one direction, one with a riding lessons advertisement, and one promoting the take-a-picture-with-Santa-while-sitting-on-a-horse deal we've got going on. I'm going to make a few more and hang them up around the ranch then go out on Tatum and Pinnacle Vista on Saturday morning to hang the "Open Ranch" signs so people can see them while driving. I'm also going to get carrots and water while Brandi's boyfriend, who works at a donut shop, apparently, will be supplying the donuts.

On another plus note, we've been getting more donations than ever. What with our new Hay for the Holidays program plus the money I've raised off of coin bins (more than three hundred by now, I'm sure), Jim said Tierra Madre has taken in over a thousand dollars. Boy, does that make me happy.

The worker that Jim was going to let go never showed up yesterday. No call or anything. Jim said that if she ever shows her face around the ranch he's going to tell her, "You know, I don't know how we'd ever survive without you but starting now, we're gonna try."

I'm so glad we've found decent volunteers and workers to replace people who don't have the decency to call and/or do a good job when it comes to mucking stalls or cleaning waters. Those horses, my best friends in the whole world, deserve better than that.

Three more days. I'm so excited!

November 26, 2009

Today is Thanksgiving, and there is so much in my life for which I am immensely thankful. Like horses.

And when it comes to horses, there are no better ones than the angels at Tierra Madre. I am so grateful to all of them for various reasons:

Thank you, Sweet Boy, for resting your nose on my hand when I fill your water, and for giving back more than you take.

Thank you, Sedonie, for your loving little nips and for transferring your kindness to me through your big black eyes.

Thank you, Chester, for your innocence and for looking for the best in people.

Thank you, Ted, for being so protective and supportive of me and for always wanting your share.

Thank you, CharlieHorse, for teaching me about life, and for allowing me to hear your thoughts when I'm with you.

Thank you, Guess, for being as stubborn as I am and for giving love away without question.

Thank you, Bella, for showing me that outer beauty truly does reflect beauty within.

Thank you, Jani, for being strong and self-supporting and for dancing for those who scratch your neck.

Thank you, Heighten, for our games of tag in your stall and for being all-knowing yet eager to learn.

Thank you, Hudson, for being my little brother, for rubbing your face against my side and allowing me to throw my arms around you in a tackle when we play.

Thank you, Cocoa, for teaching me that it is okay to be vulnerable sometimes, and for making my day when you nose dive into your food bucket.

Thank you, Akira, for your sassiness and your unbridled sweetness, and for teaching me what riding is all about.

Thank you, Mistah Lee, for lending me bits of your determination and your courage when we go for our walks.

Thank you, RustyBob, for your utter devotion and your unconditional love that you give to everybody who needs it.

Thank you, Chance, for being my brother, for meeting me at our corner with your head thrown up and your eyes soft yet piercing, for teaching me what unconditional love is every day of my life.

Thank you, Katie, for being the Lady of the Round Pen and for guiding your friends through good and bad times.

Thank you, Sundance, for gracing others with your company and for taking carrots so delicately out of my hands.

Thank you, Holly, for accepting me even though I don't know you as well as I'd like to and for looking at me with gentle eyes when I approach you.

Thank you, John, for enveloping me in your regal energy and for teaching me what leadership is really about.

Thank you, Solo, for being the nicest bully I know, for your sarcastic comments I know you make behind my back, and for knowing exactly how to make me less frustrated no matter what the circumstances are.

Thank you, Suze, for being the kind of girl that doesn't take no for an answer and for emitting your infectious confidence to everybody passing by.

Thank you, Venture, for your loyalty and your quiet strength that can never be taken away.

Thank you, Bentley, for being soft and tender despite your intimidating (yet stunning) outer looks.

Thank you, Kiss, for never questioning what is meant to be and for getting excited over grain and hay.

Thank you, Min, for being a terrorist and a hilarious one at that and for protecting your dignity at all costs.

Thank you, Charlie, for accepting any given situation and for overcoming a less-than-happy past in order to make way for friendship.

Thank you, M'Stor, for spraying me with the hose and for knocking me off my feet when I come to you with no food, for playing and loving life and everyone in it no matter what.

Thank you, Slayer, for being my knight in shining armor, for loving me and for upholding honor, faith, and loyalty – all the qualities of a true knight.

Thank you, Iron Man, for quitting at the right time and place so that you were brought into my life and for never giving up on anything after that.

Thank you, Tarzan, for being braver than anyone could ever be, for showing me how to trust and teaching me how to love again.

And for those who I don't see in body every day:

Thank you, Rusty, for teaching me about acceptance and telling me every day that I deserve to be loved.

Thank you, Mr. Steve Vai, for letting me see your artistic interpretation of the world and for your wide, innocent eyes that I've never forgotten.

Thank you, Moosie, for showing me what bravery is, for loving unconditionally, and for bestowing some of your vast knowledge upon me.

Thank you, Jericho, for allowing me to learn about true friendship and for knowing that I never was angry with you even when I pretended like I was when it came to doing NoFly.

And thank you, Little D, for teaching me to never give up when the fight has not been won and for proving that surrender is not weakness.

I love you guys more than anything. I am so thankful for you all.

And I can't forget...

Thank you, Jim, for understanding me, for teaching me what life is really about and for working day in and day out to keep those thirty angels happy and safe. You say you have heroes, and so do I. You are one of them.

November 27, 2009

Man, if today was crazy, I can only imagine what tomorrow is going to be like.

I was the first volunteer out in the morning. The sun had just risen, the entire ranch was bathed in golden sunrays, the sky was clear and everyone was happy. I knew immediately it was going to be a good day. And it was.

I helped feed the shed row then I finally got to go in where Holly, Katie, and Sundance are living to give them their grain. Jim walked with me and we both doled out the grain, giving a couple extra handfuls to Sundance as we left. That horse is a wonderful little guy. He followed me around the best he could.

Then I gave Suze and Bentley their bran mashes (Bentley has some sweet feed in his, too) as Jim and I talked about tomorrow, breaking off our conversation occasionally when Jim's phone would ring and somebody would ask for directions to the ranch (people called at least twelve times when I was there today). I got Bentley back in the field and after I brought Sweet Boy and Sedonie back into their stalls Jim asked me to put John and Solo out in the arena. "Now," he said, "remember, you gotta get John out of his pen and keep Solo and Suze out of it so you can close the door behind you. And hang onto John because you know he and

Solo will go at it and make sure that Suze doesn't tear that rope out of your hands. And when you come back for Solo make sure no one else makes a run for it through the main gate."

I almost laughed out loud as I heard this. Anyone who knew those horses would have said such a feat was impossible. But I did it.

Brandi got there sometime in between, and she was as happy to meet me as I was glad to meet her. Almost instantly we were talking about anything and everything, and I knew at once that this was a worker who belonged here.

I helped her muck out stalls and in between Jim asked me to recolor the big wooden signs outside the gate that say "Rancho Tierra Madre" and "Tierra Madre Horse Sanctuary" as the Sharpie had faded. So I went and did that. It took a good half-hour, but it was kind of nice being able to let my mind wander as I stood and colored over the faded letters, daydreaming and thinking about tomorrow. And when I climbed back through the gate and headed back up the shed row, Chance was waiting for me at our corner, standing smack against the gate with his ears pricked forward. The moment he saw that I was okay he lowered his head from where it had been resting over the bars, and looked at me expectantly.

"Hey, you," I told him as he put his head through the bars. "You probably don't want my hands on you, they smell like marker and – oh, all right!" I laughed as he pounded on the lower bar with a hoof. "Let me get your leaves, then."

Chance took them gladly and as he chewed, I couldn't help but think that tomorrow, while I'll be enjoying myself, he's going to be a nervous wreck. I'm so glad that Jim and Sam are going to rope him off. I don't want anyone to scare him.

In between walking around to get new markers, Solo and John went absolutely insane in the arena. I paused and watched them for several minutes. They reared, bucked, kicked, nipped at one another in play, then John would chase Solo in circles and Solo would whip around and charge. As they did this they kicked up so much dirt and caused so much dust to settle over the ranch that I couldn't see any of the horses in the field. But I saw the silhouettes of John and Solo, galloping in that arena with the wind pushing back their manes, and it was by far one of the most beautiful sights I've ever seen in my life. The image of those two horses charging through the fog was so haunting and breathtaking. I've never seen anything like it before.

Lynn arrived midmorning and did the waters, and Sam dragged bales of hay over to the breezeway to make a table for all of the merchandise we're going to sell tomorrow. I swept out the breezeway then drove up to CVS to get posters so I could make "Open Ranch" signs, and Jim went to ride Venture, who had been neighing expectantly at the fence for an hour. When I got back they were over in the desert area by the arena, and Sally, Sam's wife, had walked down to help set up the merchandise table. Jim usually rides Venture up to the breezeway and dismounts so Venture can walk around on his own. Venture never wanders anywhere far and always comes back when he's called. Jim has christened him the Mayor of the Breezeway.

I gave Bentley his second bran mash then Jim came over to help me wash out the buckets. Venture was standing twenty feet away with his nose in the treat bucket.

"Hey, Jim," I said, "do you think that maybe sometime, Venture would let me ride him for a little while?"

And Jim immediately turned off the hose, called Venture over, turned to me and said, "Hop on him."

I was in heaven for the twenty minutes or so Venture and I rode around. We weren't in the arena, there was not one scrap of tack on him other than a halter with reins tied onto it, and we could go anywhere we pleased. The first shaky fifteen seconds of getting used to riding with no saddle went quickly, and soon I was riding around the place in a blissful haze as though I'd done it every day.

We walked over to the main gate and trotted down the pathway down the shed row I always go through in the afternoons when I park outside the gate. We said hello to Holly and Katie and Sundance before turning back and charging through the pathway again, then walked around the arena to get to the tack room/breezeway area. I laughed out loud several times, feeling nothing but utter happiness as I rode Venture bareback all around

Tierra Madre. And when I finally got off of him so he could go home, I said to Jim, Sam, Sally, and Brandi (who were still arranging things on the merchandise table and watching from the breezeway), "I've discovered my favorite style of riding."

And they laughed and Jim answered, "Bareback is the only way to ride, sweet thing."

The hay bales were covered in homemade ornaments, books, lotions, and other nifty little trinkets that the friends of Tierra Madre had sent to us. We all talked about pricings and other details like the Santa pictures, and Jim asked me to get one of the little white stuffed horses from inside the tack room to show Brandi. Just as we decided we'd sell them for fifteen dollars each, Mike started barking and would not stop even after I put the horse away. He barked at me for five minutes until I finally figured out why he was so upset.

"He wants one of the horses," I said, and Jim shrugged and replied, "Give him one."

I went back into the tack room, got the little stuffed horse, then went out again to hand it to Mike, and he very happily trotted away with it in his mouth only to lie down with it between his front legs so he could chew at it. The five of us laughed hysterically. It was like seeing a wild bear with a pillow and blanket.

I'm so excited for tomorrow. I have to get carrots and paper bags and water and finish the signs, things I will do gladly. I have the best job of anyone tomorrow. Lynn's going to work the front gate, Sally and Brandi will be manning the merchandise table, Jim's going to be walking around talking to people and doing waters (the mucking will be done before nine o'clock) and checking in with Bre and the girls running the Santa pictures. Sam will be running the horseshoe-painting booth. But I get to lead tours of the ranch and talk about the thirty kids. I'll be able to check up on the horses and make sure they're all right, too.

I'm going to have my eye on Chance the entire time. And when I gave him my hand to nibble at today and saw gentle strength in his beautiful eyes, I pondered the possibility that perhaps he knew this and was grateful.

November 28, 2009

What a day! We had hundreds of people show up to our ranch today: elderly folks, children, parents, fellow ranchers, people who had been in the racing business, people who knew horses not at all... everyone. Overall it was a great day. Admittedly, it was tiring but not stressful at all. The horses behaved themselves well, even Min and especially Chance (I'll get to him later) and they really soaked in the attention. And best of all, the ranch brought in twenty-eight hundred dollars.

Two thousand, eight hundred dollars. Unbelievable.

We started at nine o'clock, but for Jim, Sam, Sally, me, and the other volunteers, it started much earlier. I got to the ranch around seven-thirty armed with water, carrots, candy canes, cardboard boxes, signs, and tape, and after helping Sally setting up the merchandise table, Jim and I drove up the road to hang my huge poster board signs that screamed, "Open Ranch!" We drove up to Ace Hardware after that to get grain and to the gas station to get ice.

When we got back Lynn, Brandi, and several other volunteers unknown to me were all there and everyone was running around frantically trying to get things ready. The stalls had to be mucked, waters had to be at least partway done, and breakfast had to be given before the people got there. And a little bit after nine they started trickling in.

I cannot say how many times I gave tours, how many times I said, "Be careful of that tiny gray horse!" or told Tarzan's sad tale and Mistah Lee's courageous story, how many times I watched people fall in love with John or Slayer or Charlie or Bella or any one of the horses that stuck their noses out of their pens to be patted. But there's one thing of which I am completely sure: I loved every minute of it.

At first I herded the other volunteers around with Bre who has been coming to the ranch far longer than I have. It was rather strange, having grown adults looking to me for guidance rather than the other way around, but because seniority is a factor here rather than age, I was in charge when Jim and Sam were busy. Before long, though, people started coming and I helped Sally with the merchandise table for a bit then got stuff for the horseshoe paintings and made sure Jim had everything else under control. And between visiting each and every horse to make sure he or she was all right, I gave tours and answered questions and shared stories and listened as people went on about, "how incredible this place is!" And I stood there with a huge smile on my face as I nodded, agreeing with them with all of my heart.

At one point I saw RustyBob prancing around and shifting uneasily on his lead rope, and as he had been standing waiting for kids to come and get their pictures with Santa (we had him fly south just for us), I told one of Bre's friends, who was holding him, that I'd give him a walk to calm him down. While I was walking him down the lane, the poor boy looked at me with gratitude in his eyes and let me lean on his shoulder and rub his tired face as I got him away from the commotion for a little while. He did so well, but he was very glad to have Akira come out and replace him.

Throughout this whole day I had a wonderful time, but something in my heart would shift when I'd look over at Chance. All the other horses had been getting hundreds of bits of carrots all day long, they had all been fawned over and talked about and had their pictures taken and patted to death, but because we had roped

Chance off, no one was ever with him. No one was telling him how special he was or giving him carrots except for Sam who occasionally stopped by his stall. And whenever I'd glance over at him to make sure he was okay, nine times out of ten his head would be up on the bars, facing people who were with Mistah Lee or Akira, ears perked forward and looking rather confused, as though he wanted people to come near him but he was too scared to let him.

So three or four times today I made time to go see him. And the moment he saw me coming, he was a changed horse.

"What the *hell*," was his attitude, "is going on around here, Lex? What's everyone doing here? Why are those rope things there? How come everyone down there is getting carrots and not me?"

"Oh, Chance, we want to keep everyone away so you won't be so nervous. I know you don't like big crowds, and you tend to bite people and they don't like that."

"Well, yeah, but... but..." And he seemed so lost, so relieved to see me yet so sad at the same time. I looked directly into his eyes and told him wordlessly, over and over, that I understood, and that even if no one else wanted anything to do with him, even if they refused to admire him from a distance, he was still my best boy in the whole world. Every time I stopped by his stall to spend time with him, every time I stroked his nose and let him nibble at my fingers for a while, he would calm down and gaze at me with big, almost vulnerable eyes that absolutely ripped into my soul. Around noon I was able to sit down next to his stall and talk to him for a while as he nibbled on bits of alfalfa. Eventually I was able to get my hands on some carrots and I brought him two. Chance was so, so happy to get them, but I think it was the attention he craved the most.

A few days ago I was so unhappy when I thought that I wouldn't get to see his gentle eyes on the day of the open ranch. But I did see them after all. He'd flare up around several people if they chose to ignore our sign and cross over the ropes, but when I was with him, his eyes grew soft and he was content. And that made me happier than anything.

I loved having so many guests, but part of me is happy that everyone had to go home eventually. A little after two o'clock it was just me, Jim, Sam, Sally, and Bre, and the five of us were able to sit down and recount the days' events and talk about how much we had made. It was such a great day, but I'm glad things are going to be back to normal. It would be so odd to have that many people at our ranch all the time.

December 2, 2009

The Lady of the Round Pen, Katie, has warmed up to me, I think. When I walked up the little pathway that leads to the shed row today, Chance was waiting at our corner like he usually is, but before I could get to him I heard a little whinny to my left. I looked over to the round pen and Katie was smack dab at the gate, nose to the bars and looking at me curiously.

"Well, hi, there," I told her happily, walking up to her and putting my hand on her nose. She gazed at me with boldness in her eyes and allowed me to pat her, then she turned so that her left side was facing me. In horse language, this usually means, "Scratch, please!" So I scratched her neck for a minute or two, and when I eventually left, she followed me from her pen and cocked an ear in goodbye.

What an angel.

Chance watched the entire exchange from our corner. When I finally reached him, I saw that one of his legs up to the foreleg was between the lower bars, as if he had been pawing at the bars impatiently and he had forgotten to bring it back inside his pen. I laughed at him in greeting; his ears went up and his eyes brightened, like he enjoyed hearing the sound.

"Look at you," I said as I smiled and gave him my hand. "Were you waiting for me? Oh, where are the ears, I can't see the... there they are!" His ears finally perked forward. I notice now that sometimes when I tell him to put his ears up, he does it. They always go back out of habit.

Chance played with my fingers with his lips for a long time. I pulled at his lips playfully and watched his eyes for his reaction. There was none, so I kept tickling him, occasionally bringing my palm up to rub his nose. His head stayed between the bars, and we played for a good ten minutes, only breaking off when Chance would take his head from between the bars to yawn. At one point I chided him softly for not sleeping enough, because I know he stays up so late (which is funny, because in horse years Chance is a bit of a teenager like me). But then I yawned at that moment, too, and I could see the laughter shining in his eyes.

Before I visited RustyBob and the others I gave Chance a bit of alfalfa, which surprised him, I'm sure, but made him very happy. Usually he bangs at his lower bar for food, so I'm sure he wasn't expecting such a treat. But he had minded his manners during our play time.

"You're my best boy," I told him over and over again. "My best boy in the whole world."

And days like today are the ones when I think that he is starting to believe it.

We have twenty-nine horses now, as Cocoa has officially gone home. How odd is that? When I first started in June there were twenty-nine horses, too. So many things have changed since then. Good and bad changes, small and big, but either way, time keeps on running. In this ever-changing world, I have to be thankful for its consistency.

December 4, 2009

On Fridays I don't usually stay at the ranch for too long, but today I wasn't in the best of moods so I stayed for an hour and a half, and I am so, so glad I did.

As usual I helped feed grain, fill the waters in the shed row, and feed the evening hay. CharlieHorse got his lip medicine, Charlie got his nose medicine, and Chester got thousands of pats and kisses from me. Mike carried his stuffed horse around, but he put it down a few times so he could put his wet nose in the palm of my hand, looking up at me and wordlessly asking me to pat him.

I have to talk about Mike for a minute.

Mike is the best dog anyone could ask for. He's protective of Jim and the horses, he freaks out when a horse lies down to rest because he fears they'll never get up again, and he instinctively knows things we don't. When we've had volunteers in the past who are not trustworthy (like Trent) he lets us know immediately. He keeps coyotes far from our gates and chases bunnies out of the piles of hay he have sitting around everywhere and keeps us entertained when we all sit to rest in the breezeway right after the noon feeding time. And we always know when somebody is coming in the front gates because he sends up a barking alarm each time. Once his trust is earned, he's a friend forever. He is living proof that a dog is a man's best friend.

I love that dog so much.

As is the norm for me, as I was entering the ranch today I paused to spend some time with my boy. Chance trotted right up to our corner like he always does when he sees me, his ears forward and head held high in the air. I said hello to the three musketeers in the round pen before going to see him, and as usual when I approached his stall, he put his head over the bars.

For the first time since I began writing this journal, I can say that this action *used* to be dangerous for anybody who happened to be standing next to him when his head would come flying over the stall fence. It is dangerous for me no longer.

For the first time since I began writing this journal, I am at a loss for words.

I've been able to touch on the beauty at this ranch. I've been able to find a few words for the miracles that happen here and I've been able to describe, briefly, what I've witnessed and what I've learned. But I have no words that can truly describe the simple thing that I saw today.

Because today, when Chance lifted his head up to see me, I looked directly into his eyes and saw the most beautiful thing I've seen in my life, something I have been waiting, hoping to see since the moment I laid eyes on him.

Trust.

Utter rust filled those soft brown eyes. There was no anger or fear within them, no suspicion or weariness or defeat. Instead, Chance looked at me with faith shining from the eyes that had once flashed when I got too close to him. And when I held out my hand to pat his nose, he immediately turned his head sideways to nibble at my fingers, playing our game.

I think, if I chose to do so, I could go into his stall now.

I think, at this point in time, he'd let me halter him and walk him to the arena.

I think, before another year has gone by, he would let Jim and Sam and I bring the saddle out and show it to him and grow accustomed to seeing it and, eventually, wear it.

But no matter what happens, from here on out, I'll know that Chance is starting to understand what love is. And while I know that he'll still have bad days and flashbacks and all the confusing feelings that I had to fight through when I, too, was overcoming the effects of abuse, I'll remember this moment.

Chance, the "yellow horse" that most of our volunteers have deemed unapproachable, the wild boy that nearly everyone had given up for lost, the horse that had stolen my heart from day one, is beginning to trust me.

And for now, in this moment, that fact is more than enough.

Alexis Roeckner

Winter

December 7, 2009

The cold has set in permanently. I'm starting to actually miss those brutal summer days when the sun was laughing at us from the sky and the air might as well have been from an oven. Now we are all scrambling for cover from the freezing cold whenever we can. Unfortunately for those of us at Tierra Madre, we are outside most of the day.

The horses grew their winter coats back in October and as the weather was still rather vicious back then, I thought they were crazy. But it seems like the moment the very last clump of "horse fur" was grown in, the cold struck with all of the force of a tornado and while we two-leggeds went running for our jackets, the horses were nice and warm. They knew it was going to get colder, and they knew exactly when it would happen, too. It's incredible how Mother Nature tells the horses and birds and dogs and rabbits and everybody what's coming and how to prepare for it. And it's even more amazing how there are no complaints from anybody. Just acceptance.

It was raining today, but I went to see everyone anyway. Within minutes of being outside, however, I was soaking wet and my school shoes were soggy. Jim insisted I wear his old boots if I was going to help feed in the rain and eventually I agreed. But while everybody else was snug inside their warm winter coats, I was freezing. I laughed as I walked back to my car, half an hour into the feeding. My hair was dripping wet and my hands were shaking as I offered them to the horses on my way to the gate, but they nibbled at me anyway and breathed on my aching fingers to make them warm. Solo undoubtedly laughed at me behind my back, Hudson snorted in amusement as I trotted past him and RustyBob nudged me happily as though to say, "Hurry up and get dry, Lex!"

I sat in my car for a few minutes and watched the rain pound on my windshield before I drove away. I smiled at my own craziness. I would have much rather been in the rain, getting wet with the horses, then have stayed home where I could have been dry and warm.

December 9, 2009

When I pulled up to the ranch's gates today after school, a big SUV rolled up right beside my car. I went up to the drivers' side wearily and the window rolled down to reveal two women waving at me. Their names were Terri and Wendy, I gathered, and they said they had read all about Tierra Madre and they wanted to come inside and see the ranch, please and thank you. I'm sure I stared at them in disbelief for a moment or two as they spoke. I was exhausted and rather pissed, considering that randomly pulling up to our gate and asking to come in is just about as rude as waltzing through someone's front door. Unfortunately, people did it to us all the time. Apparently nobody thinks it's necessary to call ahead of time and confirm a convenient time for them to stop by private property.

But I heard Katie and Sundance and Holly playing in the round pen and I thought of our dwindling funds. Maybe these two women would want to help provide for the angels if they met them. Maybe they'd want to volunteer. Maybe they'd want to help us.

"Sure," I said, biting back a sigh and trying to keep hold of the carrots, apples, and cookies in my arms as the women looked at me expectantly. "Come on in."

I looked down to the pathway to see Chance at his food trough, waiting for me. I smiled and nodded at him as he gazed at me. "Just a minute, brother. I promise." He went back to nibbling at whatever leftover food was around his feeder.

Because I was a bit early for the afternoon feeding and Jim wasn't out of the house yet, I showed the two women around. They loved the horses, but I was a bit irked to hear their assumptions of everybody. I had to constantly correct them.

"Oh, he's a mean one, I can definitely tell!" one of them said in oblivious fascination when we came to M'Stor. "It's so stupid that horses can be so mean!"

It was adding insult to injury, to make a disrespectful remark about one of the horses after all but barging through the Tierra Madre gates uninvited. Had I not learned what true patience was over the past few months, I am a hundred percent certain that I would have said something rude to her in that moment. Instead, I bit back my retort and calmly explained, "No, he just puts his ears back out of habit. He's a wonderful horse, really."

"He snapped at me!" the other one laughed as M'Stor gently grazed her arm with his lips. I sighed.

"No," I told her, "he's playing with you. Look at his eyes. Watch his body movement. This is his way of saying hello."

I told them all of the horses' stories and by the time we got to Chester, Jim and Mike had come out of the house. Jim shot me a look of confusion (and I didn't blame him) and I explained that Terri and Wendy had arrived the same time I did and had wanted a tour. As the two women were cooing over Chester and Ted, Jim and I exchanged an irritated look. Tierra Madre is not just a ranch, it's Jim's home. I shook my head and mouthed, "I'll deal with them." Jim smiled gratefully and went to feed Suze and Bentley their mashes. Mike, of course, had to be kept in the house.

I left after we fed the field side of the ranch, Terri and Wendy tagging along and asking questions. I was, and still am, glad that people are so interested in what we are doing and that they care enough to come check out the place. But is it too much to ask for them to call first, and to not make false assumptions about amazing animals about which they know nothing?

Either way, the horses didn't care. I suppose I shouldn't, either.

December 11, 2009

We've come very close to losing big Charlie.

For the last few months he's had a horrible sinus infection so that he can only breathe through one nostril, and it got so bad that Jim had the vet come and take a sample of what was coming out of his nose. He thought that maybe Charlie had a tumor growing in there, and he wanted to get the particles tested for cancer.

If the mucus had been cancerous, Charlie would have been a goner. But the test results came back and he's fine. Instead of a tumor, he has an infection for which antibiotics or probiotics can do nothing, so poor Charlie just has to ride it out. At least he has time to heal. For that, I am grateful. Charlie is such a gentle soul with a heart as big as he is (and he's the biggest horse at the ranch) and it hurts to see him sick.

Man, I've realized that there are so many moments like this at the ranch: heart-stopping, terrifying moments that make us fear that one of the horse is going to lose his or her life. When a normally active horse stands deathly still, when someone is pawing desperately at the ground, when a horse refuses to take a carrot, when somebody takes an off-step and limps around painfully....

Nine times out of ten those moments pass, and everything is fine, but the thing is *we never know*. And because we never know if a horse is in danger, we can't help having a constant fear of losing one of our dearest, beloved friends to colic or laminitis or a broken bone. We can't risk it.

I've come to realize that once we love and lose, we don't forget. But while these horrible moments will keep on happening, we just have to focus on what's happening in the present, be it good or bad. Right now. Now.

And right now, I'm just glad that big Charlie is going to be okay.

December 12, 2009

I was expecting harsh weather when I pulled up to the ranch this morning because of the stormy gray skies, but when I got out of my car (Mike was there to greet me) it wasn't too bad. Still, I was grateful for the two layers and the gloves and the two pairs of socks I had on.

Because the ground is so muddy now, Jim cleans and bleaches out all of the horses' feet so that abscesses – or worse, laminitis – can't develop in the horses' feet. So today, as Sam and Brandi did the waters and mucked the stalls, both of us cleaned the feet of everybody on the field side. Bre came about halfway through and entertained Suze, which was really necessary as Jim and I cleaned the "lower rank" kids in the field – Kiss and Venture – and Suze had to be distracted so she wouldn't intimidate them. M'Stor was a bit difficult as was Suze herself and Solo, of course, which was not surprising at all. What *was* surprising was that Tarzan was so wonderful about the whole process. I brought the halter to Jim after he had calmed T down and stayed by the horse's head as Jim scrubbed out T's hooves. The poor boy trembled even as I held perfectly still, but let Jim hug and pat him when everything was done.

"You're my hero, T," Jim said over and over to Tarzan, "you and Moose. You and Moose, T."

That took up most of the morning, but Sam and Brandi were fast in doing the rest of the chores, so everything was mostly done by the noon feeding time. By the way, the noon feeding time is done at about eleven o'clock, so it's not really noontime. But that's what we call it.

Before we doled out the hay, however, I went to see Chance with a brush in my hand. He's grown to like having his nose massaged, and he loves to try to take the brush from me. Today as we played I moved the brush down toward his neck, wondering if he'd object. He did, but while he threw his head up slightly and laid his ears back, his eyes didn't flash nor did he snap at me.

Progress. Sweet, beautiful progress.

There's something I've noticed here for the last month or so that I've never really mentioned. At the ranch, we don't necessarily have rank among we two-leggeds (Jim is the boss and that's about it) but there seem to be different levels of respect given to certain people. Trent, for example, had next to none. Lynn, while she was here, obtained lots more, as did Sam the Volunteer before he disappeared. And Sam is second-in-command, of course. I think that since they've all seen that I show up, work as much as I can, and that I absolutely love each horse to death, my own "status" has risen slightly over the past few months.

"When Brandi gets here," Jim told me first thing in the morning when he saw me cleaning Sweet Boy's pen, "make her muck the stalls. It's her job. You can help me do other things."

For someone who has craved respect her whole life, I think I've finally figured out how to earn it.

December 18, 2009

If there's one lesson I've learned while working at this ranch, it's that time is both a beautiful and horrible thing. Right now, at this moment in life, time is switching to that awful side. Why?

Because I think CharlieHorse's time is running out.

Doc Rollins was at the ranch yesterday to take a white blood count and to look at CharlieHorse's infection that has been going on for several weeks now. He also informed Jim that CharlieHorse has an eye disease that has caused our boy's eyes to cloud over so that he can't see too well. If CharlieHorse were younger the vet would have had more hope for his recovery. But he's thirty years old. As much as I hate to think of it, our little philosopher is starting to wind down.

He seemed fine when I stopped by after school today to see everyone, and as CharlieHorse does not like to be disturbed when he's resting, I let him be. In an attempt to put him out of my mind for the time being, I explored the new facility that is right across from his stall now, the big pen Sam and Jim made yesterday for Holly and Sundance and Katie. Jim had been worried because those three hadn't received much human interaction since they came here in November, and as the happiness of our horses is the number one priority at Tierra Madre, Jim decided that the Chocolates would be moved. For a pen that was built in a day, the new field is pretty nice; there's a pen-within-a-pen thing for Katie, like John has in the big field, and there is plenty of room for everybody.

In the shed row, Hudson and Jani were switched as well so that now the entire row goes in this order: Guess, Bella, Hudson, Heighten, Jani, Cocoa (back with us for a little while), Akira, Mistah Lee, RustyBob, and Chance. Jani hadn't been very happy next to Bella since she is very particular about her friends. But Heighten's the leader of that side of the ranch and she likes him (as Heighten does her), so switching them made Jani happier plus kept best buds Heighten and the Big Galoot— I mean Hudson together.

In my brief visit after my half-day of school (which, as usual, turned into a not-so-brief visit), I also met a really nice college student named Gwen who's staying with Jim for a little while. She grew up around horses and, being a friend of Jim's, flew out from

Maryland to spend some time with them and to get a bit of sun. I'm glad she's here; the horses love her and she is eager to help out.

Suzanne from down the road came to check on Cocoa, and, as it was around noon and the horses had been fed, Jim, Sam, Brandi, Gwen, Suzanne, and I all sat in the breezeway for an hour or so and talked. Mike lay contentedly in his spot next to Chester while the six of us laughed and told stories and talked about horses. I loved every minute of it.

It was later on in the day when I was driving home when it hit me. I hadn't had that feeling in a long time: the feeling that I *belonged*. And I'm still marveling at this simple gift that Tierra Madre has given me (a gift that has been one of many) – the realization that I am truly a part of a team.

December 19, 2009

CharlieHorse was better today, but I think everyone is looking at him a little differently and watching him a little more carefully. When Suzanne came by to pick up Cocoa for her daily ride, she winced as she saw our little philosopher standing quietly by his feed bucket. "Oh, my *God*," she gasped to no one in particular. "He needs to be put down."

My heart started aching at the very thought, and I went back to helping Brandi with the waters without saying a word, but I wondered if Suzanne was right, if CharlieHorse's time was coming more quickly than I had suspected.

In the morning when I arrived, Gwen and I fed Suze and Bentley their bran mashes and talked for a bit. After the bran mashes were doled out we put Sweet Boy and Sedonie back in their stalls after they were done playing in the arena. Right afterward, I put John and Solo out there while Jim and Gwen worked on CharlieHorse. He's getting a bunch of shots now, and while he doesn't like it, he tolerates it. He is like Bentley in that aspect; poor B banged his hind left leg and it needs to be wrapped in addition to receiving hydrotherapy. Bentley gets shots twice a day as well and though he freaked out a bit today when Jim put the needle in his neck, he calmed down the instant Jim touched his nose with a free hand and talked to him softly. It never ceases to amaze me how every single horse on this ranch knows that Jim has his or her best interests at heart.

When I trotted down the shed row to say hi to Chance, RustyBob gave me one of his pleading looks, standing shock-still at the back of his pen. His nose started quivering with silent, happy whinnies the moment he saw me coming.

"Here are my best boys," I said aloud, and right on cue, Chance came right up to his stall door to greet me. He's taken to hanging out at the back of his house, and while he always comes up to the gate when I come by to say hello, I've noticed that he's been much more relaxed and at ease. Before I could play with him today, though, I had to spend time with RustyBob.

So I climbed through the bars into his stall (it's huge now that the temporary fence that separated him from Little D is gone) and ran to him and threw my arms around his neck, kissing and patting him as much as I could. He quivered with happiness as he nibbled at my cheeks with wet lips. I burst into laughter. Chance put his head up over the bars, watching us.

"Oh, come on," I laughed, looking into his big, light brown eyes, "you gotta admit that this might not be so bad."

Chance flicked one ear back as though he was shrugging, and I patted RustyBob goodbye and went over to him. He placed his nose quietly on one of the bars and I reached in and patted it. As I often do, I had to reflect upon the fact that six months ago, I could have never done such a thing. Now I can rub his nose without fear.

Venture, in the meantime has turned into a lapdog. He still gets to come up to the breezeway every day for "Venture Time," and he knows it. Every day around ten, he trots up to the field's gate, nose to the bars, whinnying at us to open the gate and let him out. And when the chores have mostly been done, Jim goes over with the halter and reins and hops on and rides him. Some days Jim will just let him out and Venture will follow him back up to the breezeway for his special bran mash. And while we all sit and chat and rest before doing the noontime feeding, he hangs out with us, nose in the treat bucket.

Seeing Jim and Venture riding around the ranch always made me remember the time I got to ride, too. And today when I saw Jim headed to the field with the halter and reins in his hand, I pounced.

"Does Venture need to be ridden at all today?" I asked innocently.

Can I ride him, Jim?

Jim laughed and, shaking his head, went on down to the field to get Venture. Gwen was giving B his second bran mash, Brandi and Sam were doing the waters, so I thought I'd grab the brush and go work with Chance. The moment I picked up the brush, however, I heard Jim opening the gate to get the halter on Venture, and he called, "Hey, Alexis?"

"Yeah?"

"Come over here. I'll give you a leg up."

I practically ran over to them both. Within instants I was on Venture's back. And away we went.

Venture has been a better teacher than any other when it comes to riding, so when I rode today, I was able to focus on where I wanted to go and kept myself balanced more easily than the last time I rode bareback. With leg movements, a bit of gentle tugging with the reins that were attached to a simple halter, I was able to guide Venture up the lane and through the dirt pathway and down the ditch and around the arena and behind the breezeway....

Heaven. Utter heaven.

Before feeding time, I drove Jim up to the car maintenance store so he could buy a fan belt for his non-working truck, then to Chase for a money pick up and then finally to Ace Hardware so we could get a new feed bucket for Heighten (I got to pick the color). On the way back to the ranch I made Jim listen to Bryan Adam's "Brothers Under the Sun" – Chance's lullaby.

"I love it," he said as we drove up to the gate. "I like that a lot."

And when the noontime feeding had been done, the five of us sat and chatted for a little while as we rested. I mentioned how Chance was responding well to me reaching in and patting his face. Jim smiled proudly and looked over to the yellow horse. Chance had his entire head up to his ears in his trough and was eating his hay contentedly.

"When he first came here, he was a nightmare. But now…" Jim said, beaming. "He's getting there, isn't he?"

"How long has he been here?" Gwen asked.

"A year in February," Sam answered.

"He'll be as gentle as Chester in no time," said Jim happily.

Before I walked back to my car, I checked on CharlieHorse, who was eating his noontime alfalfa from his blue bin. I watched him for a moment or two, then, not wanting to disturb him, went back to the front of the breezeway to say goodbye to everyone.

CharlieHorse. If there is any trooper in this world whose patience cannot be matched, it's that horse.

One last thing: the coin bins earned us another hundred and eighteen dollars these past two weeks. Sometimes I think I underestimate the generosity of some people.

December 21, 2009

Here's a story, and it's an odd one:

Once upon a time, there was a woman named Ivy who boarded her horses at a ranch owned by Mean Woman. These horses' names were Hollywood, Cadence, and Studley, and Ivy loved them very much. She used to board other horses at Tierra Madre and paid Jim with cash and labor. In fact, she grew so accustomed to the ranch that she turned to us when a horse named Chester needed a home.

Ivy began to board Hollywood, Cadence, and Studley at Mean Woman's place, and after a while, tensions between her and Mean Woman, the owner, ran high for whatever reason. Finally, one day Mean Woman locked up Hollywood, Cadence, and Studley in a round pen, put a padlock on the gate, and said that the horses were hers until Ivy could come up with the board money for December after it had been agreed that Ivy could pay in increments throughout the month. Along with this, Mean Woman demanded money for a questionable vet bill. In total, she asked Ivy for twelve hundred dollars.

Ivy only had seven hundred.

The courts got involved, eventually siding with Mean Woman and confirming what she had already told Ivy. Mean Woman, the same heartless witch who was going to send Chester to the slaughter action for some hard cash, said that if Ivy didn't come up with twelve hundred dollars by the end of the week, the three horses were headed in the same direction. Not simply moved to another facility, not given to another owner.

Auction.

Luckily, this story has a happy end. After Ivy turned to Tierra Madre for help, Jim posted a plea for financial assistance all over social media. Within twenty-seven hours people had donated enough money to save the lives of the three innocent horses. And within another twenty-four, Hollywood, Cadence, and Studley were brought to Tierra Madre to stay.

And they all lived happily ever after. Or so I hope.

Today when I pulled in I ran to meet them at the round pen, which was empty now that Katie, Sundance, and Holly had been moved. Hollywood, a beautiful chestnut Arabian gelding, was pacing around importantly and Cadence, a quarter horse mare with a brown eye and a blue one, was eating out of a bin. Studley was just standing, looking at me. He's a dark gray with lighter gray and white splotches everywhere on his body. He was black when he was born but now he's turning white. He's only two or three years old, and he is so, so sweet. It's a shame how Hollywood bullies him and Cadence.

As I was inspecting them and saying hello, Chance trotted up to our corner and watched us curiously. When the three new kids had tired of greeting me, I walked back to him and offered him my hand.

"What do you think?" I asked him as he nibbled at my fingers. "I like them."

His answer was to turn to them and continue to watch them eating from their bins in the round pen. Satisfied, I walked away toward the barn and the breezeway.

There were a lot of people at the ranch today. Jim and Sam and Gwen were present, of course, as was Brandi along with Pat, a woman who rides Akira every Monday. Suzanne stopped by for Cocoa when the farrier was there around ten, so there was a bit of a mini-party going on as I held Solo, Heighten, and Hudson for Rob the farrier and his assistant to work on their feet. About the time everyone was there, gathered in the lane, the FedEx guy showed up and honked; Gwen went to get the package. It was a huge box of chocolates, cheeses, sausages, and various nuts, all from a random stranger in Pennsylvania. And it was all for us.

"I don't think I mind Christmas after all," Jim said later, when we were all crashed in the breezeway. He was cutting out bits of sausage as he spoke and he offered the first bit to me.

Solo was funny today. He and John had had a fight or something so when Gwen and I put them in the arena they walked away in opposite directions, but when we went to bring them out again, they suddenly started galloping all around us, snorting and rearing and tossing their heads happily as Gwen and I half-heartedly tried to catch them. Eventually they calmed down, John went home, and I brought Solo out to get his feet done. He stood irritably for a while, but for whatever reason, when I started patting his neck and kissing his cheek soundly, he stood still. He put a nose to my hand when I stopped.

Oh, Solo. He thinks he's a bully but he's not.

Solo has also turned into quite the circus horse. A few weeks ago we all caught him standing – literally standing – on the lowest bar of the arena in an attempt to reach the leaves off the tree from which Chance always eats. Sam reported that today, Solo had managed to get on the second bar. He literally had no feet on the ground; he had balanced his hind hooves on the bar second closest to the ground, and he placed his front hooves carefully on the topmost railing while craning his neck in order to get at Chance's leaves. Chance, needless to say, was not pleased.

Anyway, after Solo got his feet done, I brought out Heighten and Hudson, who were more difficult. Being the big football stars they are, they refused to stand still unless I gave them bits of alfalfa hay while Rob and his assistant worked. Heighten nearly ripped the rope out of my hands when it was his turn, Hudson stepped on my foot, both of them cantered around in circles when they were led around, and neither of them could wait to get into the arena. Eventually they were good to go, and they were let out so they could blow off some steam.

CharlieHorse, according to Jim, is improving. After Bentley gets his bran mash, shot, and hug from Jim, CharlieHorse must have his temperature taken and his Mooseshake given to him (syrup and medicine mixed together in a syringe, a combination always given to the Moose) and drops squeezed in his eyes. Poor CharlieHorse. He positively shakes when he sees Jim coming with the halter because he knows what's coming. But he lets us do what needs to be done.

Today, after Jim and Gwen had doctored him up and they had left his stall, I stayed with him for a few extra minutes. I expected him to shoo me away so he could go think by himself. Instead, I was shocked when he took a step closer to me, looking at me with his soft, dark eyes that I've grown to adore.

"CharlieHorse," I sang as I offered him my hand. When he didn't object to my patting, I rushed forward and threw my arms around him. He stood patiently. "You're such a trooper, you know that, CharlieHorse? You're the best CharlieHorse in the whole world."

He nuzzled me. "I try."

"I know you do," I answered, and I kissed his cheek. "I love you, CharlieHorse."

"As I do you, Lex. I'm gonna go eat now."

"You do that. I'll come visit you later."

Jim, Sam, Gwen, Brandi, and I all stood admiring the three new kids after we had given everyone their lunch. They were all eating their Bermuda hay contentedly. Studley in particular got a good looking over.

"He looks about two or three," Gwen observed as the three horses chowed down.

"Poor guy, he doesn't deserve that name!" laughed Brandi, and I had to agree.

"He's a beautiful horse, though," I said. "He's definitely got some Arabian in him. I see a bit of Morgan, too." It was agreed that Studley was a "mutt".

"Can you believe he was tied to a dumpster when Ivy found him?" Jim told us. "His previous owners gelded him themselves. With a knife. No tranquilizers or anything."

I winced, looking at the colt with new sympathy. He was picking bits of Bermuda out of the pin and chewing happily, ears twitching as though he was listening to our chatting. Brandi gasped, "That's horrible!"

"Yeah. And if Ivy hadn't found him I think Studley here would still be tied to that dumpster."

I couldn't believe it. The three horses had lived with Ivy for over a year before they came to us, so Studley must have suffered this abuse when he was a baby.

A baby.

What in this world would possess anyone to abuse a *baby*?

December 22, 2009

I have been volunteering at Tierra Madre Horse Sanctuary for nearly seven months now and during those seven months, I have never had to do anything as disgusting as what Brandi and I tackled today.

In several of the horses' stalls, there are these not-so-pleasant things that we call "pee-holes". They're spots where horse urine has mixed with mud and rainwater and is also full of bits of rotten hay and feces. They're unstoppable. Muck them out one day, and they reappear the next because of some horses' tendencies to use the bathroom in only one place in their stalls and because the rain aggravates them further. So there have been several unmanageable pee-holes that we've left to fester. Today, however, it was decided that it was about time we attempted to do something about The Greatest Pee-Hole In The World: in other words, the growing mound that had likely developed new species of organisms in Sweet Boy's stall.

So Brandi and I, me with a metal pitchfork, she with a rake, cleaned out the huge mass of hay, poop, dirt, mud, and other ungodly things soaked in urine in Sweet Boy's stall. The smell was unbearable. It took us forty minutes and five trips to the poop mountain to dump the cart we were using. And for all of that time and effort it took for us to use the pitchfork and rake, for all the progress we actually made, we might have been better off using guns.

"You know you love horses *when*..." I said when we were done and Brandi snorted. I'm sure we smelled great. My mom probably won't let me into the house for a week.

We mucked out the rest of the barn (thankfully devoid of pee-holes), the pen for Holly, Sundance, and Katie, and everybody's houses up to Jani. In between stalls I brought Ted and Chester out to the arena so they could play, and when they were done, Sam walked out Chance and RustyBob.

After Chance and Rusty were in the arena, I stood next to Heighten's stall, Brandi stood in it, Gwen and Jim and Sam and Mike all stood in between the barn and the arena gates. Together we watched the two horses galloping around for a good five minutes. It's wonderful to see RustyBob trotting around and having fun, but there is something so breathtaking about watching Chance galloping for all it's worth out there, his white mane flying, his head tossing, his eyes flashing with a fierce joyfulness we have all begun to notice. None of us could take our eyes off of him.

"He's changing," Sam said proudly later that day. He loves Chance as much I do. He alone can go into Chance's stall for a decent amount of time so he can muck out the stall. "I put my hand to his mouth to give him treats and a couple of times he got his teeth around my wrist. And those times he could have chopped it clean off, but he didn't."

"You notice he's starting to leave food in his bin, now?" Jim added. "He's trusting that he's not going to be fed every three days, now."

"He's learning to be happy," Sam agreed.

"Or that it's okay to be happy," said Jim.

Jim had to take Gwen to the airport around ten-thirty, and I was sad to see her go. We're going to have to find her on Facebook, I think. She was such a special addition to the ranch for the few days she was here. I'm going to miss her.

Before Jim came back and before feeding time, I took a bunch of treats, a brush and a currycomb, and trotted out to the round pen where Hollywood, Cadence, and Studley were. The three of them were gathered at the gate, close together, and I held my hands out to them as I spoke to them softly.

"Don't tell me you've never had these before," I said, grinning, as they sniffed at the treats before devouring them. "Well, you'll just have to have a few more. Studley, is that mud on your coat?"

I took the brush and walked into the round pen and in an instant the three of them ambushed me. Hollywood did his best to get the attention for himself, but Cadence and Studley got around him somehow. I showed Studley the brush and let him nibble at it for a little bit, then, one hand out to fend off Hollywood, I began to brush the mud from his right side. Studley stood, blinking, enjoying it.

"You're so young," I told him. "You've got your whole life – Cadence, give me that – ahead of you. How on earth did you end up here?"

He looked at me with gentle eyes. I saw acceptance within them, and my heart absolutely melted. I put my arms around him and kissed his soft coat, unable to tell him how envious I was of his incredible attitude despite the neglect he'd been through. And while Cadence and Hollywood trotted around me and came and went as they pleased, Studley stood right by my side as well as he could, gazing at me as if I were the only two-legged in the world.

Eventually I put the brush down outside of the round pen and turned back to the little colt. He put his nose to my hand, trust in his eyes.

"Walk with me," I said.

As I had watched Jim do so many times, I put my right arm out to the side and began to walk throughout the entire round pen. I focused only on pulling that horse's mind to mine and on the trust in myself I knew Studley would sense and be calmed by. And Studley kept his nose to my hand, following me through my twists and turns. We walked together for a long time as utter love for the colt swept through me. And that love is with me now and it will be there tomorrow and forever.

"I'll see you later," I told little Studley when I finally had to leave. "I'll be back real soon. Promise."

"Okay," was his cheerful reply. "Thanks for the treats!"

He is the true baby boy of the ranch. What a sweetheart he is. What a loving little boy.

It's as though the moment I had accepted that one of the loves of my life was going to be taken from me soon, the universe sent me another. CharlieHorse will move on to the higher, more wonderful place that he deserves, and Studley will grow up here with me and learn what happiness is.

It's amazing how the world works. And I'll thank the universe for its mysterious ways every day for the rest of my life.

December 23, 2009

Jim writes in a blog every morning, and every single day, like clockwork, I read it the minute I wake up, whether or not I'm headed to the ranch. He talks about political issues and shares daily observations, but mostly he writes about the horses and the events of the previous day around the ranch. And I love to read what he has to say, especially if I wasn't there that day.

I don't usually cry over what someone writes. But the last bit of this morning's blog had me in tears.

***

...Speaking of being turned out, yesterday when we turned out Chance & Rusty, young Chance was the best he's ever been.

He nose-dived into his halter for Sam, walked along just as pretty as you please – without pulling toward the mesquites or nipping at Sam's elbow – stood stoically when the halter was removed & then did the whole thing in reverse when it was time to go home.

He's made amazing strides over the past few weeks.

For the first time since he got here last February, you can see that he's really relaxed & confident that he'll be fed & not abused & that he's loved. Really loved.

He loves to have us play with his lips - & there are no teeth involved, either.

And his eyes.

Chance will always tell you what he's thinking with his eyes. And they've always flashed anger just before he's struck.

And, for the life of me, I haven't seen his eyes flash anger in weeks.

It's finally happening for him.

He's finally coming to the realization that life isn't a constant battle. That he doesn't need "the best defense is a good offense" thing anymore. That there'll always be food for him when he's hungry. Or, hell, even when he's not.

The faire Alexis was here yesterday. And Chance is her absolute favorite. I think, like so many people with big hearts, that she cheers for the underdog.

I stole a glance over at her when Chance & Rusty were tearing around happily.

And the look of love & pride & happiness on her face was priceless.

And then I looked at Brandi, who was also watching. And she had the very same look on her face that Alexis did.

And so did Sam.

And so did Gwen.

And so did I.

And that's why Sir Chance is feeling the way he's feeling now.

Because he knows in his bones that everybody's pulling for him. That everybody loves him & only wants the best for him. That we're all on his side.

Amazing what a little love can accomplish, isn't it?

***

I'm leaving for a family vacation tomorrow morning, and I won't be back until the second week of January. After living away from Arizona for three years from when I was twelve to fifteen, any time away from the desert is usually a misery for me, but now I've got the horses to miss, too.

I drove over during the afternoon feeding time with a plate of brownies for Jim so I could say goodbye to everybody. I climbed in

Slayer's stall and hugged him, offered my hand to Tarzan who nuzzled it, and kissed Iron Man's nose and rubbed his neck. I patted Charlie, returned the funny face Min threw me, kissed M'Stor's nose, snuck Kiss a treat when no one was around to scare him away, and then I saw Solo giving me the eye. I walked over to him.

"Hey, So-low," I said and he nipped at my hand. It's our routine; he nips and puts his ears back to show how tough he is and I kiss his nose and scratch his face to tell him how wussy I find him to be. "I'll miss you, meanie-face."

"That sucks, 'cause I'm not gonna miss you. Not one bit. When you come back you'd better have your arms full of carrots."

"Yeah, whatever. You be good for Jim while I'm gone."

I walked away. Solo pounded at the gate as though to yelp, "Hey!" I turned around to see his ears perked up. "Oh, you're... you're really leaving, huh? Well, okay. 'Bye, then."

I love that horse.

Chester, of course, let me fuss over him and the three Amigos next to Guess let me pat their noses in farewell. But when I got to CharlieHorse, I have to admit I wasn't sure what to do. Jim says that he is improving so well, but at the same time, I couldn't help but feel like my little philosopher was standing on his last legs.

I stood at the fence, not wanting to disturb him but desperately wishing I could go in and throw my arms around his neck. In the end, CharlieHorse, seeing me, turned slowly and came up to where I stood. His eyes were bright. I offered him my hand and he sniffed at it gently, and we stood together for a while, silently thinking together. I didn't say anything. I didn't have to.

There is a hidden force within every living creature that tells us when we must leave and let things be and let nature run its course, and before long, I felt the tug of the universe telling me it was time to go. I smiled at my CharlieHorse, kissing his nose softly and patting his white blaze. "Goodbye," was all I said, and my eyes stung.

And when I had taken a few steps away from him, to see the other horses, I turned back to see him gazing after me.

I hesitated.

"Go on," his eyes told me. "Go on, Lex."

"Okay," I found myself answering. "It's just... I don't want you to leave me just yet."

"I'll never leave you," was his gentle reply. "I'm healthier than I look. It's time for you to go on, Lex. It's time for you to be brave."

Brave like Moosie.

And so I left CharlieHorse and walked up the shed row, telling everyone that I'd see them in two weeks. I climbed into RustyBob's stall and hugged him. I put my hand on my Chance's nose for a moment or two, savoring how the weariness in his eyes melted into trust after he saw that it was me reaching out to him. And I patted little Studley, who seemed happy to see me.

I said before that these horses were my saviors. Well, now the angels of Tierra Madre are much, much more than that. They are my family.

January 6, 2010

Today, mere hours after I got off my plane, I pulled up to Tierra Madre as the sun was fading. I practically bolted from my car and ran for the gates the moment I saw Chance waiting for me in our corner. The familiar barn smell absolutely engulfed me and I almost laughed with the joy of being back home.

I was too excited to spend time with any one horse. I went dancing around, touching noses, speaking to all of them, savoring the quiet confidence I saw in their eyes. Spending two weeks away from them was way harder than I thought it would be.

I walked around with Jim as he did his usual evening check on everybody and I chattered away happily. I told him about my trip and he updated me on what had been going on: poor Suze had ripped her leg open on the fence but was healing greatly, Bentley was better, and CharlieHorse had just finished off his medicine for the night and was in his stall chewing on bits of hay. And when I poked my head in to look at him, CharlieHorse looked content.

Mike was insane. He pranced and jumped and whined and pawed at my legs wherever I walked, tail wagging like crazy, eyes bright and excited. I sat on the ground with him and hugged and patted him for several minutes while he looked up at me with devotion in his eyes.

"I told him, angel," Jim said later on, laughing as he watched Mike and I dancing around each other happily. "I told him that you were coming and he just jumped off his couch and I had to let him out so he could go wait for you at the gate."

And RustyBob blissfully stuck his nose out for me to kiss and Solo nipped at my hands (devoid of carrots) happily and Slayer stood while I threw my arms around him and Tarzan whinnied and nuzzled my hands and Chance's eyes softened when he saw it was me, his sister, coming up that pathway....

It is so, so good to be *home*.

January 7, 2010

I drove by the ranch after school today, relishing the fact that I could do so once again. It was wonderful to see the blue sky, to climb through the gate again to see everyone, to breathe in the familiar ranch smell I thought I'd never miss. And seeing my Chance as I approached his stall brought strength back to me in no time.

"Hey, brother," I said to him and he gazed back at me contentedly. He was watching something from the back of his house, and he seemed so at peace, so relaxed, that I turned to leave him alone. But the moment I walked away from him he trotted right up to his stall door and looked at me expectantly. So we played our game for a while before I went to check on Jim.

I ended up staying and helping to feed for a while, and when I finally made my goodbyes and walked back to my car, I saw that RustyBob had somehow flipped his bucket sideways between the rails in his frenzy to eat everything that was inside and was trying to flip it back. I laughed and set it up the right way for him. He looked at me gratefully before digging in again.

"Look at you," I told him as he ate happily, "I missed you so much, RustyBob. I missed all of you."

I had wet bran on my hands. I held my fingers out to Chance, who happily licked it off. He then went back to his food as I continued to stand next to RustyBob and fully appreciate Arizona's wild, wonderful beauty. I'd been away from it for what felt like years. I never wanted to go inside again.

I looked around me before heading back toward the gate. I could see Guess and Bella eating happily and hear Heighten and Hudson nickering at each other. Jani was quietly eating, determinedly ignoring everything going on around her. Ted had finished his food and was clanging on the gate with his hooves for more. I could see Sedona and Sweet Boy's silhouettes from a distance, cleaning each other's backs over their stall walls. Way over in the field, all the kids had begun to play musical feeders, which happens when Solo starts pushing the other horses away from their feeders so he can eat the rest and Suze gets bored of her own hay and follows suit. The result is Kiss and Venture and sometimes Bentley scurrying to other feeders to finish their dinners while John observes from his pen – his office, as we call it.

When I finally started to head toward the gate again, Chance perked his head up from his trough, looked at me for a moment, then quietly walked right up alongside me as I moved. My heart soared. There are some things words can't describe.

January 10, 2010

A slew of volunteers had come out to the ranch on Saturday and had promised they would be at the ranch today; a woman named Luanne and her friend, a man and his wife who wanted to learn about horses before they adopted, and Ivy herself, who is paying Jim in labor and cash for boarding Hollywood, Cadence, and little Studley.

Guess how many of them showed up this morning?

Jim was furious. I would be, too, had I planned my day around the expectation that other people would be there to help with the everyday chores. Is it so much to ask for people to do what they say they'll do? Is it?

Well, Sam and I got all of the stalls done and we all scrubbed out the water tubs and refilled them before the noontime-but-really-eleven-o'clock feeding. Jim pitched in in between going to the store. We all worked as hard as we could, but the day was somewhat ruined. I can't wait for the day the whole world knows about Tierra Madre and volunteers line up at the gate for the honor of helping these horses.

January 12, 2010

Some days, it's obvious to me why I come here so much: while I'm at the ranch, I don't feel the weight of depression that feels heavy enough to crush my soul.

Lately I've found myself struggling a lot with the same feelings and anxiety I've had for three years. Particularly now that I'm nearing the end of high school and facing the unfamiliar path that will be college, some days it's just hard to keep going.

But every time I feel self-conscious or nervous or sad in any way, shape, or form, all I need to do is think of the horses. And I feel better.

I talked to them a lot today. I told them about school and my family and my two-legged friends. I told them about my plans for school at ASU in the fall. And they listened, they played with me, they put their noses to my hands and looked at me with adoration in their eyes. They nipped at my arms lovingly and tugged at my sweater and performed their antics they knew I loved.

After I helped with the feeding, I headed back to the gate. Everybody was busy eating so I resisted from reaching in and patting faces, only concentrated on getting back to my car so I could continue thinking.

When I walked past Chance's stall, however, he glanced upwards. Usually he has his nose in his food bin until the moment all the food is gone, so this surprised me.

"See you tomorrow, brother," was all I said.

And he looked at me.

It was a simple thing he did, just raising his head so that it was level with mine, but it absolutely melted me. He gazed at me with courage shining in those light brown eyes of his, determination blazing behind all of the uneasiness that had evolved from anger and suspicion. And he flicked one ear to the side, a sign of something very close to respect.

"You are brave."

This belief was all I felt when I walked away from him eventually. I ran the thought over and over in my head, processing its meaning, its significance as it had come from Chance. *You are brave, you are brave, you are brave....*

And for the first time in a long time, I believed it. I can be brave like Moosie.

I've never forgotten the way the great Moose turned his head back to me that last day we had together, the way one ear had flicked toward Trent as he came walking by and how one had been back toward me. I've never forgotten the way he looked right through me all of those times or how those moments made my heart stop and my breath catch in my throat and made me believe – know – that I was understood. I've never forgotten my promise to him.

And in a flash, I remembered all sorts of things, too.

Tarzan stretching his neck out to touch my fingers with his lips for the first time.

Little Rusty lowering his head against my chest after I took his flymask off.

Me leading Sedona for the first time.

Mr. Steve Vai letting me do his NoFly after days of trying.

Venture and I riding together, alone under an enormous sky.

Little D looking at me quietly in her dying days, assuring me that all was well.

Chance, my Chance, letting me put my hand on his nose that day... that one day....

I closed my eyes.

If those horses trust me, I thought to myself as I finally walked back toward the gate, then *I can get through anything. Anything.*

And that's all the bravery I need right now.

January 15, 2010

The last few days have brought rain and muck to Arizona but today was not so bad, if only a little damp. But the sun was out. I took advantage of the warmer weather to stop by after school. It was a half-day so I had more time to check up on everybody.

Jim was on his way out to the store when I got there so I opened the gate for his truck. He leaned out the window and stopped right next to me.

"Hey, baby girl," he said. He looked exhausted. "How are you?"

"How are *you*?" I asked, concerned.

Just as I couldn't ever lie to him, Jim couldn't lie to me, or anybody. "It's just a struggle," he responded quietly. I had to lean in a bit to hear him. "This. All of this. It's just... " He trailed off, then he smiled. "But I'll be alright. Just been a rough day, is all."

I said nothing.

"What's the matter?" he asked. "You look worried."

"I'm worried about you," I said honestly, and he shook his head.

"Never worry about me. We fight on," he told me. "I'm off to the store, sweet thing. Ivy's around here somewhere if you want to meet her. Email me later, okay?"

"Okay," I said, and he smiled again as he drove off.

I closed the gate after he left and walked down the pathway. There are times I don't really appreciate the fact that Jim is practically on his own when it comes to these horses. But he does a lot of the labor in the morning plus the fundraising for medical bills, food, equipment.... It's amazing to me how he shoulders it all, how much he sacrifices to keep the horses alive and happy.

When I got to the breezeway, I saw a woman sweeping Jim's front porch step. I walked over to her and called out cheerfully and she whipped around, surprised. "Oh, hi there!" she said.

"Hi – I'm Alexis," I said. "You must be Ivy."

"I am," she said, putting the broom down. "Nice to meet you. You're the one who wants little Studley, aren't you?"

I smiled. I had mentioned it to Sam, the fact that I wanted to buy Studley from Ivy so I could train him, ride him….

"Well, I do," I said truthfully, "but realistically, that won't happen. It's enough for me just to be around him every day, you know? The cost alone would kill me, anyway."

"Yeah, it's sorta killing me," she answered. "I'm just lucky that Jim helped me get my horses away from that bitch and that I can keep them here. It's great what he does. I'm glad I can be a part of it."

I nodded. She seemed very nice but also a person that dealt with no nonsense. She was tough, and I immediately respected that. I could see how she had saved Chester's life.

We walked up to the breezeway and I looked out at the horses in the shed row. Everyone had been fed lunch earlier and some of the kids were still eating. I was still watching them when Ivy picked up a halter and turned to me.

"You're the one who loves Chance."

Most of the other volunteers already knew: I was the crazy girl that was constantly talking to the wild yellow horse, the one who rubbed his nose and gave him carrots and the one to whom he trotted when I went up to his stall.

"Yes," I said, and I smiled at my own craziness. "He's my brother."

She nodded. "I cleaned his stall the other day and he nearly killed me, like, twice. What the hell kind of person would do that to an animal? Make 'em so scared they'll attack anybody who walks by?"

I thought of Trent.

"I've been asking myself that for years," I answered with a sad smile, and she snorted.

Ivy turned her three kids – Hollywood, Cadence, and Studley – into the arena before I left, and I ended up holding Hollywood for her as she got Studley back on his feet after his legs got stuck in the fence mid-roll. Studley galloped to the other end of the arena in shame the moment he was free, head lowered. Cadence trotted after him and I let Hollywood charge through the gate to join them.

"No one saw, you crazy boy," Ivy called after Studley as he stood, ears twitching, in the corner. "We still love you. Now go have fun."

I like her. I'm glad Tierra Madre has found a worker who understands the horses like Jim and Sam and I do.

January 18, 2010

It rained all morning today. The sky was one big gray cloud and the air was damp and the horses were muddy. I sighed repeatedly during the drive over. So much for the sun.

I met Luanne, a friend of Brandi's, for the first time. She was like most of the volunteers we've had – nice, did work quietly, liked the horses enough – and she mucked out most of the shed row stalls while Brandi and I tacked the barn and the pen where Katie and Sundance and Holly were. And I tell you, when we got into that pen, all hell broke loose.

The three horses went crazy. They pranced around and jumped and bit each other repeatedly and ran around us like they were toddlers on a sugar high. Their energy was contagious: their neighbors Guess and Ted started dancing too which made CharlieHorse, who had been hanging in the "out" portion of his home closest to the Chocolates, waddle into his stall to be away from the noise. I had to lock Sundance in the little pen in the corner and hold the two girls off while Brandi made a run for the stall door, dragging the half-full poop cart behind her. When she was safely out, I dove for the gate the instant I let Sundance loose and he lunged for the girls. I'd like to say I kept my cool during the entire time, but I was shaking when I got out of the pen. Almost getting trampled by three fourteen-hundred pound animals was a bit of an ordeal. My guess is that their energy was up from the cooler weather.

After that I mostly emptied out the water buckets in the shed row. Hudson amused himself by nibbling the back of my neck, my hair, my cheeks, and my shoulders, all the while "helping" with the hose that I was using when I did his water. Eventually I gave up all together and launched myself at him, roughhousing the best I could for someone who was less than ten percent of his body weight. He was calmer after that. Luanne and Brandi said they felt sorry for me, but I didn't mind too much.

Before I left I was in three layers and still shivering. The horses kept on acting up so they were warm from running (not to mention their winter coats), but I and the other two-leggeds were freezing. I just hope this cold snap doesn't last.

January 21, 2010

A huge storm is brewing on the horizon. Tornado possibility. Wind. Thunder. Lightning. Rain. Lots of rain. The trees are dancing uncontrollably. The sky is a ghastly, eerie shade of gray.

I wish that every one of those horses were under safer shelter. An enclosed barn, something...

***

I Facebook messaged Jim earlier:

7:35; Alexis Roeckner: *Jim – I'm worried sick about you guys. Are you okay? Are the kids okay?*

7:37; Jim Gath: *Alive....everything's flooded....the mesquite across from Akira's has fallen.....the wind is blowing the tarps & all the hay is getting soaked....everything's blowing all over hell's half-acre....my drier's been running non-stop since early morning....the kids are* hating it....according to TV, 3 inches of rain so far today.....that's supposed to double by tomorrow.....tired.....worried.....

January 22, 2010

This morning when I drove in, the first thing I saw was Tierra Madre's giant tan trashcan on its side in the wash area between the gate and the arena, contents strewn across the desert brush and dirt. The bulldozer we borrowed from the neighbors every now and then was in what partially resembled the arena. As I parked and headed up toward the breezeway, swearing under my breath in astonishment, I realized that the storm had done more damage than I thought possible.

The chairs and tables in the breezeway were knocked over. Half the hay was in ruins, some of it molded into the mud for fifteen feet around the huge stack. The ground moved when I walked in muddy places. The lids off trashcans had fallen off. Cocoa's food can, outside her stall, was destroyed, contents watery and wasted. The tree outside of Chance's stall and the one outside of Akira's had apparently fallen and Sam was lifting them back up with ropes and the bulldozer. There was a river of mud and horse poop and water flowing from the house all down the driveway. The arena looked like a giant swimming pool. And the stalls were indescribably filthy. As were the horses.

I had stayed up late last night, worried out of my mind, staying online in the official Friends of Tierra Madre forum where our friends all across the country were equally frantic. They had all heard the tornado warning on the news and begged us to tell them what was going on. I gave everyone updates on the weather and watched all hell break loose outside my window and Facebooked Jim until he lost power a little before eleven. Then he called me to give me an update.

One woman on the forum had asked if there were trailers available and higher ground to get to if the horses needed to be evacuated, and I panicked, realizing that if the worst did happen, the horses were stuck out in one of the worst storms Arizona has seen no matter what. I was glad when I was there this morning, seeing everyone, touching noses once again, letting the horses' breath warm my hands, relief flooding through me when I saw that everyone had weathered the storm.

My friend Anne from school had answered the plea I posted on Facebook, a plea asking for volunteers to help Tierra Madre in the morning. She helped me groom the horses that were the filthiest, clean up the breezeway, and muck out bits of moldy hay and mud from around the haystack. Brandi and Luanne mucked stalls as well as they could and Jim and Sam, armed with buckets, bailed out the pools of water that had collected in stalls, occasionally having to dig and rebuild the stall ground. Ivy came and helped with the mucking and the waters, too.

Anne groomed Iron Man while I scraped mud off of Slayer, using the hoof pick to get the dirt off the outside of his hooves. We were going to clean Hudson, who was completely mud-caked, but he kept nipping and biting and playing as he always does and since I was not on my own during that time, we let him be. We went in to see Chester then I cleaned Jani while Anne worked on Mistah Lee. I groomed RustyBob, too, but I made the mistake of giving him the small green brush to chew on and he tried to swallow it. I scolded him roundly for that, and he was embarrassed. But like we always do, we made up not a few minutes afterwards.

Chance kept trotting around in his stall, watching John and Solo moving around out in the mud-soaked arena with shining eyes. His palomino coat was smeared with mud and his hooves were filthy and his white mane and tail were matted, but to me he was still the most beautiful horse in the world.

When we were grooming the horses I snuck over to him after I had finished with my RustyBob. He was watching Hollywood, Cadence, and Studley in the round pen, but when he heard me coming, he trotted over to his stall door, studying me.

"Hey, brother," I murmured. "I wish I could go in there and brush you off."

Chance looked silently upwards, raising his head so his nose was above his ears, and I realized he was looking up at the tree. Instead of banging on the lower bar for leaves, he was asking for them in a politer way.

I had to reach up a bit more to get to his leaves, as Sam had raised the tree higher up than it had been, and I picked off the freshest, most dew-soaked leaves I could find. Chance's eyes shone as he watched me, and he took his snack from my fingers as gently as Chester takes his carrots. I watched him eat with pride in my heart.

"I thought about you all last night," I whispered. "I dreamed about you. Half of me wished you were safe in a barn. But the other half of me wished that you and I were out riding in the storm."

He chewed slowly as though processing this, then he placed his hoof gently on the lower bar of his stall door. I offered him my hand and we played our lip game until Anne finished brushing Mistah Lee.

The ranch looked much better than it did when we left. I'm so glad that everyone is okay.

January 28, 2010

Several more people seem to be becoming aware of Tierra Madre. I tell the families for whom I babysit all about this place and they are all alive with the magic these horses create. Another man I talked to wants to volunteer, and now several of my friends are becoming involved. One, Carrie, wants to volunteer Saturday mornings.

This is great. This will bring attention to the ranch, to the horses, to Jim.

I keep wondering what else I can do, what more I can give to the ranch besides simply going there and helping with the chores and hanging out with everybody. The more people we find, the better. Jim and Sam can't run the ranch by themselves.

January 29, 2010

Brandi and Luanne have been dismissed temporarily, but not because they are bad workers. On the contrary, Jim says they are some of the best the ranch has ever seen. Apparently, the ranch's funding is slow right now. Costs that have to be cut must be cut. The place is hurting financially, and it makes me worry.

I keep hoping more volunteers show up. I hope more people see this place and fall in love and donate funds. The horses need every friend they can get.

I counted eighty dollars from the coin bins this week. And that's all we're going to get for a long time because of the crisis in Haiti. I'm glad the victims of the earthquake will be getting funds, but things are going to be tighter for us.

January 31, 2010

Carrie and I were the only volunteers this morning, besides Ivy, who is working off her board for Cadence, Hollywood, and Studley. The two of us mucked out the barn and everybody's stalls in the shed row up to Jani, then we got to take Mistah Lee and CharlieHorse for a walk.

Carrie worked well. I wanted to do most of the work so she could spend time with the horses and get to know them and get to look into their eyes and see the secrets they were willing to share, but she did all of that while doing a heavy amount of labor. Mucking stalls is not easy for a newcomer, but she helped me clean stalls like a pro.

Jim was pleased with her, too. She's going to be volunteering Saturday mornings when she can, and he said he would be glad to have her back.

In the meantime, we're all brainstorming for fundraising ideas. In the meantime, as much as I hate to think it, we're all worried.

February 1, 2010

Solo was tubed tonight.

Colic.

Jim thinks Solo is fine now, but I know, miles away, that he's scared. Things like this are rattling and bone-chilling. I said before how horrible these moments are, these moments that happen all the time that terrify us and leave us uncertain about the fate of one of our family members. Tonight was one of those times. Luckily Solo pulled through. Luckily he's okay.

Our horses are priceless; there is no monetary value on any of their lives, but there was a vet bill for saving Solo's: $535.

It's getting tougher. It's hard to run a donation-funded ranch during this recession and not go insane. I don't know how Jim does it.

I'm so grateful for the friends of Tierra Madre that are scattered all over the country that send us what they can, when they can. I hope every one of them knows that if it weren't for them, we'd be lost.

February 5, 2010

Jim has an idea for advertising for this place. As we sat brainstorming several different ideas this afternoon, he asked if I'd be willing to help him with a project.

I told him last Sunday about how my laptop came with a cool movie-making software called iMovie and how it has the ability to burn DVDs. What if, Jim said, we made a DVD of the horses and sold them? People would get to take a look inside the ranch and see exactly what it is we do.

I think it's a great idea. I said I'd love to help and would get started right away.

Jim told me to have at it. "You know the horses," he told me. "You know what to do."

When I walked to my car later on, Chance eyed me with a glimmer of hope behind his eyes, and, smiling, I turned around and picked off a few bits of alfalfa to give him. He took them quietly and munched contentedly.

How great would it be for everyone to know his story? And Tarzan's? Mistah Lee's? Iron Man's and all the stories of our ex-racers, from M'Stor to Bella to John? The triumphant stories of those like Akira and Suze who found loving homes when they needed them most? How amazing that would be. Maybe this DVD will help do that. I really hope it will.

February 7, 2010

The DVD is coming along, and I think it will actually work when it comes to raising awareness for the ranch. It's going to be a slideshow with Jim talking in the background about the sanctuary, with pictures of all the horses flashing up on the screen.

Jim wants to sell it across the nation. "Not the town," he said today, "not the state, but the whole freaking country."

In other news, there was a relatively new volunteer there today called Beth. And let me tell you, she's a volunteer at another place that rescues smaller animals, and I'm sure she is great with them, but she does not understand horses. I had to walk her through basic horsemanship lessons I would have thought were common sense: how not to wave her arms around and startle them, how not to approach them from behind, how not to screech suddenly in their ears or move quickly when she was close to their faces. Little things she did nearly drove me mad.

"You have to be firm with them," I kept saying when she was walking some of our gentlest horses, who were having none of her.

"A horse herd is two or more. It's the way these guys' brains work. When you are with them, they are in a herd, and you have to be in charge."

But she didn't get it. Not with Bentley, who got so pissed off at the antics she did around him that he nipped her hard enough to make her shriek, not with Jani, who flicked an ear and glared at her with something close to incredulity in her eyes when she was near, and especially not with Chance, who wouldn't even spare her more than one ear-pinned glance in her direction. When I approached him to give him his leaves, Beth cackled, "He's gonna come and eat 'cha!" as though the prospect was the funniest thing in the world. And I had to go in, multiple times, to re-clean the stalls after she declared herself "done". She was lovely to talk to but I wish she had a little more horse sense.

Ah, well. I shouldn't talk. I still don't know all there is to know about horses, and I probably never will. Besides, beggars can't be choosers. Beth's willing to help us when we need it, so for that I am grateful.

I just sure wish she knew that dancing around like a maniac around sanctuary horses is probably not the best idea. Jim's probably quite relieved he had her sign a waiver.

February 10, 2010

I'm sitting next to Slayer and Iron Man as I write this. The two boys are separated from Tarzan by a little hallway with a tree at the end of it under which I'm currently sitting. Iron Man's neck was stretched out to inspect my laptop earlier, and as I was working on the DVD I showed him bits of it. His response?

"Do you have any food?"

I love that little boy.

Slayer is looking at me right now, watching my every move, and Tarzan is standing quietly on my left, head rising and ears twitching at every little noise.

It's so peaceful here. I'm under the biggest, bluest sky, my best friends are all around me, and there are no cars rushing by so I can hear all the snorting and occasional pawing of hooves and the whisper of the wind. I put my head to Slayer's chest a few minutes ago and I could hear the rhythm of his steady heartbeat.

This place is so alive around me. Spring is on its way and everything is growing. I know there are a few birds' nests up in the roof of the breezeway full of eggs. The horses are losing their winter coats. I know this because I just got up to scratch Iron Man's neck and dark bay hair started coming off faster than anything. My jacket is covered in it.

***

Jim came out of the house eventually, so I went to talk to him about the DVD and help him with the feeding.

On my way out, I stopped and looked at Chance as per usual. I look at Chance every day, and there is not one moment during which I don't admire the arch of his neck, the golden hues of his coat, his slender legs and his soft, soft eyes. Oh, his eyes. Once filled with hatred and fear of me, their gentleness has been permanently embedded into my heart.

It's crazy to me when I look back to last June. There's no logical reason I fell for him the moment I saw him, but I did. Honestly, there's no logic for a lot of things, but maybe that's how it's supposed to be.

Chance will be as gentle as the rest of these guys (excluding Min) someday. I promised him I would wait, and here I am still waiting. But I understand perfectly. There's no logic for what he went through, either, nor is there logic behind what any of these horses went through before they came home.

February 13, 2010

The DVD is done!

I went to the ranch yesterday to do the recording and finished it up last night. After days of editing, shortening, recording, rearranging, I premiered it today for Jim, Sam, Carrie, Brandi, and Ivy. They loved it.

It's going to be big. It's only five or six minutes long but when people buy it I know they're going to want more videos of the kids. That's what I'm hoping, anyway. I hope people watch it and fall helplessly in love with the ranch at first sight as I did.

There is only so much that pictures can say, but really – how can you not fall in love with these angels once you've looked into their eyes and seen the world in its entirety?

February 14, 2010

Today is Valentine's Day, and I'm actually not upset about it. Who needs Valentines when you have thirty-two wonderful friends waiting for you with open arms... er, hooves?

Over the last few weeks, people have paid for raffle tickets for the Valentine's Day painting, and today we did the drawing. Min, elected by the friends of Tierra Madre (for some reason), chose the winning ticket. We put the tickets in front of him and he put his nose on the number 20. I can't remember the winner's name, but she is one lucky gal. The painting that all the horses did is absolutely gorgeous.

These past few days, I have really been noticing a ranking system we've got going on here. Not amongst the horses, mind you, but the humans.

Today we had Ivy and Beth and my friend Carrie here. While Ivy mainly works by herself, the other two came to me when they had questions. I'm a good twenty years younger than Beth and she constantly asked me if she was doing things right, what horses' names were, etc. If I asked her to do something she obeyed without question. Even Katie, a nice college student who stopped by today to apparently do a project about Tierra Madre for school, understood that even though I was younger, she was to do as I asked and come to me if she had problems if she couldn't find Jim or Sam.

I, unfortunately, was born power hungry and wanting to be in charge. But here, knowledge of the horses and the amount of respect Jim has for you determines rank. I think that is really something special. No one gets to come in here and demand respect, like Trent tried to do. It must be earned. And it is a privilege to earn it from these guys.

I've gotten so fast at mucking out stalls and doing waters that I've had lots of time to spend with the horses. And today in between doing everything, I visited with each of my friends. Iron Man nibbled playfully at my hairline and Slayer put his forehead against mine for several minutes, breathing gently into my face and washing my worries away. I scratched mud off of a very happy Katie; gave treats to Ted and rubbed his nose as he chewed happily; watched Venture as he hung out in the breezeway and occasionally tugged him out of the treat bucket; offered Tarzan my hand and scratched his nose; played with Hudson; hugged and kissed RustyBob, brought Akira home from the arena and talked to her for a while; rubbed dirt off of Solo's face; savored the few moments of attention John gave to me; offered a ton of treats to a very happy Chester; scratched Guess's neck and Sundance's shoulders as I watched their waters fill; and played the lip game I have with Chance. And Studley, turned out into the arena for a while, followed me around, trying to get as close to me as he could while there was a gate between us. I went over to him at one point and walked along the gate of the arena and he followed me cheerfully, just like he had in the round pen some months ago. I keep telling myself it wasn't purely because I had treats.

So I don't have a one Valentine this year, and that's all right with me. Right now, I have thirty-two, and that's a whole lot better than one.

February 21, 2010

This past week has been a blur of school, babysitting, the ranch, and staring at my computer screen burning DVDs. We have to find a brand of DVDs that works on Jim's computer but other than that, everything's coming along fine.

Yesterday the rain started up again and the temperature dropped. The horses' think winter coats – back with a vengeance – certainly did their jobs. I have to marvel again at how incredible it is how the horses take everything in stride. They all have shade structures to retreat under if it's too hot or too rainy, but the majority of them simply stand and let the rain fall down on them. No complaints. No irritable swishing of tails or shaking of heads. They are simply and undeniably one with Mother Earth.

Humans run from nature if it is not to their liking. Horses take it exactly for what it is and as it comes.

March 2, 2010

I miss summer.

I miss being able to be with the horses every day. I miss the freedom that it represents.

School is dragging me down. Now I can only stop by twice or three times a week. I'm lucky if I can make it out to volunteer Sunday mornings. And instead of writing about my adventures when I get home, I have so much homework to do instead that I don't have the will to write.

During the days I'm not at the ranch, I'm scared that the horses will all forget me. I know horses focus on the here and now, and if I'm not there with them every day…

Well, there I go focusing on the future. The best thing I can do is focus on the present, and right now, school *is* my present. And even if I'm not around as often as I want to be, I know that the best horseman there ever was is caring for everybody.

March 12, 2010

A new horse has come to Tierra Madre! His name is Buddy and he has been dubbed "George Clooney" since he is just a handsome. He used to work at a local horse rescue that helps children and adults with special needs through enabling them to ride. It's extremely therapeutic for them and those horses have healed many a broken soul.

Buddy worked at the rescue for years ferrying kids on his back, and one day just a short while ago he started limping. Everybody fussed and worried over him and when it was decided that if he couldn't work, he couldn't stay, there was a rush to find another home for him as soon as possible. The owner called Jim and asked if there was a place available for a horse with a bad foot. Jim, being Jim, told them to send Buddy over.

Needless to say, Buddy is now home for good, and he seems absolutely thrilled about it. Only thing is for sure though: he definitely does not walk with a limp. Hmm.

Jim, laughing with approval upon this discovery, said Buddy must have gotten tired of working all day long. Therapeutic that place might be for the humans, but the horses don't get to have a whole lot of fun.

Smart horse.

March 18, 2010

There were so many people at the ranch today. Jim, Sam, me, Brandi, a lovely past volunteer named Helen, and a guy from ASU named Patrick. Suzanne from down the road also brought her white horse (also named Solo) over for a bit. I was reminded of Jericho, Venture's old friend, when the white horse was let out in the arena with Venture. The sight made my breath catch in my throat more than once. Part of me wished Venture would run and play with the white horse, but Venture wasn't having any of it. He turned his back to Solo and ignored him until Jim got the halter on him and led him out of the arena, softly apologizing to Venture for putting him out with a horse he hadn't liked. No horse would ever replace Jericho.

Jim's been riding Buddy lately so he can re-train him a little, and that horse definitely doesn't limp when he's being ridden, which I find hilarious. Once Jim is satisfied that Buddy will do well without a bit (we don't use bits when we ride here), Buddy will join Akira as a lesson horse. Akira will be pleased, I think. They already get along so well, as do Buddy and Jani, of all horses. She's so standoffish with everyone else that we were all surprised when she didn't seem to mind Buddy at all.

I think Buddy looks a lot like Mr. Steve Vai, but he doesn't have his eyes. It's been seven months and I still remember Mr. Steve Vai's beautiful eyes. I imagine I'll remember his eyes for the rest of my life.

The last few times I've come to the ranch, I've noticed that John follows me around whenever I'm in the arena. While it's possible he's been standing close to me and looking at me intently in search of food, I like to think that he's grown to appreciate my company. And let me tell you, to be noticed and respected by the king himself… that is truly something. How I could get lost in that horse's regal eyes. Somehow when I leave John, I'm always questioning things about life and about myself. He reminds me of Moosie in that he seems to know more about me than I do.

I sprayed down M'Stor and Suze today while doing water tubs. It's starting to get warm again, and neither of those horses can ever get enough water. Soon we'll be doing NoFly once more, just as I did when I first began here. Looking back, I can't believe that I've been at this ranch for over nine months.

March 22, 2010

Today I needed the angels of Tierra Madre more than ever. They have a way of melting away the stress I've been feeling lately over school and finally deciding on a college for the fall. As always, I find so much comfort in all the horses here, but it's always, always my yellow horse I look to when I need courage to see me through the day.

I've come to understand that no one can ever truly explain the connection that he or she has with a horse. It's not an understatement to say that such connected beings, both human and horse, simply see each other from the outside in. They have a nameless, soulful thread that strings their thoughts, ideas, hopes and dreams together. At least, that's how I feel with Chance and how every horse here must feel with Jim, a horse whisperer if there ever was one. In all the other horse places I've been – various riding facilities and shows – never have I felt such a present, powerful energy. I suppose that comes with Tierra Madre.

I've never known a place that allows such a powerful connection to exist.

Today I looked back through this journal and I realized that I don't write as much as I did during the summer and the start of my senior year. I realize now that it's a result of the stress I've been under lately. Instead of writing about the way these horses have been helping me, I've been spending more time savoring their comfort and learning from them. Instead of spending time finding words, I've been spending time finding answers.

And when I look ahead at the future... well, my school project, the one that brought me to the ranch in the first place, is officially done. I give my presentation in May, during which I'll tell my peers about where I've worked, what I did, and what I learned.

Two of those questions are easy to answer. But how can I really sum up what I've learned and how I've changed since the first of June to any audience?

Maybe I'll just have to say what was apparent to me from day one: even though this volunteer work was originally only a school requirement, even though I only had to give a hundred hours of my time and have already surpassed those by far, I did not, could not, and will not ever stop coming to this sanctuary.

Just as each and every one of these horses found a forever home in Tierra Madre, so did I.

Spring

March 28, 2010

We have yet another new horse! Her name is River, and she's a baby at barely three years old. Two days ago her life could have gone two ways: sanctuary or slaughter.

She's beautiful. She almost as tall as Suze but she's pretty skinny and much slimmer as she is fresh off the race track and full of energy to boot. Apparently she broke her front left sesamoid bone while she was being exercised a few days ago, and the person who called Jim said she could probably never race again, but would he be willing to give her months of stall rest in order to save her from going to auction? Jim told her to send River his way.

I have to say, River has an enormous pen considering she isn't allowed to run around for several months. All of the horses live in huge stalls, really. For now we're putting her next to RustyBob, who can't get over his gorgeous new stable mate.

When I met her today, River was too excited to stand still. She was quivering and shifting around and whipping her head back and forth to investigate the sounds of the world around her, eyes curious and bright. I laughed as I watched her. It's amazing to me, the disbelief some horses seem to have when they come here. It's like they can't believe that their new home is real, like it's too good to be true.

Well, it's true.

Welcome home, baby girl.

May 11, 2010

It's unbelievable how I haven't written in a while.

So much has happened. So much is happening. I've worked more in school this past month than I have the entire year, and it has hurt my ability to be at the ranch.

But now, for updates. First and foremost is Heighten.

About four weeks ago, Heighten started limping on his hind left leg. It turns out there is a hairline fracture in his hock and numerous infections to boot. He is starting to shed pounds and cannot put a lot of weight on his injured leg. Jim is worried sick; the rest of us are scared as well.

But Jim says he doesn't care how long or how hard the battle is. They will fight. Together with the best veterinarians in the Phoenix Valley, they will fight for Heighten's life.

I can see it in his eyes how drained that boy has become, how tired he already is from fighting the infections and the fatigue and the pain.

But he's pulling through. And he will pull through in the end, because he's Heighten.

Hudson is still as goofy as ever. A little while back Sam and Jim built a little fence between his and Heighten's fences so that they couldn't roughhouse as much. Heighten needs to conserve energy and keep as much weight off his leg as possible. Hudson wasn't very pleased about this at first, but now, he's just happy he can still be next to his friend and check in on him.

Guess and Bella and Jani are still angels. Guess, of course, is still the gorgeous queen bee and Bella a beautiful example of grace. Jani is still a little standoffish and reserved, but I love her all the more for it. Her new friend Buddy continues to amaze me with his wit, his charm, and his street smarts. It still cracks me up how he faked his limp to get out of working.

Katie and Sundance and Holly are still rambunctious and they still band together like the team they are. Cadence and Hollywood and Studley are still happy as clams in their round pen. Hollywood bosses the other two around, and Cadence and Studley take it all in stride.

Mistah Lee and Akira are still in love. Mistah Lee still gets his walks and his hip, once completely useless to him, is healing more and more every day. The strength he possesses is otherworldly and uplifting. Little Miss Akira, of course, is still sweet and demure but always guarded in her love for other humans besides Jim. Broken hearts, after all, do not mend so easily.

RustyBob continues to be my cheerleader and one of the sweetest boys in the whole world. River is still beyond thrilled to be in a new home where she gets all the carrots and treats and love she wants. Chance, of course, is still and will always be my brother. We still play our lip game, and I always make sure he gets leaves and a few minutes of loving words when I'm with him. But he has a long way to go, and I want to be there with him every step of the way.

Chester, the sweet teddy bear of a horse that he is, is so loved by everyone here and is so content to just hang out with anyone that goes into his stall for hugs. Ted, my first friend at this ranch, still bangs incessantly on his stall bars for food any time someone is within twenty feet of him. The poor boy will need his back fixed again soon. But he is still faithful and still one of the most tender, loving souls I'll ever meet. CharlieHorse, my sweet little philosopher, is quieter than ever these days. We think he's winding down for good this time, to be honest. For the time being though, he is happy, content, and peaceful.

Sweet Boy and Sedona are still delightfully loveable and completely codependent – one does not go anywhere without the other. Sedonie is on a bit of a diet now, and he compensates by stealing Sweet Boy's food whenever he can. Sweet Boy only minds a little.

John continues to be the king; not by vote, not by popular demand, but purely because of his regal, awe-inspiring confidence and his intelligence that I've yet to see matched by any horse. His second-in-command, Solo, is still convinced he's superior to everyone (but John) and is a total punk to the other horses, but he is still somehow innocent and likeable all the same. Suze, a queen bee if there ever was one, is still our big, gorgeous girl and is forever trying to take the hoses out of water when we fill the tubs. Bentley, our big black warhorse, is still such a gentle little boy and continues to battle various ailments due to his bad immune system. The Mayor of the Breezeway, also known as Venture, still hangs out with us before the noontime feeding and gets a bran mash and treats (and sometimes gives rides in return). And Kiss, at the bottom of the herd hierarchy, is making friends with Venture, slowly but steadily. He's happy to get attention when he gets it and is constantly, quietly nickering for one of us to sneak him treats.

Charlie and Min are still the sweet, odd couple. The biggest horse and the littlest. Forever friends. Min still has absolutely no idea how small he really is and continues to be what Jim lovingly calls our resident terrorist. Charlie, forever a gentleman and a wise soul, is recovering from the infection he had in his nose. Our vet calls Charlie's nose infection the greatest medical victory of his career.

M'Stor is still a goof and a rambunctious one at that. He still gets a kick out of spraying me in the face when I'm filling his water bucket since he can never get enough of playing with the hose. I'm still amazed at how far he has come from the days he could barely walk due to his broken leg. When he first got to the ranch his life hung in the balance. Not anymore.

Slayer and Iron Man continue to be the gentle beasts who are by now very good friends. Slayer will forever be my knight in shining armor and Iron Man is still the most wondrous, happy boy who quit at the right time in order to come how to Tierra Madre.

Tarzan is still a hero in all of our eyes. Abused badly enough to still be cautious of the world around him, he simply takes each day as it comes and has the biggest, bravest heart of any creature I've ever had the honor of knowing. He might tremble when people are near him, but his courage to love despite what he has been through is the most humbling power in the world.

Mike is still just about the most intelligent, loyal, protective and devoted creature on four legs, the heart of Tierra Madre and Jim's partner in crime.

And that's it. All 34 horses and an amazing ranch dog. My brothers and sisters. My family.

May 14, 2010

Something crazy happened today. Today was my senior presentation at school, the presentation I knew I would have to make when I first started volunteering. It was the entire reason I walked through the ranch's gates in the first place. It was what brought me to Tierra Madre.

So maybe that doesn't fit the definition of crazy. (I would be a better example.) But to me, giving that presentation was surreal.

As I stood in front of my classmates and teachers to talk about the ranch, I found it very difficult to fully express just how much the place meant to me. I told them what my duties had been. I told them about some of the horses and what I had done to help fundraise. But I couldn't really put into words what lessons I had learned, and to be honest, I don't think I ever can. I walked through those gates that first day expecting to learn a few basic lessons about horsemanship, put in my hundred hours then be done. Boy, did all of that change.

Today as I left the ranch after making a brief visit, after two weeks of not seeing me, Chance followed me to our corner and nicely asked for leaves. The first day I met him, he wanted absolutely nothing to do with me. Today, even though I hadn't seen him in a while, I saw within him recognition and the beginnings of trust.

I'm going to college in the fall. Last summer will probably never repeat itself as I will be starting a summer job here in a few weeks and will be working a lot of the time. I won't get to be at the ranch every day or even as often as I want. But I know now that when I do come back, my brother will be here waiting for me. And Jim. And Mike. And Sam. And all of my friends that I've grown to love over this past year. Their journeys, and mine, have been and will always be woven together no matter where I go.

And as I held my fingers out for Chance to nibble, I knew that *that* knowledge is enough to keep me going. Just like every horse in that place has had to go through numerous journeys to get to where they are today, I've grown in ways I never dreamed were possible. And when I'm at Tierra Madre, I remember. When I'm here, I'm home.

I guess I didn't mean for this to be my last entry, but it certainly seems like the time and place to close this journal. These horses will continue to heal and truly *live* at this sanctuary, and while the words might cease in this journal, there will never truly be an end.

It has almost been an entire year since I walked through those gates. I still call humans "two-leggeds". And horses?

They are and will always be my saviors.

Alexis Roeckner

Epilogue

August 4, 2014

To say that the horses of Tierra Madre Horse Sanctuary gave me my life back is the understatement of the century. When I first walked through those gates, I was more spiritually lost than even I knew at the time. Carrying deep wounds from my past and convinced that people I let into my life would only end up hurting me, I quickly learned that if the horses that surrounded me were able to heal from their traumatic experiences and look for all that is good and beautiful, there was no reason I couldn't do the same. How lucky were we all to end up at Tierra Madre? How lucky am I that all of our paths were intertwined?

Looking back over this journal, this account of the first year I experienced at Tierra Madre, I find it hard to believe that so much time has passed. Many things have changed, of course, in the four years since I ended this journal in May 2010.

CharlieHorse joined the Great Herd two months after my last entry. Chester, like his soul-brother Moosie, peacefully died in his sleep in November 2011. The brave, great Tarzan joined them in April 2012. Mistah Lee headed off to his next adventure at the start of 2013, and Charlie, after heroically fighting cellulitus and a horrific leg infection for many months, gracefully decided it was time to run with his friends in the Herd at the end of July of 2013. Just recently, this past July, Ted – my first friend at Tierra Madre – told us it was his time to go after patiently coping with his bad back for so long. And on the same day, John, our king of Tierra Madre, coliced badly just as he had many times before, only on that horrible day, we couldn't save him.

One of the most devastating losses of all was when we lost Mike, Tierra Madre's loyal ranch dog and Jim's partner in crime, in May 2011 to cancer. The ranch will never be the same without him, without any of them.

But the balance of Mother Nature's plan is so perfectly executed, for with every heartbreak we've endured there have been countless miracles and wonderful occurrences. A beautiful gray horse named Nibz came to live at Tierra Madre in 2011. Katie, Sundance, and Holly – the three exceptions to the rule that once horses walked through our gates they would never leave – went to a loving home together where they would have a little more room to run around and be happy. In February 2013, another ex-racer named Bourbon was welcomed to the ranch. The great racehorse Zenyatta's former stable mate, Sarbonne, also came to live with us in August 2013. Then, in February of this year, we got two new horses: a young, spirited paint named Jazz and another older, gentle soul named Wild Bill. Every horse, every single one of them, is happy and home forever.

Throughout the past four years, these horses have seen and done it all. The medical issues they have endured and survived together are astonishing: Hollywood fought laminitis – the practically incurable hoof disease that claimed the lives of Little D and Mr. Steve Vai – and *won*. Heighten overcame a broken leg after fighting certain death for fourteen months. After losing several hundred pounds and fighting pain that I cannot begin to imagine for over a year, Heighten's recovery is a true miracle and a tribute to the dedication Jim shows to each of his horses.

Colic has taken hold of several of our horses these past few years, but the fact that so many of them fought through the worst thing a horse can endure is absolutely, breathtakingly incredible. Cellulitis and a poor immune system have been issues for Bentley but he continues to take it in stride and is still the sweetest, most loving little boy. Min might have chronic laminitis, Venture might have Cushings, and Kiss and Jani might have ringbone, but they fight on with unmatched courage and determination. Studley gets summer sores, Sedona had parts of his legs that swelled recently, and Heighten now deals with bone spurs as a result of his broken knee, but they march on with their heads high, never complaining, never slowing. The medical care that each of these horses receives is top notch and I have to say, the vets that service this ranch are incredible.

As for Chance, my amazing brother Chance, he continues to fight his demons and is completely different from the horse I met five years ago. Others can go into his stall now and walk him around the ranch – including me. We do groundwork together. I give him bran mashes and scratch his face all over and sit outside his stall and sing to him. And he listens with gentleness in his eyes. My brother just goes to show that despite the forces of anger and hatred in this world, love wins. Love always wins.

March of 2013 brought another amazing ranch dog named "Levon" to the sanctuary, a loving German Shepherd mix that was found on the side of the road. "Sam" left the ranch permanently to pursue other interests in November 2012, but we have gained absolutely incredible volunteers and workers that will be around for years to come. We have developed new practices and ways of doing things. Jim no longer runs the place alone; some of the day-to-day stress of keeping the ranch afloat is off his shoulders. At the end of the day, Tierra Madre Horse Sanctuary is still the ranch it always was, the ranch that works magic on every horse that calls it home and the place that brings people from all walks of life together. And as always, Jim continues to show each and every horse nothing but kindness, understanding, and utter devotion. The connection he has with his "kids" continues to be more powerful than anything else I have seen and will ever see. The love he has for every one of those horses will forever be proof to me that there is still good left in this world.

During the first year of my volunteering, I did my very best to help heal those horses and considered it an honor to do so. Instead, they ended up healing *me*. Whether they are here with me on

Earth or running high above in the Great Herd, the horses of Tierra Madre continue to guide me every day of my life. They define my purpose and the choices I make and the standard of happiness by which I live. Whenever I am scared to reach beyond my comfort zone or whenever I feel my self-confidence slip, I think of the quiet, unbreakable strength that dwells deep within their souls. Whenever I focus far too much on what has happened in the past or what has yet to occur in the future, I think of the way they live for each and every moment.

Above all, I think of Moosie.

I've never forgotten my promise I made to him. I had no idea that on that day, as I promised to be brave just like him, I was making a promise by which I would live for the rest of my life. And not one day goes by that I don't miss him. Not one day goes by that I don't miss my baby Rusty or Mr. Steve Vai or Jericho or Little D or CharlieHorse or Chester or Tarzan or Mistah Lee or Charlie or Ted or our great, regal king, John.

But Tierra Madre Horse Sanctuary has taught me that it is because of that kind of grief we all keep on living. Through feeling such a profound sense of loss do we really know that we have loved so strongly and will continue to love for as long as we are here. The pain of losing the beloved horses we've welcomed home runs deep. But the love we have for each of them is even deeper.

Jim says that when Father Sun rises in the morning, the Great Herd is there pulling him across the sky. And if I listen carefully as the sun begins its journey upwards at the start of every new day, I swear I hear the thundering of hooves.

And every day as I hear the Great Herd charging on the horizon, I realize that life throws us so many gifts if we are open to receiving them, for it is a privilege and a responsibility to gratefully take what has been given to us, both the good and the bad; to open the gate and run at whatever is there; to be brave even in the face of the unknown. To understand a fraction of what life is all about is to know that in the end, we only have each other, and we only have today.

Today, the horses that call Tierra Madre their forever home gallop around the arena as fast as they can. They fight through their pasts and their ailments and they live with joy in their hearts. Today and every day, they are free. They are loved.

With every morning sunrise, Jim and I and all of the Tierra Madre family listen for the triumphant sounds of our angels that are in the Great Herd, and we rejoice for them.

And today and every day, we march on.

A Year With Angels

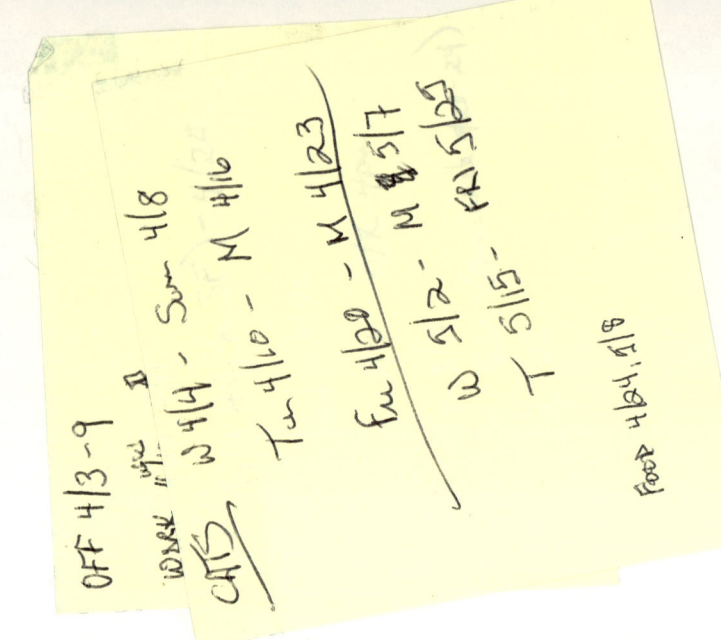

OFF 4/3-9
WORK night II
CATS W 4/4 - Sun 4/8
Tu 4/10 - M 4/16
Fri 4/20 - M 4/23
W 5/2 - M 5/7
T 5/15 - FRI 5/25

FOOD 4/04, 5/8

About the Author

Alexis Roeckner was born in Scottsdale, Arizona and raised in the next-door western town of Cave Creek. Her love for the beautiful Sonoran Desert and for horses, the ultimate symbol of the Wild West, undoubtedly came from her upbringing. After a whirlwind few years of living in the Bay Area in California and in Bradenton, Florida from 2004 to 2006, Roeckner now lives back in Arizona with her ornery calico cat, Gypsy.

She graduated from Foothills Academy College Preparatory in June 2010 then pursued her education at the Walter Cronkite School of Journalism at Arizona State University. She later switched to the Julie Ann Wrigley School of Sustainability and graduated with her degree in sustainability in May 2014. Roeckner is currently the director of curriculum development for SmartRoots Global, a nonprofit organization that seeks to create sustainability curriculum for elementary schools in developing nations and educate young minds about caring for Mother Earth.

Roeckner loves to write and has wanted to be an author since she learned how to string words together to make sentences. She also loves coffee, the sun, and Kenny Loggins.

Roeckner continues to volunteer at Tierra Madre Horse Sanctuary and is constantly in awe of the horses she considers to be her family and her saviors. She is the ranch's official videographer.